2020

THE PUBLICATIONS OF THE BEDFORDSHIRE
HISTORICAL RECORD SOCIETY
VOLUME 96

THE BEDFORD DIARY OF LEAH AYNSLEY

1943 – 1946

Edited by Patricia and Robert Malcolmson

THE BEDFORDSHIRE HISTORICAL RECORD SOCIETY

THE BOYDELL PRESS

First published 2020

A publication of
Bedfordshire Historical Record Society
published by The Boydell Press
an imprint of Boydell & Brewer Ltd
Bridge Farm Business Park, Top Street, Martlesham, IP12 4RB
and of Boydell & Brewer Inc.
668 Mt Hope Avenue, Rochester, NY 14620–2371, USA
website: www.boydellandbrewer.com

ISBN 978–0–85155–083–1

ISSN 0067–4826

The Society is most grateful for financial support from

The Wixamtree Trust

who have helped make the publication of this volume possible

Details of previous volumes are available from
Boydell and Brewer Ltd

A CIP catalogue record for this book is available
from the British Library

The publisher has no responsibility for the continued existence or accuracy of
URLs for external or third-party internet websites referred to in this book,
and does not guarantee that any content on such websites is,
or will remain, accurate or appropriate

This publication is printed on acid-free paper

Printed and bound in Great Britain by TJ International Ltd, Padstow, Cornwall

Contents

Illustrations

Maps

The editors and publisher are grateful to all the institutions and persons listed for permission to reproduce the materials in which they hold copyright. Every effort has been made to trace the copyright holders; apologies are offered for any omission, and the publisher will be pleased to add any necessary acknowledgement in subsequent editions.

Acknowledgements

Our first debt is to our friend Barbara Tearle, who told us about the existence of Leah Aynsley's diary. Without this information, we probably would never have learned of this appealing primary source and decided to edit it. So, our warm thanks to Barbara. Second, the fact that this diary was entrusted to the Bedfordshire Archives and Records Service is a result of the initiative of her nephew, John Aynsley (son of Leah's younger brother, Jim). Personal papers are often at risk of destruction. We are grateful to John for ensuring that his aunt's writings have been preserved.

John Aynsley was also of great help to us in 2018 when we were hard at work on this book. He showed us a number of family photographs (three are reproduced below); answered questions by email; and met with us in Bedford one day in May 2018 to talk more about his family's history, answer various questions, and help us better understand the context of his aunt's life. We are much indebted to John for his constructive contributions to the making of this book.

Our other major debt is to Nicola Avery, Editor of the Bedfordshire Historical Record Society. She reviewed the typescript we sent her with impressive care. She spotted many errors in it that we had overlooked, along with passages that called out for clarification. She suggested numerous useful editorial changes and, overall, was a notable help in polishing our presentation of the diary. Her colleague, Stuart Antrobus, also read the typescript and pointed to a number of places where we could (and did) make improvements. We very much appreciate the contributions of both Nicola and Stuart. Stuart introduced us to Maurice Nicholson, an authority on the Queen's Park district of Bedford, where Leah lived, and he kindly advised us on local sources. Ann Stephenson did valuable family research on our behalf, for which we are (as usual) grateful. The Nelson Public Library in British Columbia dealt very efficiently with our requests for books through the province's Inter-Library Loans service. We are also indebted to the archivists at both the BBC Written Archives Centre and the Royal Voluntary Service Archive and Heritage Collection for help in using their collections. Finally, Pamela Birch and her colleagues at the Bedfordshire Archives and Records Service provided all sorts of timely assistance for our work, both while we were working in Bedford in May 2018 and, by email, while we were working at home in British Columbia. Our hearty thanks to all these people.

On a more personal note, one of us (Robert) would like to record the help he received as a beginning research student in 1966 from the late Patricia Bell, then Assistant Archivist at the County Record Office. Her friendly manner, patience and generosity were key reasons for his satisfying engagement with research on primary sources and his later decision to become a historian.

Nelson, British Columbia
August 2019

Introduction

'I think I know why I keep a diary', Leah Aynsley wrote on 3 May 1954. 'Being single I want something of mine to live after me; I intend bequeathing it to Bedfordshire Records Office[1] and being written by a working-class person among whom I suspect not many will keep such diaries, it may be interesting in future centuries; also I find great pleasure in reading it occasionally.' She thought, too, that her diary 'is often useful to settle arguments as to what happened on such and such occasions.' This was the second time in her writing that she had wondered about her reasons for diary-keeping. 'Perhaps I hope that it will be published after my death', she remarked on 11 June 1948, when she also speculated on her possible desire 'to perpetuate myself, seeing I have no children' – Samuel Pepys, she observed, had also been childless. (She had read Pepys' diary in 1930, just after finishing and enjoying the diary of his contemporary, John Evelyn.)[2] 'Or perhaps I am like the person who carries a camera; I like to reproduce experiences on paper so that I can go over them at some future time and savour them again.'[3]

Leah's self-identification as working-class is both noteworthy and apt. Her father, Michael, was an engineer's pattern maker. He and her mother Mary (née Richardson) – the former living in Sunderland, the latter in North Shields – had married in Tynemouth in October 1898. Both Leah's grandfathers were shipwrights. Seafaring and other forms of labour were well represented in both extended families, whose members had homes in various parts of the North-East. Leah was born on 16 January 1902, her two brothers, John and Jim, in August 1904 and December 1905 respectively. Given the depressed economy of the North-East after the Great War, Leah's parents had moved in 1921 with their three children (all then in their teens) to Bedford in search of better opportunities. Michael Aynsley, Leah's father, did succeed

---

[1] A note dated 6 September 1977 inserted at the beginning of her diary repeats her desire that the diary be deposited in the County Record Office. The diary comprises thirteen books and is now catalogued in the Bedfordshire Archives and Records Service (BARS) as Z1606.

[2] Diary, 18 July 1930.

[3] The metaphor of its volunteer 'Observers' as 'cameras with which we are trying to photograph contemporary life' had been used by Mass Observation a decade earlier in justifying one of its fundamental approaches to social investigation (Charles Madge and Tom Harrisson, eds, *First Year's Work, 1937–38, by Mass-Observation* [London, 1938], p. 66). Each person's 'subjective' take on what was observed mattered. If Leah knew about Mass Observation's work, she never said so. While she certainly possessed some of the qualities of a perceptive 'Observer', had she written for Mass Observation she would have lost control of her diary once she put it in the post – it then became Mass Observation property – and her desire to see it published someday would probably not have been fulfilled. By communicating her desire to family members (this was unusual), its preservation was ensured and the chances of eventual publication were increased.

in finding employment and for around a decade he worked at Vauxhall Motors in Luton.[4] From 1931 he was unemployed. Leah, and Michael's younger son, Jim, were probably from that time the main supporters of the household. John was then married and living in Luton. Leah's mother, Mary, had died of cancer in February 1928.

Immediately or almost immediately upon their arrival in Bedford in 1921, the Aynsley family took up residence in the Queen's Park area of the town, which was to the west of the main rail line from London to the North (see Map 1). Their home was at 66 Marlborough Road, a standard smallish terraced house built at the beginning of the century (where Leah continued to live until near the end of her life). The 1939 *Directory of Bedford* testifies to the working-class character of this neighbourhood. Of the forty-one households on Marlborough Road numbered between 56 and 80 on the west side and 47 and 101 on the east side, all those headed by men whose occupations were identified were, without exception, working-class, or perhaps at a stretch lower middle-class (such as one storekeeper). Four households were headed by labourers; the rest were more specific. These occupations included a printer, a carriage cleaner, a baker, a wireman, a groom, a french polisher, an ironmonger's assistant, a porter, a plate-layer and a carpenter; two each of moulder, electrician, fitter, and train driver; and three pattern makers (in addition to the retired Michael Aynsley).

By far and away the biggest employer in this district of Bedford was the W.H. Allen & Sons Engineering works, which were located adjacent to the rail tracks and just north of the River Great Ouse. Their existence in Bedford dated to 1894. This factory, as maps and aerial photographs reveal (see map 1 and illustration 4), was very large, and a dominant local presence in Queen's Park. Leah worked at Allen's during most of the war, as did slightly more than 3,000 other people at the peak of wartime employment. Queen's Park, Bedford, was close to a one-industry community, loosely speaking, though of course many of the district's residents worked elsewhere and many of Allen's workers lived in other parts of town. The factory was a major supplier to the Navy and merchant marine, especially of turbine-driven generators and their components.[5] Most of its workers were deemed 'essential' to the war effort, including Leah herself, a secretary. It is likely that many of those who lived near these works ventured only occasionally – perhaps once a week or less frequently – into the centre of Bedford.[6]

This is the basic background to understanding Leah Aynsley's wartime life and writing. Her diary offers – as do many diaries – a portrait of a chunk of the author's life; often there is little evidence on that life before the diary begins or after it ends. A diary can often be seen as disclosing a chapter or two of what the diarist must later have thought of as a life of many chapters; most of these are now little known or completely unknown to posterity, and are likely to remain so in the absence of documentation. But whilst keeping a diary, an otherwise obscure person is able to shine a light (for a while) onto both her individual life and the times in which this life was led.

---

4   Her father had a motor bike and may have he used it to commute the rather long distance between his home and his work. He may also have cycled there and back. His elder son was a very keen cyclist.

5   BARS, Z450/1; W.H. Allen Engineering website; Michael R. Lane, *The Story of Queen's Engineering Works, Bedford: A History of W.H. Allen & Sons Co. Ltd.* (London, 1998), esp. chap. 6.

6   On the verge of war in 1939, and just before evacuees arrived, Bedford probably had a population of close to 50,000. No census was taken in 1941. The town's population in 1951 was 53,065.

* * * *

Leah Aynsley had kept a diary, intermittently, during the 1930s,[7] but she wrote nothing during the almost four and a half years following July 1938. This volume reproduces everything that she wrote as a diarist during and immediately after the war: starting in January 1943 and concluding in March 1946.[8] Nothing has been omitted. There has been no editorial making of selections – except in terms of choosing when to start and when to end.

Our annotations are designed, first, to add to the text pertinent facts that Leah, who was writing a private diary, had no reason to include; and second, to enlarge on events and topics, usually public ones, which she mentioned but did not elaborate on. Our key objective is to offer a portrait of a life and times, and we strive to present her 'times' more fully than she does herself (all diarists leave gaps in their accounts) by means of references to other sources, such as local newspapers, trade directories, and relevant secondary works. Her reactions to public occurrences can be better appreciated when the basic facts of these events and their contexts are suitably acknowledged and understood.

As for Leah's character, outlooks, and domestic circumstances, rather than remarking on them in this Introduction, we prefer to allow details about them to emerge as the diary unfolds. Our prime concern is to let Leah speak for herself, to enable her to reveal what she wished to reveal at any given time. Our own interpretative comments are rare and reserved mainly for a handful of footnotes and the Epilogue, where we draw together some of the major strands of her temperament and way of life.

Since Leah's writing is largely error-free, there has been little need to alter her prose – punctuation, as is commonly the case with diaries, is the main exception, though with her it is not an especially notable exception. She tended to be a close observer of rules, grammatical and otherwise. Occasionally she misspelled a proper name, and normally we have silently corrected these errors. She occasionally and deliberately omits certain words, notably 'the' and 'of'; and her spelling of 'realize' (rather than 'realise') is not standard British usage. Whenever possible the illustrations are linked to relevant passages in the diary. Map 1 shows the Queen's Park neighbourhood in 1950. Map 2 of the surrounding area, 1946, shows Leah's home in relation to her garden allotment in Thistley Green, Bromham.

Almost all of Leah Aynsley's life during these years was experienced within cycling distance of her home. Domesticity, broadly conceived, and gardening were at the centre of her daily life, with access to the countryside being a major complement to her urban existence. Still, as her diary discloses, she had a life beyond home and garden that connected her to a broader and outward-looking culture. Hers was in some respects a limited life (e.g., in terms of travel), in other respects expansive (e.g., through books). A full reading of her diary allows an appreciation of one woman's existence that resists simplified generalisations.

---

[7] We have occasionally drawn on passages from these first two books of her diary (BARS, Z1606/1-2) to help understand her life during her first forty years and her family's history.
[8] These are workbooks catalogued BARS, Z1606/3-6. Leah had numbered them in pencil as books 1–4.

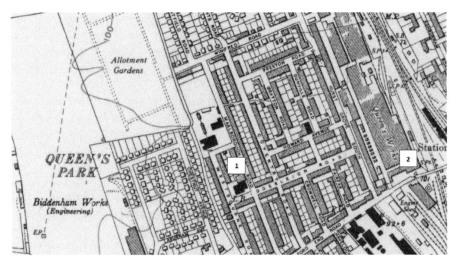

Map 1 Queen's Park, on the western edge of Bedford © Crown Copyright 1946
The main north-south rail line may be seen at the far right edge of the map. The Bedford
passenger station was and still is located just off the top right corner of the map.

1 The Aynsley home, 66 Marlborough Road   2 W.H. Allen & Sons Engineering

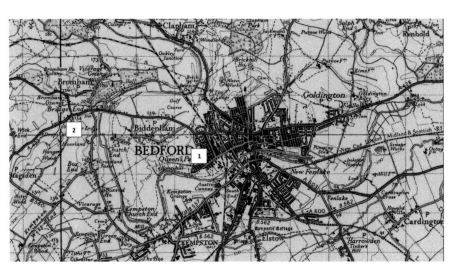

Map 2 Bedford and Surrounding Area Ordnance Survey © Crown Copyright 1946
1 The Aynsley home, Queen's Park, Bedford   2 The Aynsley allotment, Thistley Green, Bromham

1943

Wednesday, 4 January.
I am keeping this diary especially for you Winnnie.[1] I find I have to write such stilted letters to you in Canada, on account of the censor, that you will know very little about us during these war years. So I intend, D.W., to send what I have written after the war is over.

We had a very nice Xmas, but no jollification of any sort. We had the Friday, Saturday and Sunday holiday, which was much better than having to go straight to work on Boxing Day as we have done for the past 2 years. I went out to tea Boxing Day, and on Sunday John [her brother, from Luton] arrived just as I was serving dinner and stayed until after tea. We let him hear my new records, 'Variations on a Theme of Handel's' by Brahms, played by [pianist] Solomon; it takes 3 12" records. Also [her other brother] Jim's new records: Schubert's 'Impromptu in A flat' and a Polonaise of Chopin's.[2]

Before I go any further, Winnie, I must tell you that we are able to have a very good musical education in Bedford. After the intensive Bombing of London the BBC musical section moved to Bedford. They commandeered the Corn Exchange, various Sunday Schools, School Halls, and even the Gas Works recreation hall in Queen's Park.[3] Some of the concerts, such as the fortnightly Symphony Concert, are public. Others are by invitation only. Just before Xmas I was at a Symphony

---

[1] Winnie, a first cousin, was born in 1899 and emigrated to Canada with her family in 1913. She was then Winifred Patterson. Later she married Stan Davis and had one son. Her home town in Canada is never revealed, though it was probably somewhere in southern Ontario. Most of the details concerning Leah's various relatives are provided in the last two volumes of her diary in the Bedfordshire Archives and Records Service (BARS), Z1606/12 & 13.

[2] Leah played the piano; and she sometimes taught students, though not (apparently) in the several years after 1942. Much earlier, on 10 August 1930, she had recorded her gratitude: 'that my mother had taught me to play [piano] fairly well (considering that we are only working people) so I always have this pleasure to fall back on when the weather is bad and I am without companions.' She was also 'glad and thankful that I am very fond of good reading.'

[3] In fact, the BBC's Music Department and Orchestra had first evacuated to Bristol, which was expected to be safer than London, but Bristol was hit hard by heavy raids in 1940–41 and thus safer and more reliable quarters were sought out. Bedford was chosen, partly because it is near London, and in late July 1941 a special train brought the musicians to Bedford from Weston-super-Mare; heavy orchestral instruments were transported by van. The move is described in an appendix ('The BBC Symphony Orchestra Moves to Bedford') to our edited volume, *A Soldier in Bedfordshire 1941–1942: The Diary of Private Denis Argent, Royal Engineers*, BHRS, vol. 88 (Woodbridge, 2009), pp. 184–6. There were already 436 BBC staff members in Bedford by September 1941 (BBC Written Archives Centre, file R13/223). The Music Department made use of several studios, though not all of them full-time, including the Corn Exchange; St Paul's Mission Hall, All Hallow's Lane; Bunyan Schoolrooms, Castle Hill; Bedford School Hall; Co-Partners Club Hall, Lawrence Street in Queen's Park; and Trinity Chapel, St Paul's Church for religious broadcasts (BBC Written Archives Centre, file R35/123). See also below, 29 June 1945, note 38.

Concert conducted by Sir Henry Wood, and on the Sunday evening I was at an invitation concert conducted by Adrian Boult in the Bedford School Hall. This is called a studio concert and you are not allowed to applaud.[4]

John says he has just bought a piano. I am anxious to go through to Luton to try it.

I spent last weekend at the garden.[5] The 2-mile cycle ride to it was very peaceful, with no cars on the road.[6] Two herons were flapping about near Bromham Bridge, and I got off my bike to watch them, also to take breath after fighting a high wind. When I opened the door of the garden hut what a sight met my eyes. Rats had been having a Christmas party with our potatoes. What wasteful creatures they are. There was a pile of potato crisps made by the rats by the door. They had gnawed a hole the size of an orange in the box to get at the potatoes. I do not know where they can have come from as there are no houses near.

Thursday, 7 January.
In the blackout last night Jim was knocked off his bicycle by an army lorry. Fortunately he was not hurt, but as it was raining he got covered with mud when lying on the road. The lorry never stopped. Also at 8.30 p.m. Father went out for ½ hour to get some fresh air. He was out over an hour. He had lost his way in the blackout

---

4   In his memoir, *My Own Trumpet* (London, 1973), p. 120, Sir Adrian Boult recalled that Bedford: 'already overcrowded, welcomed us in a very friendly way, even though some people wondered whether we should attract air raids.... The authorities let us alter the platform of the Corn Exchange, and it made a reasonably good studio, but a rather overpowering concert hall, and when it was used as a Corn Exchange, we moved to the Great Hall of Bedford School. This place with its wooden galleries made a fine sound-box, and the school authorities were most cooperative, only asking that the boys might have access to the galleries, while we often had several hundred troops, American and our own, on the floor.' He also remembered the convenience of the Corn Exchange's location, in the centre of town: 'at the mid-morning break, or the tea interval, it was easy to get sustenance quite near. I used to go across to Woolworths where a friendly Welsh lady would always have a beaker of Ovaltine ready for me.'
5   This garden was an allotment, 100 feet long and 50 feet wide, surrounded by similar garden plots on the south-west outskirts of Bromham. It was just off Thistley Lane, which still remains, and runs south from the main road from Bromham Bridge to Stagsden. The field to the east in the 1940s was 'Thistley Green', which no longer exists: this land is now entirely occupied by postwar housing. In her diary for 23 February 1943 Leah drew two maps of her allotment and its setting. She described Thistley Lane as 'leading to the woods' with a 'hillside rising to South'. To the west was a 'Quarry overgrown with scrub', and there was a poultry farm on the south side of the High Road just west of the lane. The allotment, running east-west, included a hut, tank, and compost bin (see illustration 3).
   Gardening of hardy, nutritious vegetables and fruit was actively encouraged as part of the war effort on the home front to minimise the need for imported produce. By the war's end there were around 1,500,000 allotments under cultivation: Margaret Willes, *The Gardens of the British Working Class* (New Haven and London, 2014), p. 288. Fuller accounts of wartime 'Dig for Victory' campaigns and practices (including allotments) are found in Ursula Buchan, *A Green and Pleasant Land: How England's Gardeners Fought the Second World War* (London, 2014) and Daniel Smith, *The Spade as Mighty as the Sword; The Story of the Second World War 'Dig for Victory' Campaign* (London, 2013).
6   Since petrol for private motoring had been banned since mid-1942, road traffic, aside from military vehicles, was by now very light.

and had to ask his way home! It certainly was very dark – no moon nor stars. I stayed at home – the best place on such a night.

Friday, 8 January.
Nothing to report. One piece of information I would not be able to write you is about all the American soldiers we have stationed near Bedford. At least they are really airmen [members of the US Army Air Force] but they wear khaki like our army. I have been told that they have taken over en bloc most of the aerodromes in the district.[7] They certainly are a thrill to all our flappers. Things came to such a pass with them ringing up the girls at our Works [W.H. Allen & Sons Engineering] that all females were not allowed to have phone calls. The Yanks blocked all the lines for hours!![8]

Monday, 11 January.
Saturday was very frosty so I did not go to the garden. Instead I did some shopping and went to an exhibition of pictures [lasting a fortnight] in the Boys' Modern School gymnasium. It was called 'An Exhibition of Contemporary Paintings' given by CEMA. (Council for the Encouragement of Music and the Arts) but the stuff at that exhibition ought not to be *encouraged*, in fact it ought to be *suppressed*. I have seen some of the modern art, including Surrealism, but never such a collection of tripe as I saw on Saturday. The most discernible thing was a fish's head with some ice on a plate, but who wants to gaze at a fish head on their walls? One picture that looked like a vivid green fish was called 'Fallen Tree at Sunset'.[9]

---

[7]   US air crews were plentiful in north Bedfordshire from later 1942, though not nearly as prominent as they were in East Anglia: airfields of the Eighth Army Air Force are shown on a map in D.A. Lande, *From Somewhere in England: The Life and Times of the 8th AF Bomber, Fighter and Ground Crews in WWII* (np, 1991), p. 10. The main US bases in the county were in Podington and, in particular, Thurleigh (Graham Smith, *Hertfordshire and Bedfordshire Airfields in the Second World War* [Newbury, 1999], chaps 12 and 15).

[8]   Allen's employed some 500 women, around a sixth of their workforce, about ninety percent of them full-time (BARS, Z450/1).

   American servicemen first arrived in Bedfordshire in the summer of 1942 and, as Graham Smith has observed: 'made an immediate impact…. Suddenly, as if by magic, many scarce goods that had all but vanished from the shops, began to filter out from the PX stores – razor blades, cheap cigarettes, sweets (or candies), tinned fruit and ham, chewing gum, and a new commodity – nylons. Soon the lanes and roads were crammed with their large lorries and little omnipresent jeeps. The streets of the nearby towns echoed to the sounds of American accents and became crowded with servicemen…. Bedford, especially, became an off-duty mecca for the GIs with its several Red Cross clubs, and, from the summer of 1944, as the base for Glenn Miller's band.' (*Hertfordshire and Bedfordshire Airfields*, p. 270).

   Another Bedford diarist, a married woman (b. 1898) who volunteered for Mass Observation (no. 5451), wrote on 10 October 1942 of observing: 'a little drama today. A rather coarse type of girl and an American soldier were overtaken by a young civilian in labouring clothes. He made signs of speaking to the girl, but she seized the American's arms and brazenly glared at the Englishman as if to say "See, you are not wanted." He looked crestfallen and hurried off. Not a word had been spoken but a whole tale had been unfolded.' See also below: 29 January 1943, note 15.

[9]   The *Bedford Record*, 5 January 1943, p. 5, described the background to this exhibition. These circulating collections of modern painting and craftsmanship: 'are varied. Six collections by War Artists' pictures are on tour in this county. Other collections are works by living

Crockery is very difficult to get hold of, and the other week I paid 2s 6d for an odd cup and saucer, the only ones in the shop. It was white with narrow blue bands. Saturday I tried to get a white or white and blue plate to go with it but could not. I happened to see a very small bakelite mug, no bigger than a small teacup, so I bought it as I am using a thick ware ½ pint pot for my afternoon tea at the Office, the juniors having broken successive cups and all I could get was this great mug. The little mug was 1s 6½d. I had a cup and saucer given me for a Christmas present, so besides a complete set of 12, we have in the house only 3 odd teacups and 3 breakfast cups. I bought 2 weeks' sweet ration – 6 ounce liquorice all sorts.

On Sunday the frost changed to rain and again I did not go to the garden. I went to see a friend in the afternoon and had a visitor in the evening. Jim went off to fire-watch for his firm at about 9 p.m. Fire-watchers are supposed to go on duty at blackout time, but his firm are lenient and provided there is no raid warning they go what time is convenient as long as they sleep on the premises.[10]

Tuesday, 12 January.
M.A.M. offered me her ticket for the BBC Symphony Concert tomorrow night, but as Father is not too well, and the woman [who helped Leah with housework] has not been in for over a week, I did not accept it.[11]

When I got home from the Office I found a Xmas card from you Winnie, postmark 23/11/42. It had on it 'letter following'; that letter arrived 28/12/42.

I attended the weekly lecture at The Adult School [Co-operative Hall, Midland Road] on 'Living' or 'How to Live' or something like that. There was a lively discussion afterwards. The lecturer, a young clergyman, was the most angelic looking man I've seen. He just needed a white robe and a pair of wings and he would have flown off to heaven!

Scottish artists, of modern French painting, of British landscapes, contemporary portraiture, and allied artists, to mention only a few.' A fortnight later this paper (19 January, p. 1) offered more charitable views than Leah's: 'A lively interest has been shown in these works by artists of today, and many questions have been asked, particularly about the more abstract pictures. These have been readily answered by CEMA [Council for the Encouragement of Music and the Arts] representatives ... [and] the result has been that numbers of visitors have taken at any rate the first step toward the new language in which they are addressed by the more advanced painters of the present day.' (Many Mass Observation diarists expressed a dislike for modern art.) Not all was avant-garde: 'Much of the exhibition has given immediate delight to the visitors, for most of the pictures, of course, use a familiar idiom.' The paper also asked (p. 5) 'Is Bedford really becoming art-conscious at last?' and urged the opening post-war of an art gallery – which in fact happened: the Cecil Higgins Museum (later named the Higgins Art Gallery & Museum) opened in July 1949.

[10] The haphazardness of fire-watching is a prominent theme in Terence H. O'Brien, *Civil Defence* (London, 1955), pp. 595–609, a volume in the *History of the Second World War, United Kingdom Civil Series*, edited by W. K. Hancock.

[11] These public performances in Bedford by BBC musicians were usually advertised in advance and almost always enthusiastically received - 'sheer pleasure' was the verdict on a concert at the Corn Exchange conducted by Adrian Boult (*Bedford Record*, 12 January 1943, p. 5). The BBC Orchestra in Bedford gave both full evening performances and lunch-time concerts (the latter were not broadcast). The location of the site of the musical broadcasts was censored, partly in deference to public fear that to do so would invite an aerial attack on the town (BBC Written Archives Centre, file R61/17, letter of 31 July 1941).

Thursday, 14 January.

Yesterday I called to see Mrs Simpson (the woman who chars and cooks) and find out whether she was back from London. She told me she would have to give up work as she is going to have an operation in London. So I will have to look for another woman. We have had Mrs S. since September. She was a good worker.

I was wondering during the night whether I should try to obtain my release from work and only work afternoons but as that would be only 20 hours a week and at my rate of pay, less the income tax deducted each week for last year, I would only earn £1 a week. I could just manage on that while Father is alive, but Jim has had notice this morning to undergo his medical on Saturday (my birthday), and if he goes in the army I will be the sole support of the house as there is no army allowance for a bachelor's dependents. So it is no use my thinking of part time work yet. I must wait and see.

Monday, 18 January.

As the woman had not turned up all the week up to Friday, and the house was getting in a dirty condition and there is a lot of cooking to do Saturdays, I stayed away from the Office on Saturday morning and got on with it. I cleaned the stairs and passage, scrubbed the front, scrubbed the yard and lavatory and the kitchen, and then I baked. I did feel tired by lunchtime with the unwonted work, and lay down afterwards for more than an hour. Anyway, the place looked fresher. Meanwhile Jim had been for his medical exam. It took nearly all the morning. He passed Grade II as he has bad eyesight and varicose veins. I never knew he had the latter, but apparently he was aware of them himself. Most of the exam seems to have been an intelligence test.

With all the instructions etc. Jim is giving me about the garden, one would think he was going out East in a week or so's time. Actually I have known men not yet called up a year or so after their medical. He is certain he will be called up in a fortnight at the latest. It is unfortunate that he has bought all his seeds for the garden including about ¾ cwt [hundred pounds] seed potatoes. It looks as though I'll have my work set. And who is going to consume the produce when grown?

On Saturday I raked over some of the rough dry ground and on Sunday I planted a row of broad beans as it seems a very mild winter. Also I staked out a new path I have had in my mind for months. I feel that I have done a good bit of work this weekend. On Sunday night we had a raid warning, the first for about 6 months. It only lasted about ¾ hour and I heard no bombs.

I had a letter from my Aunt Tiny in Sunderland. She says she had 2 friends to tea last Wednesday when 'her friends', as she always calls the enemy raiders, came over and they had to finish the tea party in the air-raid shelter. She says my cousin Jessie (who lives with her) is expecting a baby. How awful for her when they are continually having air-raids and her husband is in the bomber command.[12]

---

[12] Aunt Tiny (b. 1878) was an unmarried sister of Leah's father. Jessie Aynsley (b. 1917) had lived with Aunt Tiny after her mother's death in 1921 and until her marriage to Noble Hugill in 1939 (volume thirteen of Leah's diary). One presumes that after Noble joined the RAF, Jessie returned to live with the Aunt who had (more or less) raised her.

Thursday, 21 January.

There was a daylight raid on London yesterday. A school was hit and the 1 o'clock news today said 40 odd children killed, 50 injured and some not accounted for. Reprisals for Berlin I suppose.[13]

Your letter, Winnie, of December 20th arrived this morning. You ask on various points of English speech. That is a safe subject to write on; I need not worry about the censor.

Friday, 22 January.

Last night I was at the Folk Dance Party at the Dujon Restaurant [34–36 High Street]. I enjoyed it very much. This sort of dancing needs every bit of your attention to do it correctly, so that your mind is taken off every worry and I always find it a tonic. There was a Yankee soldier looking on. He said he was a specialist in American Folk Dancing, but he could not be persuaded to take part in our dancing.

This morning a Government envelope came for Jim. I was sure it was his calling up papers and my knees began to shake, but it was a fee they pay them for lost time having their medical exam.

Monday, 25 January.

Not much to record for this weekend. I had friends to tea (Trixy Prentice and Flossie Clark) yesterday and we had music, draughts and solo whist afterwards. Jim went off to fire-watch for the chapel.

Wednesday, 27 January.

I was at the Adult School Christmas party last evening and had what you may call a 'riotous time'. Usually after these affairs I cannot sleep for the first part of the night afterwards (as was the case last Thursday after the Folk Dance). I put this down to drinking tea or coffee during the evening (which I never do at home) so last night I kept strictly to water and slept as well as usual. I bought a fruit cake left over from the refreshments which will do very well for afternoon tea at the Office. I owe them cake for my birthday (on the 16th) but have been unable to get enough cake for 12 people up to the present.

Friday, 29 January.

Nothing much to report. Jim had a letter from Stella [Young]. She is still in bed but sounds cheerful and hopeful. Jim persists in acting as though he would be called up any day. As we will have no army allowance for him (being a bachelor) he has arranged that I am to have the rent of a house he owns. Of course, exactly half of it will go in income tax, but the remainder will be a great help towards keeping our home going. He has even arranged for the tenant to bring the rent to me once a

---

[13] Sandhurst Road School in Catford, south-east London, received a direct hit, killing thirty-eight children and six teachers. There is a detailed account of the raid and its victims, including numerous photographs, in Winston G. Ramsey, *The Blitz Then and Now,* vol. 3 (London, 1990), pp. 204–14. On 16 and 17 January 1943 the RAF conducted its first major raids on Berlin since November 1941.

month. Also he has sold some of the seed potatoes, so there won't be quite so many to have to plant.

Ken Liller, one of the younger engineers in our Department, has left today. He has been longing to get into one of the Services for 2–3 years but the company would not release him. At last they have released him and he has got a commission in a new electrical section of the Royal Engineers. It seems a pity for the Company to have the power to hold back young men who are eager to be off to serve their country. Of course, they are supposed to be helping the war in our Factory, and we get representatives of the Navy, Army, and RAF, telling us how useful we are, but a lot of us have idle time on our hands and the young men don't like it.[14]

We have had American airmen stationed near the town since about last September. The local paper has been having a lot to say about the poor hospitality the town has offered them. Apparently something is being done about it in the way of recreation/clubhouse for them, with sleeping accommodation if they get stranded in the town. Of course private people have entertained them, but I used to think it was awful when I passed through the town on a dark wet night, to see them mouching about (or rather hear them) with nowhere to go.[15] I suppose Bedford having had 17,000 official evacuees,[16] other evacuees, foreign refugees, several thousand war

14 Leah worked as a secretary for W.H. Allen & Sons Engineering in Queen's Park, which was a major supplier to the Navy and merchant marine; the former took 60% of the company's production (W.H. Allen Engineering Association website).
15 The Bedford woman mentioned above (note 8) wrote on 12 September 1942 of local tensions concerning the recently-arrived Americans: 'Today I heard children mocking at American voices and I thought it a great pity that their ignorance goes unchecked. Some of the young Americans look rather forlorn and I often wish I could invite them to my home. There should be some organisation to act as a go-between our Americans guests and ourselves.' The Women's Voluntary Services (WVS) was already attending to some of these Americans' needs and would continue to do so. WVS Narrative Reports indicate that members assisted the American Red Cross with an information desk and supplied helpers at Bedford's busy multinational canteen, which many Americans made use of (March and June 1943); and as early as July 1943 the borough's WVS was cooperating with the American Red Cross 'in recommending solicitors to help Americans who are in trouble, for example, wanting to divorce an English wife!' (Royal Voluntary Service Archive & Heritage Centre, Devizes, Wiltshire. Jennifer Hunt kindly gave us access to this material for 1943.) This observation points to the existence of at least a few over-hasty Anglo-American marriages.
Hospitality for Americans a few weeks earlier had already served as a signal for the future. On Friday, 19 December 1942 local school-teachers held a Christmas party for fifty to sixty American troops; and around 100 Bedford families 'shared their homes with American Servicemen during Christmas tide' some entertaining two or more Americans (*Bedford Record*, 22 December 1942, p. 3 and 29 December, p. 1).
Several weeks later there were further signs that appropriate hospitality was being extended to these American visitors: 'It will no doubt please those who have been giving hospitality[in private houses] to the Americans to hear that they really do appreciate it even if they don't keep writing letters saying so.' 'We are treated just as if we were the sons' some of the young Americans had reputedly declared (*Bedford Record*, 9 February 1943, p. 5). They could also relax in the lounge of the new American Red Cross Centre in High Street (*Bedford Record*, 16 February 1943, p. 1).
16 This was the estimated number of government-sponsored evacuees in early September 1939, most of them London schoolchildren, many of whom returned home during the following half-year. Still, Bedford in 1942/43 remained a congested place, as many sources attest.

workers from other towns and a host of B.B.C. artists and technicians billeted on it, the town's resources have got rather sucked dry.[17]

Monday, 1 February.

This has been a weekend of high winds and rain. On Sunday morning the trellis in the backyard threatened to blow down so it had to be tied to the apple tree to relieve the strain. In the afternoon I felt I needed to go out so wrapped up well and set off for the garden to get a week's supply of Brussels sprouts. I had to walk most of the 2 miles as the wind was so high, but I enjoyed it. I stopped at Bromham Bridge. This is a Roman bridge with 26 arches and a water mill next to it.[18] It is a lovely scene with the trees of Bromham Park in the background, the weir where boys are fond of bathing, and a row of willow trees near the mill, and a large low-lying meadow in the foreground that is a carpet of buttercups in Spring. Today the river was in flood and racing in streams across the meadow. When I reached our garden I found the roof of the hut had blown right off! There was a jumbled heap of corrugated iron sheets and beams of wood that had been holding it down. As Jim cannot get up in daylight until next weekend I arranged with a man nearby to replace it, but apparently I have done the wrong thing and should have left the matter to Jim. To crown all a terrific rainstorm came on and I was soaked to the skin. My mac was still dripping water by supper time. When I got home the rain stopped and there was a magnificent orange sunset with a complete rainbow in the east.

Tuesday, 2 February.

Last night I had a fit on and turned out the pantry that runs under the stairs and scrubbed the floor. That is all I intended to do at first, but I went on and cleaned 3 shelves by the gas oven, the top shelf of the delph-rack with 3 huge meat plates that adorn it (but never get set on the table) and the floor in the corner next the gas oven was very dirty so I scrubbed it with strong soda water. After that, 8.30 p.m., I was dog tired and wished I'd only done the pantry. I can still feel the effects this morning.

Thursday, 4 February.

Life rolls uneventfully along. I went to lecture on 'Raw Materials' on Tuesday night, and to Folk-dance class last night. They were two starry moonless nights and as I have read there is a new comet about, I keep star gazing as I am walking along. It is a wonder I don't get knocked down in the 'blackout'. I have not seen any comet.

One of the engineers in our Department is a Home Guard 'Commando'. They have to go through a strenuous training, and late Saturday night, wearing plimsolls they had to jump over what appeared to be a 4 foot wall but there was a 10 foot

---

[17] When the BBC's music department arrived in Bedford in May 1941, the town – as Adrian Boult recalled – was 'already crammed with refugees'. The BBC needed forty offices and was allowed to take over two residential hotels, thereby squeezing further Bedford's capacity for housing (*My Own Trumpet*, p. 119).

[18] While this bridge went back to the Middle Ages, most of it was a result of rebuilding in 1813.

drop on the other side and he broke his ankle. The hospital says he has broken bones that very rarely get broken and it will take 6–9 months to mend. At the end of 3 months they hope to put his foot in irons so that he can get about. Poor Gerry – he'll go mad with inactivity for so long, as he likes to be always on the go and is no bookworm. So with Ken Liller leaving last week we are 2 engineers short. The rest will have to 'pull their socks up'. I don't know whether I have mentioned it, but Jim is in the Home Guard – not in the commando section, however. They have made him a stretcher bearer; he had asked to be in the Signals section.

Friday, 5 February.
All yesterday morning and again in the evening and during the night there was the incessant drone of 'Fortresses'.[19] I said to myself yesterday morning that some poor humans were going to have a hellish time in 2 or 3 hours – and sure enough this morning's paper says the Americans attacked Germany yesterday; some say there were 500 planes. It is a direful sound when perhaps early in the evening, plane after plane wends its way east or south-east, and then you are wakened very early in the morning when they are all coming back. You wonder what has happened somewhere, and whether the boys in the planes are badly wounded, because sometimes the engines have a very lame sound. In the early years of the war, when they were enemy planes that throbbed endlessly, the main sensation was fear; and early in the evening you wondered whether Coventry or Birmingham were 'for it' this time, and when they were returning later you hoped there were no spare bombs they'd unload over you.[20]

Monday, 8 February.
Saturday afternoon was stormy so I went shopping instead of to the garden. I spent the last 11 [ration] points of the period on biscuits and sago. There were tins of fruit about but were not to be sold until the next rationing period – today. On Sunday the weather was lovely – quite spring-like when sheltered from the wind and of course I spent the afternoon at the garden, mainly doing landscape gardening, trying to get new paths level and such like.[21] Imagine my surprise to find a heavy frost this morning and the ice so thick on the rainwater tub that I couldn't break it. The vagaries of the English climate. Frost all went and rain at night. Turned out bookcase.

Wednesday, 10 February.
I think I have found the comet. On Saturday night I found a 'smudge' near one of the stars in the 'Great Bear'. It was starry again last night (but moonlight) and I

---

[19] She added a correction in a space beside this entry: 'They could not have been Forts during the night.' (These US planes, Boeing B-17s, were used mainly or entirely for daylight bombing.)
[20] It was routine for German planes on their way home to jettison any bombs not used against their principal target, and occasionally the result was inadvertent English casualties.
[21] Gardens were not only utilitarian; they also had aesthetic and recreational dimensions, and were a source of much personal satisfaction. Leah was often concerned with the design features of her garden (as were others: Willes, *Gardens of the British Working Class*, chap. 12). Gardening was a common outlet for creative impulses, then as now.

saw this smudge had moved away from near that particular star. I wish I had a telescope. Jim lent his out. Wrote S.A.

There was a full house at the lecture last night including 2 Indian students. It was on our 'Political Liberties'. The lecturer had lived for years at the Hague, and seems to have lived in a good many other countries, including U.S.A., and told us about some of the funny laws in some of the States in this last country. With the Indian students being there I thought it was going to be rather awkward when he said that backward people should not be allowed to have a democratic government. He gave instances where such rule had failed, and luckily he kept off the Indian question altogether. Nobody mentioned it in the discussion that followed either.

On the way home from work I tried to buy a pair of lisle stockings, as follows: 1st shop shut, 2nd shop no 8½", 3rd and 4th shut, 5th shop no lisle stockings, 6th shop I got a pair – 3 coupons. Even now they are not what I want, but I don't want to give up more coupons on stockings at present – nor waste a precious Saturday afternoon hunting.

Friday, 12 February.
Weather very spring-like. Washed hair last night. This book is going to be useful for keeping records of letters etc. Wrote Mrs Leedham and Lily [her sister-in-law in Luton].

Monday, 15 February.
This has been a very nice weekend. Spring is in the air. At the garden I got one of the paths levelled to my satisfaction, and planted radishes and a lupin plant; also pruned gooseberry bushes. I see that one of the gooseberry cuttings I planted in autumn has taken. Jim planted an onion bed and some rows of parsnips. On Sunday afternoon I spent an hour at the garden and raked the other path level. I feel pleased with myself as that is a nasty job off my mind. Although fallen somewhat, the river is still in flood and at Bromham Mill [dating from c. 1800] I was surprised to see a man and 2 children trying to get a canoe upstream. They were having a tough time when I crossed the bridge. After tea I went to see my friends Flora and Bernard Arnold [at 14 Oak Road]. She is 39 and going to have her first baby in the summer. They do not know whether they are glad or sorry. I think it is a good thing. She is still at her work where she has been for 25 years (her cousin's stationery and printing business) and I think she will welcome the change of getting away from there. Here, married women under a certain age who have no children under 14, have to go to work for at least half-days.[22]

Wednesday, 17 February.
Had a card from Lily yesterday. She says it will be O.K. for me to go on Sunday. Her sister Vera is getting married on Saturday. Lily has been in bed with rheumatism in her foot. There *is* a lot of rheumatism about for all it's been such a mild winter. These last 3 days mine has spread from my back down the right thigh to behind the knee, and sometimes I feel it in the calf. I have been taking Boots Rheumatic Saline

---

[22] However, they would not have been required to leave home to take up 'essential' work.

for the last month and my back has felt worse since. I thought it was because the Saline was driving the rheumatism out of my system that made it feel worse, and I have bought another bottle to give it a good trial, but I am certainly not getting any relief. One of the neighbours has had sciatica and asked my Father if I could tell him a cure for it. I said 'tell Mr. Billing that it is just what I want to know myself now.'

For my own record I must mention that on Monday I cleaned cupboard shelves, chiffonier, and cutlery drawer; I am trying to do some turning out of dirty corners every Monday night.

I had a letter from my Aunt Sarah at Worthing this morning. She says they had 2 raids last week; 9 killed and 30 taken to hospital. Worthing is 10 miles from Brighton on South Coast. She sent me a blue wool scarf and a pom-pom ornament for a coat or hat.

Monday, 22 February.
Cleaned out chiffonier and scullery drawers.

Saturday afternoon was spring-like again but as I felt the rheumatism bad I did not reach the garden until nearly 4 o'clock, but that was partly due to calling at the village shop on my way for some chocolates. I had never been in before. It is a lovely tiny little shop; the sort I should like for myself. All the fittings were highly varnished and all the goods neatly placed and labelled. Outside the window was a garden as neat as the shop, with coloured primroses and crocuses in bloom and a blackbird hopping about. I had to wait about ¼ hour watching the village people getting their odds and ends (including paraffin oil for their lamps) before it was my turn.

At the garden I thinned out turnips (planted in the autumn), planted out pansies at the 4 corners where 2 paths cross, and sowed some spinach. While I was busy a little elderly lady (about 50 at least) passed. She wore very townified clothes and thin high heeled shoes. I wondered what she was up to as there was nothing but ploughed field and hedge the way she was going. She stood at the hedge a long time and then came back. She stopped and spoke to me and got very chatty. She has bought a bit of land in the far corner of the field (bog at present) and is going to cultivate it herself. She either does not know what she is in for, or she is very plucky. She is looking forward to a nice lawn with fruit trees and bringing her tea on a Saturday afternoon. She has no hut for her implements and no fence up. She says all she needs is a fork and she is going to bring that with her every time. She lives 3 miles away on the other side of Bedford, so she'll have that fork to carry 6 miles every time. She has a very high hedge on the *south* side of the land (the land is 40' x 50'). She is going to trim it with a pair of secateurs!!! It is the sort of hedge that Jim tackled with an axe and a saw. She talks and looks far too refined for all the rough work that will be needed on that bit of land, but she seemed enraptured with the lovely air and the birds singing and she will probably be happy pottering on a little bit of land of her own away from the town. Good luck to her. At this point I think you ought to have a sketch to see the 'lay of the land' near the garden.[23]

---

[23] She attached two pages of maps she had drawn of the gardens and fields near the High Road in Bromham.

On Sunday afternoon I went to Luton [her brother's house at 61 Carlton Crescent]. How those girls [her nieces] grow. Jacqueline (9 last month) is as tall as her mother. I could easily have worn the raspberry pink frock she had on. I said to them 'I don't know where you spring from – both your Mummy and Daddy's people are small.' Janet said 'Perhaps we are starting a new line'!! Janet had new blue frock in the same style – both made by Lily. They looked very elegant. [See Illustration 2.] The reason Lily has been in bed is she has had rheumatism in her feet and it has made her heart bad. Her sister was married on Saturday and Lily made and iced the cake. John made the pillars between the tiers and silvered them. The piano is rather nice, but it wants someone to practise scales on it a few hours a day. Coming home in the train, which was full of men and women in the services, a Land Girl offered me her seat. I must be looking old [she was 41] as this is the first time a grown woman has offered me her seat. I did not accept it but stood all the journey.[24]

Tuesday, 23 February.
On the strong recommendation of my Aunt Tiny I have started sodium salicylate for rheumatism every morning. I will continue to take Boot's Rheumatism Saline twice daily – it will be kill or cure. Wrote C.M.C.

Monday, 1 March.
Last Thursday I asked Miss Barber if I could work on a ¾ time basis, i.e. come in at 10.30 a.m. instead of 8.30 a.m., as I cannot get any domestic help. She said only the National Service Officer could decide that and she did not think he would agree. When I pointed out that it might be only temporary, until I could get a woman, she said she would look into it. I have not heard any more. On Friday I was racked with rheumatism and felt so ill I went straight to bed from the Office. Saturday morning I felt better in my head but stiff and weak and got up to go to the doctor but as I moved around I felt better and went to the Office at 9.40 and gradually felt better as the day went on.

I did not do much at garden – but planted some Lily of the Valley. Broad beans are pushing through. Wrote S.A. regarding scarf.

Tuesday, 2 March.
Miss Barber told me that my request to be put on ¾ time has been granted. I am to have 2 hours off every day for household jobs. The snag is that I have to do *all* my office work in ¾ of the time with ¾ of the pay, but I think I'll survive that.

Wednesday, 3 March.
When I got home last night I found a letter from William Forsyth saying that Aunt Isabella [Forsyth, of 16 Adelaide Square, Bedford] died on Monday and the funeral is today (Wednesday). She is 73. My Mother, your Mother, and Aunt Lil all died in February; Aunt Eliza was killed at end of January and was buried in February,

---

[24] Members of the Women's Land Army in the county are the subject of Stuart Antrobus's detailed and informative book, *'We Wouldn't Have Missed it for the World': The Women's Land Army in Bedfordshire, 1939–1950* (Copt Hewick, 2008).

and now that last sister has just cleared February – in fact if it had been Leap Year would have died in February. Strange isn't it?[25]
Later.
I went to Aunt B's funeral: a very simple service in the cemetery chapel and only the family and Jim and I present. The syrens went during the evening but I heard no bombs dropped. I understand that our cousin, Lily Richardson, lives at a Royal Ordnance Factory (called Chimney Corner) near Bedford. Her policeman husband was transferred to duty at the factory. She is a complete stranger to me and I would not know her by sight, but Mabel served her in the shop. Washed hair.

Thursday, 4 March.
Warning at 5 a.m. I heard a bomb drop in distance after the syrens sounded but I did not get out of bed. There was a dreadful catastrophe in London last night – 178 people were crushed to death in the entrance to an air-raid shelter. Apparently a woman with a baby tripped and fell, an old man fell on her, and all the incoming crowd followed suit. It is increditable [incapable of being believed]. Either there must have been no light so that no-one could see what was ahead, or there must have been a dreadful panic among the crowd seeking shelter. There were 19 steps down to the shelter and the woman fell at the bottom.[26]

Monday, 8 March.
Spring is getting into full swing. The almond trees are in bloom and so is the yellow forsythia. Snowdrops, crocuses and double daffodils are blooming. My gooseberry bushes have some leaves. I planted some carrot seed yesterday. It was very hot up at the garden and I did not need a coat to work in, but this morning white frost and fog until 10 a.m. I am on ¾ time and don't start at Office until 10.30. It is killing doing all this housework first. I wish I could stop myself doing so much.

Jim, Father and I went to tea at my friend's Trixy Prentice [at 28 Kingsbrook Road] on Saturday. There were 3 other guests and we had a very jolly evening. Trix had managed a very good spread – almost prewar in variety, if not in quality: cress, crab paste, 2 sorts of jam, buttered (?)[27] tea cake, jelly, stewed prunes, tinned plums, little cakes, and 2 large cakes!! She said she had been saving up for the party. Since her Father and Mother died recently she has had her old Aunt (Miss Prentice or Aunt Alice) living with her. She is 86 and reads and darns without glasses. I asked about her sister (aged 93) in New Zealand and she said 'Oh she's very well and she's buying a lot of new clothes'!! On account of having her old Aunt, Trixy need only work afternoon, so she has mornings to hunt for foodstuffs.[28]

---

[25] 'All bad luck happens in February', she wrote on 27 February 1931, when her father was dismissed from his job at Vauxhall Motors.
[26] The story of this tragedy at the Bethnal Green Tube Station shelter is presented in detail in Ramsey, *The Blitz Then and Now*, vol. 3, pp. 220–9. Some people blamed the tragedy on Jews, a reflection of the widespread anti-Semitism of the period (Wendy Webster, *Mixing It: Diversity in World War Two Britain* [Oxford, 2018], p. 145).
[27] Perhaps Leah wondered if margarine had been used.
[28] In other words, because she needed to care for a dependent relative, the Labour Exchange only required her to work part-time.

Friday, 12 March.
I have had a week of this ¾ time. It is tough job. I am hard at it from 7.45 a.m. to 9.45 a.m. and then I have 10 minutes to rest, and change and get off to the office.

Monday, 15 March.
This diary is going to be very dull I can see. Lovely weather over the weekend and I did some gardening, but I do wish it would rain: it is weeks since we had any. During the last fortnight the army have been having maneouvres all over the Bedford district. They have slung all their own cables along the streets and along the hedges, and trees to Bromham (2½ miles). Yesterday the men were taking all the cables down and reeling it in on drums. Talk about getting wool in a tangle; the men had those cables in a hopeless mess along the Bromham Road. That lovely field below Bromham Bridge near the mill is all churned up with tanks and there is a fearsome looking gun in a cabbage field nearby. Jim has made me a nice chair for the garden and I sat sewing in it yesterday afternoon. I planted the Christmas rose given me by Flossie Clarke in our back garden yesterday.

    Father was very poorly Friday night. Was very sick. He looks terribly frail and I wish I was at home altogether. At any rate I did everything possible this morning and he only had to cook greens and potatoes and warm gravy [for his mid-day meal].

Thursday, 18 March.
A Mrs Simmons called last night and offered to work mornings for me, so I have arranged for her to start Friday and I will show her round. Father was very sick Monday and again yesterday. He went to the doctor this morning but would not let me go with him (to see about diet etc.). Neither would he let the doctor give him an injection and did not tell him how long he had been sick, so I am afraid we are in for a packet with Father. His craziness makes it difficult. As soon as he stops being sick he is ready for a good meal – and has it. He won't give his inside a rest.

Friday, 19 March.
Cold, gray[29] day with north wind (got called away and forgot what I was going to say).

Monday, 22 March.
It is now spring. They say down here 'There are as many frosts in May as fogs in March.' We are going to have *very* frosty May if that is anything to go by – fogs every morning, but lovely afternoons. I planted foxglove seeds by the hedge on Saturday. Have you ever seen foxglove seeds? They are as fine as pepper. Certainly, there need be no fear of the birds pecking them as they would never be able to see them spread out. A boy went down the lane at the back of the hedge with a lovely bunch of primroses, so yesterday I quit gardening and went to the wood instead. I picked a small bunch of primroses and then sat on a bent tree and just looked round, with the place all to myself. It was heavenly. There is going to be a vast carpet of bluebells soon. I must go again, as it is only 10 minutes walk from the garden.

---

[29] Leah here deviates from the customary British usage 'grey'.

From what I could see it is not so pretty as 'my' wood. This is a wood I often go to alone and always refer to it as 'my wood' as I never knew its name. It is about 4 miles from Bedford. It is on a hill and has wide grassy sides and clearings and the primroses look so pretty all among the grass (instead of poking out of dead leaves and twigs) and there are *banks* of violets and wood anemones – and being on a hill you get a wide view down the rides. In the early days of the war when they stopped bank holidays, to make the most of Whitsun I got up on the Sunday morning and went to the wood *before* breakfast just to see the bluebells and I had all that wood to myself. I came home with bluebells, buttercups and white May got from near Bromham Bridge. The following Easter Sunday I went again, and in one of the prettiest glades I found a bomb crater, with all the trees and shrubs round it blackened and dead with the blast. Jerry certainly made a miss that time, but it was a desecration.

I am reading another Yankee book, *The Happy Mountain* [by Maristan Chapman, 1928]. It is about 'homemade' boys and girls who have never seen towns and cities and live in the mountains. I should never have believed there were such people in America in the 20th century. It is very enjoyable now that I can understand the language. They use a very queer English (and so does the writer), not a bit like you hear at the movies.[30] I recently read an American book called *Village Chronicle* [by James McConnaughey, 1936] about a small university town in Georgia, but it was horrid – all lipstick, matrimonial troubles, nigger baiting etc., just like we imagine America to be from the films and magazines. I like the mountain people much better. Some years ago I read *The Country of the Pointed Firs* [by Sarah Orne Jewett, 1896]. I forget who it is by. It is an American classic I think, and I liked it.[31]

I had a letter from Sunderland this morning with newspaper cuttings. They had their worst raid of the war last week. St Thomas church destroyed, town hall, secondary school and children's hospital badly damaged. There were not many casualties. They have had a time since the war began up there. My Aunt Tiny says food is hard to get and some days they have to go without dinner. I do not know whether that is because of dislocation through the raids, or whether it is always difficult in the large towns. I am certainly thankful we moved to Bedford where you'd hardly know there was a war on (except for hard work). Did I ever mention

---

[30] *The Happy Mountain* is the tale of a young man who sets out from his remote mountain home to learn more about the world, and returns home to marry his beloved (not without a dash of American violence). The writing is evocative of simpler times, with much topographical description, local turns of phrase, superstitions and folk customs. To some English readers it might have seemed like an exotic version of Thomas Hardy's *The Woodlanders*. A man described as '"a shambling moldwarp"' (p. 80) could easily have fitted into Hardy's world.

[31] *Village Chronicle* is actually set in North Carolina – during the years of Prohibition. The novel is a colourful portrait of life in a small college town, including fraternity initiations (some violent), football, faculty politics, plagiarism and infidelities, most well-lubricated with bootlegged alcohol. *The Country of the Painted Firs* is a gentle tale of a summer spent by a writer in a small port in Maine, learning the residents' stories and manners. The writer's landlady grows medicinal herbs, dispenses tinctures and advice and scours the forest in search of a secret patch of pennyroyal and other wild plants – a feature of the book that Leah surely enjoyed. This paragraph suggests the range of Leah's reading, as do numerous later diary entries.

that our old house at 11 Hendon Burn Avenue was burnt out with incendiaries last Autumn? I thought yesterday afternoon when I was walking on a grassy path over the hill to the wood, 'Fancy me, with all my cares behind, enjoying this lovely place, when there is so much suffering in the world.' On the way down again, however, there was terrific roaring although I could not see a thing – and then over the edge of the hill came 12 planes and [it] seemed as if they were coming straight at me.

All the engineers at our factory, 45 years old and under, have to re-register as there is a great need for engineering officers in the army. We have already lost Ken Tiller, and now they want his substitute, Ian Ord, and Gerry Goodwin (who is away with a broken ankle). Also Mr Burditt, an older engineer, has not been replaced when he left 3 weeks ago to go to a factory in Gloucester. It is a wonder they ever let him go, but they did not realize there was going to be this 'comb-out'.

At lunch-time they were all talking about Churchill's speech broadcast last night. None of them were pleased with it; I did not listen to it as I take no account of speeches – talk is so easy to some people.[32]

They have been collecting for a wedding-present today for Mr. [Henry James] Garrard and Miss [Kathleen] Rogers. He is a man of about 55 and is Head of the Sales Department; he is a widower with two grown up sons. She is his typist aged 26. She will certainly be an old (and rich) man's darling,[33] but I do not envy her.

---

[32] Almost at the beginning of this major speech the Prime Minister cited a view of the war that he was keen to reject: 'It was clear to me that a good many people were so much impressed by the favourable turn in our fortunes which has marked the last six months that they have jumped to the conclusion that the war will soon be over.' However, his main focus was on 'post-war and domestic issues' (matters that he generally preferred not to discuss). While many people were already looking forward to post-war reforms that would make Britain a better society (for example, the welfare changes proposed in the Beveridge Report of December 1942, which had been enthusiastically received), Churchill expressed caution: 'we must be aware of attempts to over-persuade or even to coerce His Majesty's Government to bind themselves or their unknown successors, in conditions which no one can foresee and which may be years ahead, to impose great new expenditure on the State without any relation to the circumstances which might prevail at that time, and to make them pledge themselves to particular schemes without relation to other extremely important aspects of our post-war needs.'

Churchill's reluctance to make any firm commitments to plans for post-war social improvement was probably the main reason for these listeners' displeasure with what he had to say. He did, however, endorse the idea of a Four Years' Plan 'for the period of transition and reconstruction which will follow the downfall of Hitler.' This Plan ('no promises but every preparation', dependent on sound finances) – and here he was setting the bar fairly high - 'would cover five or six large measures of a practical character which must all have been the subject of prolonged, careful, energetic preparation beforehand, and which fit together into a general scheme.' And he offered strong support to 'national compulsory insurance for all classes for all purposes from the cradle to the grave.' But it would have been hard not to conclude that his overall sympathies were, like those of his Conservative Party, more with individual freedom and enterprise than with government planning (Robert Rhodes James, ed., *Winston S. Churchill: His Complete Speeches 1897–1963*, vol. 7 [London and New York, 1974], pp. 6755–65).

[33] Trained as an electrical engineer, Garrard lived in a flat at 43 Shakespeare Road, a large Victorian house in an affluent neighbourhood just north of Queen's Park. See also below: 16 June 1943, note 56.

She wants to work half days only of course. But the Ministry of Labour says she must keep on full time. Rather hard lines for her, as I know there is no fun in keeping house and being out at work all day – and it would be still worse if you had been used to an easy life as I am sure she has.

Tuesday, 23 March.
My last night's weekly job was turning out the store cupboard. It used to be the 'sideboard bed'. Do you remember it? The bed was taken out and two deep shelves put in, as well as the bottom. I keep all the war stores in it and glass and china on the top shelf. I still have the tin of strawberry jam you sent, and the tin of lemon juice and one jelly. There were 20 lbs. sugar, the result of my not taking sugar in drinks and of having dinner at the canteen. I will be able to make some more jam. There were 13 lbs. of Jam, jelly, and marmalade. We are each allowed 1 lb. preserves per month, which we usually have in marmalade, but we had mincemeat in December.

It is a month today since I started taking sodium salicylate, but I still have rheumatic pains. The leg pains usually start mid-afternoon. They vanish when I get to bed.

Except for saying that Lily Richardson lived there, I do not think I have mentioned the Royal Ordnance Factory near Bedford. It was built shortly after the big blitzes and Bedford fully expected to receive a share of the bombing the next winter, but apparently the Germans have not heard of it. It is 7 miles long, and is supposed to be partly underground, or at any rate it is banked up with earth and turfed so it looks like the fields. Thousands of people were billeted on Bedford to work there, and lots of Bedford girls were forced to go and work there. You can tell them by the golden sheen on them; their skin and hair gets covered with a golden powder; it is explosive. Now the tale goes about that they have made enough of that sort of ammunition to last the war (how long is that I wonder?) and the work-people are being drafted elsewhere. It was the dread of all the girls and women not in Government controlled jobs of being sent to 'chimney corner', the R.O.F.'s unofficial name. The work was monotonous, the pay *small*, and there was the danger of explosions. There has only been one of these last, and a pretty girl I know got her face badly burnt, but she looks all right again now.[34]

[34] This Royal Ordnance Factory (ROF) was opened in February 1942 south of Bedford, between Elstow and Wilstead. It was managed by agents of the catering company, J. Lyons, and was responsible for filling and packing munitions – one of some sixteen such factories in the country. The hazards of working in these factories are documented in Jack Hyams, *Bomb Girls: Britain's Secret Army: The Munitions Women of World War II* (London, 2013). *Rules of the Danger Area, Elstow Ordnance Factory*, a pamphlet published in 1942 by J. Lyons, was a local attempt to deal with these hazards (a copy is held in Bedford Central Library, Bedfordshire Heritage Library). Elstow's ROF produced some 100,000 tons of bombs, in due course specialising in the huge 4,000 pound bombs, some 25,000 of which it delivered to Bomber Command. At its height the factory employed more than 3,000 people (H.E. Bates, *The Tinkers of Elstow: The Story of the Royal Ordnance Factory run by J. Lyons & Company Limited for the Ministry of Supply during the World War of 1939–1945* [privately printed, 1946]; *Bedfordshire Times*, 15 February 1963, p. 9).

Thursday, 25 March.

Last night I made myself a brew with celery seeds. It is supposed to be good for rheumatism.

I had a letter from Lily; she is in bed with pains in her back and chest. The doctor does not know what it wrong and she is going to hospital for an exam. Wrote to Lily. Also I had a letter from my old friend Cissie in Sunderland. She too has been in bed a month with congestion of the lungs and nobody to look after her but odd people coming in. She had to stay in bed when Sunderland had its worst raid on March 14th, and the doors were blown open with the blast and the knobs flew off. I had a 3rd letter from friend near Stockton-on-Tees. She was in Sunderland on the 15th March and her expression of it is 'what a mess'.

The reason Cissie has more than one door to her bedroom is that they live in a flat like you did, Winnie, in Trevor Terrace [Sunderland], but she used the middle room for bedroom. The poor souls on the coasts have had raids the whole of the war; they must be nervous wrecks.

Monday, 29 March.

Yesterday Bedford and District went on to the Milk Distribution Scheme. That is, every district has to have only one milkman to save petrol, tyres, time etc. instead of a number of men having customers in the same street. We used to have ours from a farm in the country but now we have it from a dairy at the end of the street. Luckily he sells fresh milk and not pasteurised. I am not in favour of pasteurised milk. I thought the new man would put us on to the bare ration (2 pints per week per person) but he says we can have 2 pints a *day* for the family. Our old man let us have 1½ pints a day and I always kept mum about it as I read only the other week that any dairyman found exceeding the ration would be punished.[35] To balance this improvement our baker left word that he cannot deliver any more cakes. He has been leaving us one (sometimes very poor) every Saturday.

I went to the garden on Saturday afternoon. I planted another row of onions, and climbing nasturtiums near the posts; also some young rhubarb plants from back garden at home, where I have been raising them. Some of my friends walked by on their way to the woods and hailed me.

On Sunday I had a real day of rest for once in a while. In the afternoon I went to bed with a book, a biography of D.H. Lawrence. I am afraid he is somewhat incestuous, but he sent me to sleep.[36] After an early tea I went to meet a crowd who were going to a concert by the BBC. Theatre Orchestra and Singers. We met early

---

35 The new arrangements for the retail deliveries of milk, as one authority has observed: 'provided for the allocation, by exchange of customers, to each dairyman of exclusive delivery rights in a block of adjacent streets.' The objective was to avoid waste of time and materials. At their peak these rationalisation schemes covered almost eighty per cent of the British population: 'They were estimated then to have saved approximately one-third of the total vehicle-miles employed in milk delivery at the time of their initiation, and comparable savings in manpower and rubber tires.' (R.J. Hammond, *Food and Agriculture in Britain 1939–45: Aspects of Wartime Control* [Stanford, CA, 1954], p. 107). Rubber was precious, especially after Japan's conquests from late 1941 cut off supplies from traditional sources in the Far East.

36 This book was probably by Catherine Carswell, *The Savage Pilgrimage* (1932).

as the concert was in Bedford School Hall and no seats bookable. In our crowd were Mr. Clutterbuck (an Englishman who has lived all over the world and, until the war, only the first 5 years of his life in England), and his French wife and two Hindu students. The concert was lovely, all light classical stuff – opera, overtures, Sibelius' *Valse Triste*, Mozart's *Magic Flute* etc. – and there were 2 solo singers. It was a charity concert and a collection was made for the welfare of the Services in Bedfordshire.[37] Coming home after the concert I absolutely sped along. I felt I could walk miles with ease. I suppose it was after having a restful day.

I have bought you *Monarch of the Glen* [1941], a book by Compton MacKenzie [1883–1972], that I enjoyed reading very much. I hope you have not already read it. I didn't know we could send parcels to Canada but I found we could, so think you deserve a little return for the parcels you have sent us.

After the usual news at lunch-time they announced that the German fortifications in North Africa, the Mareth Line, are in our hands. We have had a Major St John in the Office today discussing with Mr Townsend machines for making heavy wire mesh. This wire netting is for laying on the sand (or any rough ground) and is all that is necessary for planes to take off and land on (instead of all the concrete runways they made in France). After discussing the Mareth Line [fortifications in Tunisia] with his customer, Mr Townsend got a bit worried and suggested that as we were driving the enemy out of Africa the wire mesh machines would not be needed!!! I felt quite ashamed of him showing such a mentality, but the other man laughed and said 'We will probably want the netting all the way to Berlin – carry on with it.'

By-the-way, all down the outside of the offices we have wire netting hanging (fine chicken run stuff). It is about 18 inches away from the wall, and looks like a veil over the building. It is supposed to be some sort of protection in case of invasion, but Heaven help us if it was all the protection we had, as the wind wafts it anywhere and it looks just like a lace veil. At first it made one feel like a monkey looking out of a cage at the zoo.

Tuesday, 30 March.
This is Stock-taking and I ought to have started work at 8 a.m. I thought it funny that everybody had arrived before me and all the bike racks were full; then in the cloak-room nobody was about and all the clothes hanging up. As I am not actually Stock-taking (everybody has to work overtime whether taking stock or not) I never remembered anything until the girl came to offer me refreshments which we only get in the mornings on this special occasion. I came to with a nasty bump then, as it means working late and I have not let them know at home.

Wednesday, 31 March.
This morning, while I was typing I heard a terrific thud that shook the place. I stopped typing to listen but heard nothing more and thought it might be someone banging about on the flat roof. At lunch I found most people had heard it in widely

---

37 The *Bedford Record*, 30 March 1943, p. 1, reported that: 'The chief work of the evening, and the most outstanding, was C.V. Standford's setting for chorus and orchestra of Tennyson's immortal poem "The Revenge".'

different parts of the factory. For a long while during the morning Fortresses were droning as though there were dozens of them but they were above the clouds. At teatime Jim said 2 of them collided at Wellingborough (about 15 miles away). They must have been loaded with bombs to have been heard that distance.

I went through all my music and put all what I did not want into the salvage bag, and made a pile that Janet might like since they have a piano. I came across lots of traces of mice. I have 2 traps set in the front room but mice won't go near them. I am afraid of their finding their way to the stores in the old sideboard bed – so Jim has promised to have a mouse hunt tomorrow night. I hope he does not want me to help in the hunt.

Friday, 2 April.
Jim had all the furniture moved last night but could not find a mouse. This morning there were fresh traces. I wish I had helped in the hunt now. There must be some spot he has missed. Posted *Monarch of the Glen*.

Tuesday, 6 April.
On Saturday night we put the clocks forward another hour. It is now 'double summer time'. It is light until 9 in the evening but dark when I get up in the mornings.[38] It was very hot on Saturday afternoon and I did not have a coat on at the garden. I planted more carrots, and set out chrysanthemum shoots. Something has eaten the tops of the lupin plants so I sooted the remains. The pansies are in bloom, but the wallflowers are still only on their way. The Worcester Pearmain apple has 30 clusters of flower buds and the tree is not much taller than myself; the plums and gooseberries are blossoming.

On Sunday Jim had to go to Yelden [some 14 miles north of Bedford] for shooting practice with the Home Guard and had to take his dinner; so I took my dinner to the garden and left Pa to fend for himself. I worked in the garden for about an hour; it was all fresh and dewy. I read a book while I was picnicing and after a good laze I went up the hill to the woods. I gathered 4 bunches [of] primroses and dug some roots for the garden. Two bunches I packed up straightaway to send to my friend in Sunderland. I intended taking the parcel to the GPO before I went to tea, but I saw the Post Office van in the country and gave the driver the parcel, so the flowers were off to Sunderland within an hour of being picked.

I was pleased to find a mouse in one of the traps. Both my neighbours now have mice. There must be a plague of them.

Wednesday, 7 April.
After the perfect weather of the weekend we are now having terrifically high wind. It is dreadful at present. Yesterday it snapped one of the posts keeping up the trellis.

---

[38] Standard time was no longer observed. The clock was always put an hour ahead except between around early April and sometime in August when it was put two hours ahead. The objective was to link more closely 'normal' waking and working hours with the hours of sunlight, and thereby reduce somewhat the demand for energy, which was needed to support the war effort. See also below, 17 August 1943, where Leah complains about this policy's consequences.

I should imagine all the trellis is down by now. And the hut that lost its roof in the last high wind is probably blown away.

One of the girls that I sit with at lunch says she has just made the acquaintance of cousin Sybil [Cuthbertson, at 16 Adelaide Square]. She had a notice by post that she had to attend a course in fire-fighting lectures. Sybil lives in the same district and I expect she too had a notice, as it was at the first lecture she met her. I expect I will be getting a notice. All women between the ages of 18 and 45 had to register for fire-watching and now they are waking up to the fact fire-watchers ought to know a bit about fighting fires. Jim, along with a good many men, has been fire-watching since its inception, but has never been taught anything of fire-fighting!![39]

Later.
Well, the trellis is still standing but 8 slates had blown off my bedroom roof (the roof was reconditioned last summer). Mrs Simmonds, who looks after the house mornings, is quite good. She came round this evening and we discussed spring-cleaning. She is going to do 3 bedrooms and stairs and passage before Easter.

I was at a friend's this evening, who has a cousin at the R.O.F [Royal Ordnance Factory]. It is true about them closing down – at least half or two-thirds are being closed down but they are keeping on the bomb section. I thought it must be true because lots of people are losing their lodgers. It seems strange after all the commotion that factory caused here. First there were the hundreds of builders and navvies – a real rough lot. Lots of buses were chartered to take them to the site, which made travelling in the winters very bad for other workers. And there used to be dreadful fights and even murders among the men – the sort of thing entirely foreign to Bedford. Then they gradually went and the actual munitions workers came along and people with room had to put them up.

Tuesday, 13 April.
Nothing much to report. Garden flourishing. Took carpet from Pa's bedroom last evening and Jim beat it, and cleared the room as much as possible for Mrs. Simmons to spring-clean today. The great cleaning orgy has begun.

The budget is out today: beer, whisky, tobacco, amusements all to have increased tax. Tax on fur coats and jewellery to be doubled. None of these things affect me.

Wednesday, 14 April.
Just after sunset last night the air was filled with droning. I went outside to see what it was and at first could see nothing; then the man next door pointed them out. The sky was full of tiny specks like moths and gnats. The planes were not in formation but scattered over the whole sky and only high up, all going south west, and as

---

[39] Jim's experience was not uncommon. New regulations of 15 January 1941 required persons of both sexes 'within prescribed ages to perform part-time civil defence duties', including fire-watching. But training for this was not particularly successful. Responsibility for the training of new fire-watchers was spread among the Fire Brigades, the Auxiliary Fire Service, the Wardens' Service, experienced members of Supplementary Fire Parties and private businesses that employed their own instructor; and there was sometimes minimal cooperation between independent businessmen and government departments in organising fire-watching and preparing to respond to actual fires (O'Brien, *Civil Defence*, pp. 593–4).

they disappeared more were following on. All the neighbours were out watching them and trying to count them. Mr Bowyer remarked 'Somebody is going to have a rough night.' It would be France that would get it. There is no mention of it in the newspaper this morning. *Later.* It was given out on wireless that the planes had been over Italy.

Friday, 16 April.
Nothing much to report, except this is the warmest spring I remember for many a year. We have stopped hot water bottles and fires, and last evening I was reading in the garden for a short while without a coat on. I was reading a book out of the library on herbs. Nearly everything is good for something. Rosemary is good for headache and improves the memory, so as we have a hedge of that bush I have had three lots of that tea this week (after pulling the rooms about for spring-cleaning) and I certainly find it refreshing. The book says rosemary grows best where a woman rules the house. When I announced that fact to the family Pa said 'That must be why ours grows so badly.' He won't be beaten – that man. That very stickly stuff we used to trim our hats with when children – we called it Stickly Jack – the book calls it Clivers or Goosegrass; [it] is good for cancer and also for slimming. That ought to suit you Winnie. It is something you cannot get rid of in our garden.

The apple tree in back garden is buzzing with bees, and a girl brought a bunch of wild hyacinths to the Office. The usual time for these is 10th May onwards.

There is a notice up that we are to have a Works Doctor, as well as the usual nurse. Lots of jokes about that. I also heard he is to look after 6 other factories in the town, so a fat lot of attention each factory will get.
Later.
I see women and children go by in frocks and no hats, like summer.

Monday, 19 April.
Primrose Day.[40] Father's birthday; he is 73. Saturday and Sunday were like the height of summer. Father went to Luton yesterday. He had a nice time, but came home looking very white and faint and is the same this morning. He blamed having to walk home from the station but he really was not fit to travel in the first place. He said Lily was a lot better. The weather was so grand that Jim and I had our tea at the garden. I went exploring in the wood. The bluebells are out, but do not make the carpet of blue it is my dream to see. At some crossroads in the wood I decided to go along one to see where it led. Although I kept on for 20 minutes there seemed no end in sight so turned back. It must be a very big wood (for England). Primroses, bluebells, celandines and wood anemones were all out but they had a thirsty, height-of-summer appearance.[41] They will be getting a drink today as it is cold and raining – and they have stopped the heating in the Offices.

I had the stair carpet up in the evening and stripped my bedroom ready for spring-cleaning tomorrow.

---

40 The anniversary of the death of Prime Minister Benjamin Disraeli, 19 April 1881. The primrose was his favourite flower. The Primrose League, founded in 1883 to propagate Conservative ideas, still existed.
41 The *Bedford Record*, 20 April 1943, p. 1, published a pleasing photograph of trees in blossom.

Thursday, 22 April.

I forgot to mention that there was an air-raid warning during last Friday night. I did not get up, but I read in the local weekly paper that a village church (no place name given) had its windows blown out. A good many people heard the bombs drop but not 'yours truly'. The Government say we are to have 2 days holiday at Easter but our mean firm are only giving us Saturday morning and Monday. We are working tomorrow, Good Friday. Last year and year before we only had the Easter Monday. Some friends have beguiled me into going hiking on Easter Monday. They want to walk among the Barton Hills (15 miles from Bedford [part of the Chilterns, south of Barton-le-Clay]), and as I know the district well and they have never been, they want me to act as guide. I only hope they don't walk me off my feet. They are both 10 years younger than I am and with lots more vigour. It is a beautiful district and I am looking forward to seeing it again after some years, but I vowed once before I would go no more [on] long hikes as it takes me a few days to get over the fatigue. However, I have promised I would venture once again.

Although they say that every age has its compensations, and I believe it has, I frequently long for a return of youth and strength and [to] be able to crowd all the things into a day that I used to. I remember the time when we would bathe or go on the river before breakfast – breakfast out of doors – and then have off to the Office, and in the evening play tennis until dark, strenuous tennis matches on Saturday afternoon, and set off on the Sunday mornings at 6.30 a.m. for a day at the sea or elsewhere and keep that sort of life up all the summer. If I bathed before breakfast nowadays I should want the rest of the day in bed. And the winters – dancing until 1 and 2 in the morning and theatres, whist drives and everything that was going. To think that we went 50 miles to see shows in London and came back on the midnight train. Air-raid warnings cannot keep me out of bed after 10.30 nowadays. But sometimes, when I am feeling very well for a few hours, and I hear the younger ones chattering about their doings (although poor things they have not quarter the opportunity to enjoy themselves as we had owing to the war) I get an awful urge to do it all again.[42]

Tuesday, 27 April.

Easter is over once again, and the weather was typical Bank Holiday weather. Good Friday was cold and wet and I was glad I had not holiday. On Saturday I went to the garden after an early tea, but no sooner had I arrived than 2 friends came and asked the way to the wood, so I went with them and helped to gather flowers. We

---

[42] Some four years later, on 2 June 1947, Leah wrote again about her life when she was in her twenties: 'I have been reading some of my old diaries, about 1924–6 [these have not survived]. How I *lived* in those days, it makes me breathless, the amount of pleasure I used to crowd into evenings, weekends and holidays: tennis, bathing, folk dancing, theatres, ordinary dancing, P.T., choral society practices, numerous visits to Bourne End and Wilden, river picnics and long walks. Not to mention people to tea or supper and cards till midnight.' Of course, during these happy times not only was she young and energetic, her mother was still alive and her father had a job. The depression of the 1930s and her father's unemployment must have caused the Aynsley household distress, though Leah said almost nothing about domestic hardships (she was not given to complaining).

had an air-raid warning on Friday night and Saturday night and some people heard bombs, but I barely roused.

I had a restful day Sunday – and was quite fresh for yesterday's walk. There was a high wind all day and my face is very red and stinging but that is all I had to complain about the weather. In fact the cold just suited me for walking. We arrived at Harlington Station and, with the help of the map, arrived at a lovely hollow in the hills, sheltered from the wind, and ate our lunch in hot sunshine. The only other people we saw were two girls gathering flowers high up on the hill opposite, a female figure that appeared on the hilltop, and two elderly scoutmasters (the sort that might be County Commissioners) who climbed the hills. I should not have minded staying there all the afternoon it was so lovely and quiet, but the others wanted to see as much as possible so we too found an easy way up the hills, and found that what the girls had been gathering were cowslips. Arrived at the plateau at the top – we had a grand view of Bedfordshire towards the north. We walked along a country lane, across the main Bedford-Luton Highroad and to the Barton Springs in another circle of hills. Here there were trippers, boys camping, and such like. This is not so much to my taste. We could not get tea anywhere in the village, so we sat on one of those seats that surround a tree and ate all the food we had left, in front of a pub, and hoped the pub people would invite us in for a drink of tea – but no such luck. I remarked that this was the first time we had had tea in the street since being in France. It so happened that we 3 had been in France together and one of them answered 'Except we have no tea to pour in the gutter.' You see in France the cafés are just tables and chairs set out in the street and when they never gave us a slop basin it used to amuse us to empty our cups into the gutter. We made our way back to the station by a different route and got lost in the fields, but as Harlington church is on a hilltop it was a good guide. Arrived at the station we found that they had *taken off* some of the trains because it was holiday, so we had an hour to wait on the station. I was pleased that I stood the exercise pretty well and feel none the worse today.

Thursday, 29 April.
This diary was begun with the intention of telling you how we live in wartime, as the censor would delete anything I told you in a letter, but I notice I say very little about the war – more about the weather, the garden, and housework.

Well, I suppose I would not be bothering to grow vegetables if there was no war. The onion bed is a blank; I do not know whether because of bad seed, the dry hot spring, or insect pests, but as onions are things you cannot buy in winter, and friends in Sunderland were glad of parcels of them, it is a very necessary crop. We are planting some more, but it is very late to get a good crop. Another worry is the early potatoes. Jim covers them up at night if there is going to be a frost. Last night he risked leaving them (as it means cycling 4 miles) and there was frost. They will be damaged. Apparently potatoes are very tender things. I got a book out of the library called *Garden Foes*[43] to see what had destroyed the onions. It is a marvel

---

[43] *Garden Foes: Insect, Animal and Fungoid Pests ... With all the latest remedies for their eradication ... Illustrated* (London, 1911) by Thomas William Sanders.

to me that any garden exists considering the millions of foes it must have. Do you know that one bean aphid can have 7 hundred odd *million* offspring in summer!!

Also the fact that we could not buy tea on Monday and that they reduced the train service on a Bank Holiday instead of running extras are both the result of the war. They did not want us to travel at all at Easter.

Do you know I have not heard a word from Stella since the week after Christmas. I have written since and have sent parcels of periodicals. To be sure she wrote to Jim late in January and said she would write [to] me soon but I am still waiting.

Tuesday, 4 May.
It was so wet on Saturday I went shopping instead of to the garden. Lately I have been to nearly every shop in Bedford for fully-fashioned lisle stockings size 8½". What strikes me is the way assistants look so glum when they think they have to serve you, and how they beam all over their faces when they can say 'Sorry, we have none.' It was just the same when I asked for a toilet roll on Saturday. The man beamed all over when he said he had none. I nearly beamed back, but I thought he might have been smiling because it was a T.R. [toilet roll] and I thought I had better keep my dignity. You have to give 3 coupons (instead of 2) for fully-fashioned hose. All during the cold weather I kept asking for thick lisle and could not get any at all, and now I cannot get fine lisle but managed to get 2 pair thick. That was 6 coupons and I bought a pair on Friday for 2 coupons but they are so baggy round the ankles I will have to send them to Aunt Tiny to wear in the house. Eight coupons gone and still looking for fine lisle. You probably wonder why I don't get art silk. It is no use wasting coupons on them as we only have 40 coupons for the whole of next year. I have 2 pair silk and 2 pair art silk for special occasions. Pure silk is now unprocurable.

I went up to the garden on Sunday morning to make up for Saturday, and heard the village bells ringing for church. Which reminds me that bell-ringing was reinstated at Easter for all Sundays and special days. The little children think they are something new. On Christmas Day, Tony, aged 3, who lives on one side of us, said 'Do you hear that noise? That's a bell.' At Easter Michael, aged nearly 7 and lives on the other side, said, when the church bells in our street began to toll, 'That's a bell ringing because it's Easter.' They seem to look on them the same as we do air-raid syrens.[44] Michael would not believe me when I told him a bell like that used to be rung at his school.[45]

On Saturday evening when the rain stopped I went for a walk. I passed a blockhouse. Every road leading out of town has its blockhouses, built when the invasion was expected. They are pill-boxes built right across the footpath and you have to step onto the road to get by (very dangerous for people with prams). As I was

[44] The spelling 'sirens' was also in use by Leah and other writers in wartime.
[45] Bell-ringing had been banned in the spring of 1940 and only revived (by some churches, if they had enough bell-ringers) after the Allied victories in North Africa in November 1942. Bell-ringing is mentioned in a report on Home Guard celebrations – 'proclaiming to the world the Allies' latest victory in the cause of freedom' (*Bedford Record*, 18 May 1943, p. 1). Another writer this month (*Bedfordshire Times*, 7 May 1943, p. 8) observed that: 'church bells, after nearly three years of silence, are coming into their own again'.

passing the blockhouse there was also an American officer, an Englishman and his daughter. The American remarked 'These things are very annoying' and then the Englishman started about 'the invasion' we nearly had. I bet he told the Yank a yarn. I overheard him say 'We were all expecting it', which was not true. I myself was, however. We have also tank traps here and there in the main streets but they are underground affairs and I do not know how they are worked. Also there are things that I always thought were cisterns of water to put out fires – but I found out on Sunday they are bases to mount big guns, if necessary.

I had the front room carpet up last night and we beat it at 10 p.m. I hope the woman has cleaned the room. When I strip a room for spring-cleaning I always dread that the woman has not yet turned up to do it and that I have to set to and do it myself when I get home. Mrs Simmons has not let me down so far. She is one of the best helps we have had.

Reverting to the small children, some of them do not know what a banana is like. Tony's uncle sent him 3 from Gibraltar. He was allowed to eat one, one was sent to the school to show the children and one was raffled off for a charity!![46]

Wednesday, 5 May.
After saying what I did about bananas, it is a funny thing that last night I saw in an *ironmonger's* window 2 bright green bananas labelled 'Genuine Article. Not for Sale. Lent by a member of our Staff.' Which reminds me of when I stayed in France [in August 1937]. About 7 a.m. they would bring to our bedrooms a cup of tea, coffee, or chocolate, and 2 rolls and butter, and that is all we had until 12.30 lunch. So I thought we would like some bananas to have with the rolls. There were none in the village and I searched all over Dinard [in Brittany] for them but only found a bunch of bright green ones. In that shop pears were 10 francs *each* (1s 6d). I thought at the time how empty and poor the shops were compared with English shops. It was the same behind the show streets in Switzerland. I do not think the English realized what rich and fortunate people they were, before the war. I read an item in the newspaper the other day on how badly off the French people were with (among other things) no cream. We used to say in 1937 that their ices had no

---

[46] The scarcity of bananas in wartime was often remarked on and later remembered. The subject is imaginatively discussed in C.M. Peniston-Bird, '"Yes, we have no bananas": sharing memories of the Second World War', in Mary Addyman, Laura Wood and Christopher Yinnitsaros, eds, *Food, Drink, and the Written Word in Britain, 1820–1945* (London, 2017). Almost three years later, after the war, bananas still featured prominently in Bedford's public awareness. According to the *Bedford Record*, 12 March 1946, p. 3: 'Thousands of Jamaica bananas will be on sale in Bedfordshire tomorrow (Wednesday) and Thursday. They arrived at the wholesalers in Bedford last Thursday, and there were amusing scenes during the unloading operations. Crowds of children, on their way home from school, saw the lorries, piled high with the fruit, and gathered around excitedly. The police had to be called in the afternoon to one shop to disperse the crowd of youngsters, many of whom had never seen a banana before.' An accompanying photograph shows two children admiring a bunch of bananas, which they looked at 'with wonderment'. (The bananas were to be 'fairly distributed throughout the county, and anyone below the age of 18 years will be able to obtain one pound of them.') Another, and more vivid, version of this photograph featuring children is in Nigel Lutt, *Bedfordshire at War* (Stroud, 1997), p. 118.

cream in them – also 1s 6d each. By-the-way, we have not been allowed cream in England since the beginning of war. It is all made into butter or cheese.

Thursday, 6 May.
I have written to my Aunt Sarah at Worthing to see if she will have me for a week's holiday. The factory is closing August Bank Holiday week but I am one of the skeleton staff being retained that week and can have my holiday when I choose. We are only having one week and an extra week's pay – wartime measure.

Saturday, 8 May.
News in this morning's paper that Tunis and Bizerte [Tunisia] are in Allied hands. It seems as though the African campaign is nearly finished. When I arrived at work I expected to hear them discussing the victory, but all the girls in the cloakroom could talk about was – we are only to have 36 clothing coupons in the new ration books, to last at least a year. The 60 in our present books are to last 14 months.

Monday, 10 May.
Another wet Saturday so I went shopping. Jim's curtains had big slits in when they came from the wash and I went to look for new material. You have to give coupons for it and I intended to use Father's, but judge of my disappointment to find that although he buys hardly any clothes he had only 21 coupons in his [ration] book. He had been letting outsiders use his book. I told him when he did it with his last book that it was illegal and that we needed all our coupons for ourselves as the clothing coupons have to cover household things like towels, sheets, curtains. It is very annoying, but I am afraid Father is gradually becoming more senile and we must just put up with it. Some curtain material *without* coupons was 22s 11d per yard and Mabel (Belfast Linen Warehouse) showed me some at 17s 11d. It was the heavy brocade for drawing rooms etc. I am used to giving 3s 11d per yard for bedrooms. The cheapest I have seen with coupons is 6s 11d per yard. I will wait and look around more. Jim says he does not mind doing without curtains! Lace or net curtains are unprocurable. Two people have advised me to get the gummed net (that is used for sticking to glass to prevent it splintering during raids) and soak out the gum; but I am not needing net curtains just yet.

Thursday, 13 May.
Tunisia fell completely yesterday. Today it is 8 years ago since I started to work at Igranic Electric Company Limited [Elstow Road].

Friday, 14 May.
Air-raid warning during the night. After getting house rid of mice, they are back again.

Monday, 17 May.
After two very sweltering days in middle of week, Saturday and Sunday were perfect, bright sunshine and a cool east wind. May is the month of all months in Bedfordshire. In spite of my thinking that all the flowers had come out in April and there were none left for May, the scene of Bromham Mill on Saturday was Arca-

dian. Imagine a bright blue sky, and a little brook running to the river with a few children fishing and paddling in it, a bright gold carpet of buttercups right to the river's edge and on the river a lovely swan; all the hedges and dozens of odd trees and bushes dotted about the meadow simply white with hawthorn. The scent of May and blossoming bean fields was heavy, and cuckoos were in nearly every tree.

Yesterday was the 3rd anniversary of the formation of the Home Guard and there was a big parade in the town. We had to have dinner just after 12 so that Jim could be at rendezvous at 1 o'clock, although the salute was not until 2.15. It was amusing in the morning with the men all furbishing up and getting their uniforms ready, trotting around to each other's houses for advice etc. Harold [Bradley] next door [68 Marlborough Road] had taken something he wears to pieces and could not put it together again. Jim could not help him as he had not owned one, so Harold had to trot off elsewhere. Jim had been issued with a gun for the occasion. Actually when practicing shooting they take turns with one or two guns.[47]

Wednesday, 19 May.

Yesterday and today the newspapers are full of the damage caused in the Ruhr Valley by the breach our aircraft have made in their great dam. The tables seem to be surely turning for Germany. It must be hellish with all that water let loose on an industrial area. I can just imagine word going round that the dam might be breached, and thousands fleeing for safety and the brave and devoted ones staying by the disabled and infirm. What a world![48]

I went to the dentist's last night. The tooth I thought was wrong is O.K. and had already been filled, but he found a large cavity in a tooth supposed to be sound. I thought he would never stop drilling and I have developed slight neuralgia today on that side.

After reading the papers properly I find there were *two* dams breached.

Thursday, 20 May.

Papers full of Churchill's speech in America. He is a wonderful man, the way he hops round the globe.[49]

---

[47] The ceremonies were described in some detail in the press: *Bedford Record*, 18 May 1943, p. 1 and *Bedfordshire Times*, 21 May 1943, p. 5. In Bedford and in most other places such public events embracing patriotic values and national solidarity were well publicised.

[48] These dam-busting raids on 16–17 May were heavily publicised, with much emphasis on the challenges faced. One authority on these raids has concluded that they: 'resulted in some flooding in the Ruhr valley and caused great temporary concern among the population. Complete success would have resulted in considerable loss of life as well as a major reduction of production. The obvious possibility that other dams might be breached added to the worries of the population. But neither the raids on the cities nor those on the dams produced the loss of life that was anticipated by the attackers and rumored among the victims.' (Earl R. Beck, 'Under the Bombs', in Igor Primoratz, ed., *Terror from the Sky: The Bombing of German Cities in World War II* [New York and Oxford, 2010], p. 62). The dams, major sources of electricity, were quickly repaired.

[49] On 19 May, a little over a week after arriving in the United States on the *Queen Mary*, Churchill made a masterful address to Congress, broadcast live by the BBC, which both avoided dwelling on potential pitfalls in the US-UK relationship and evinced a new confidence that the war had reached a turning point (James, ed., *Winston S. Churchill: His*

I have had a letter from Aunt Sarah at Worthing. D.V. [God willing] I am going there for a week's holiday on June 19th. I have not seen the sea since war broke out.

Friday, 21 May.
Had a letter from Sunderland with a cutting about last weekend's raid. There are many dead and some industrial damage. My Aunt T. says she had never known such a night of terror.[50] My cousin Jessie [Hugill] is expecting a baby this week, which would make things worse for them.

My friend Flora, aged 39, is expecting a baby in July. I saw her a week ago and she was very distressed because the doctor had told her (after an X-ray) that there was a growth which would have to be removed first. She was on her way to have further advice when I saw her, and it turns out that there is nothing more wrong with her than twins!! Her husband was telling me he was going to keep pigs. A cow or goats would be more useful in these circumstances.

Monday, 24 May.
Father is ill. The doctor injected him with liver on Friday. He won't stay in bed, however, and seems worse after the injection. Pa is what you might call 'cussed'. The doctor has wanted to inject all the time, but Pa has refused and he has been gradually getting worse since a month before Easter. He has been imagining he was getting better. He would not let me go to the doctor with him, neither would he let the doctor come to the house, so on Thursday I wrote to the doctor and asked him to insist on giving him an injection next time he called for medicine. Pa went on Friday and the deed was done. I have this game every time – persuading Pa to go to the doctor, then asking the doctor to do the necessary. If the doctor was worth his salt he would do it at first as he has told me time and time again that medicine is no use for Father and only live injections will help him. Because it is *liver* Pa resists every time, and the doctor cannot be bothered with him and lets things slide until I step in. He was quite bad tempered about it just before Christmas so I wrote a letter instead of seeing him. No wonder my hair is quite white at the temples. Father is very very difficult and now that he is feeble-minded he is worse. The doctor to me called him a devil, so you know I am not exaggerating. I don't approve of the doctor and would change him but Father would never consent, and as he is a panel doctor I cannot change him without Father's signed form. This has been going on since 6 years next September. The doctor told me then he would not live long and

---

Complete Speeches, vol. 7, pp. 6775–84). On 26 May Churchill continued his travels, from Washington to Algiers, with stops in Newfoundland and Gibraltar, involving some seventeen airborne hours. This was a time when long-distance air travel was gruelling (Churchill was pushing seventy), usually uncomfortable and often dangerous – and thus was seen as noteworthy by citizens such as Leah who had never set foot in an airplane (and the vast majority had not) and rarely slept anywhere but home. The prime minister's travels this spring, consuming a little over a month, are detailed by Martin Gilbert, *The Road to Victory: Winston S. Churchill 1941–1945* (London, 1986), pp. 395–426. In mid-November 1943 Churchill asked an aide to calculate the total mileage of his travels since September 1939. The answer was 111,000 miles: 792 hours spent at sea, 339 hours in the air (Ibid., p. 552).
[50] These raids on 15/16 May caused heavy damage – perhaps 200 houses were destroyed – and left some seventy-three people seriously injured and seventy-five dead (www.ne-diary.genuki.uk).

I never expected him to come out alive from the hospital he was in 9 weeks, but the liver injections saved him. He was told to have one once a month to keep well, but he has gone, at times, as long as a year without any and then he is so bad he has to have a course of them.

We put in 18 tomato plants on Saturday. Everybody's roses are in full bloom. June is the usual month for roses.

Thursday, 27 May.
Called to see the doctor last night as Father's feet and legs are very swollen, but he still persists in going about. The doctor says we can do nothing about it, but if Father has not called for another injection by Saturday I am to let him know and he will call at our house.

I have just started salicin [an anti-inflammatory] for rheumatism. The medical dictionary says it is *the* thing. It is an extract of willow bark. The bottle says 'to be taken as directed by physician' but the chemist's assistant and I decided that if I take 2 tablets a day I won't be killed. Salicyclate of soda that I have taken for many weeks is a mineral drug, from coal tar I think; it has not improved me.
Later.
Jim got his calling-up papers today. He is to report at Bury St Edmunds [Suffolk] training camp for 3rd June.

Saturday, 29 May.
Father had another injection yesterday and he seems a little better. Four people I know had their calling-up papers on Thursday, including the husband of the woman (Mrs Simmons) who works for us. I must say that she has been very helpful while Father has been bad.

Monday, 31 May.
I read a letter sent to Father Saturday night, saying what a dreadful raid there was at Sunderland last Sunday night – property destroyed and underground shelter received a direct hit. An incendiary made a dent on Aunt T's shelter. At 11 p.m. on the Sunday the ambulance came for Jessie and she had a baby girl at 5 a.m. after such a fearful night. Four churches were badly damaged and 2 hospitals had to be evacuated. Aunt T. said there was a riot at the Town Hall and men threatened to do no more work until the town had more protection. Now they have barrage balloons.[51]

A Sunday school (Germans say Torquay) had a direct hit and 15 dead children have been found. They are still searching for others.[52]

---

51 This was the last major raid of the war in Sunderland (23/24 May) and caused the most deaths – eighty-four. Thirteen people were killed in one public shelter, eight in two others. Among the dead was a group of joiners from Glasgow who were there to repair earlier bomb damage (Ibid).
52 In fact, twenty-one children were killed. The raid is described in Ramsey, *The Blitz Then and Now, vol. 3,* pp. 275–7. The incident was also recorded in a diary written this day in Tuscany by a woman the same age as Leah: 'the BBC reports that yesterday's German raiders over England bombed a country church in which a Sunday school service was taking place, killing twenty children, and machine-gunned children playing on a beach.' This is

Thursday, 3 June.

I had two teeth filled at the dentist's last night. It is a gruelling business, especially as old fillings had to be drilled out.

Jim and I were up at 6 a.m. this morning as he wanted to get the 7.30 train to Cambridge for Bury St Edmunds. He left the house well before 7 as St John's Station is 2 miles away, but he was back again at 7.15 as he had forgotten his gas mask! The next train is not until 10.50 and it means a 3 hour wait at Cambridge.

Tuesday, 8 June.

Had a P.C. [postcard] from Jim on Saturday saying 'Well fed, well clothed and well worked.' Also a letter yesterday morning. We had our first garden peas on Sunday. They are 1s per lb. in the shops. And we had a gooseberry pie from our own bushes. Since Jim went away we have had simply torrents of rain. There is a saying here:

> If the oak before the ash, then 'twill only be a splash.
> If the ash before the oak, then it sure will be a soak.

I have always found the oak trees come into leaf first, but this year during the hot dry early spring I found the ash trees in leaf while there were no oaks out, and I wondered if there would be any truth in the saying. We have certainly had a soak from Thursday until today, and the sky is still heavy for rain.

Mr Markham is coming to do the kitchen on Thursday. Next Sunday is Whit Sunday and we are having Monday and Tuesday holiday. This [is] what we had pre-war. Three years ago we had no holiday at all [after the German invasions of France and the Low Countries].

Wednesday, 9 June.

I had a letter from Stella yesterday. I am afraid she is in a bad way. The operations she has had, and the tube she has had in her chest, have not done the trick. They are going to cut some more rib away (at the front this time). She is still only allowed up one hour a day and she only weighs 6 stone 12½ lb. Before she goes through the next operation she is having a week's leave at home, which she is looking forward to.

I also had a letter from Lily, offering to have Father if ever I wanted to go away for a holiday, and also a scrawl from John saying he is coming to Bedford on Saturday.

I dug some new potatoes last night.

Friday, 11 June.

Mr Markham coloured the scullery walls yesterday and last night I started in on cleaning some of the paint and getting some of the dishes and pots and pans back into place. Mr. M. remarked to Pa on how nice our garden looked. Its main glory at present is honeysuckle and blue flax. This reminds me of yesterday, when we went to view the Igranic shelters. At the beginning of the war underground shelters

---

testimony to the impact of British broadcasts to the continent – which this English-Italian diarist records on several other occasions (Iris Origo, *War In Val d'Orcia: An Italian War Diary 1943–1944* [London, 2017; first published 1947], p. 57).

were made for the work people on some spare ground adjacent the factories. When the factory was extended a lot of our bike racks were pushed among the mounds of earth over the shelters and the place looked a regular rubbish heap. Then somebody started scattering flower seeds over the shelters and at present they are a blaze of colour with all sorts of flowers, but mainly poppies. Every mound and hole and corner has poppies – red, pink, white striped, double and single. They are glorious and we stroll round at lunch time. Yesterday we met one of the managers, a soulful old gentleman who always talks very high-flown, and he remarked when passing 'Isn't it wonderful how nature covers up the graves?' I sincerely hope our air-raid shelters are not our graves!

These shelters are awful things and we used to spend hours in them when the sirens[53] went; but now we do not go down for sirens but have our own 'Spotters' on the roof and go down (willy-nilly) when they signal. If enemy planes are too near when they 'spot' them, they sometimes give a 'crash' warning when there is no time to go down the shelters and we have to get under desks or any other covers in the Offices. There used to be some funny scenes: men with their heads in safety but their sterns sticking out and legs and boots poking out in all directions. I, being small,[54] could tuck myself away easily and watch the others' efforts. We all used to feel like sheep when we scrambled out again. We rarely get warnings now.

Wednesday, 16 June.
Well, the Whitsun holiday is over. It seems to be correct about the 'oaks and ashes'. We have had 'a soak' this Whitsun, together with large hailstones and thunder-storms.[55] John came on Saturday and stayed the night, while Lily and the children were at Grandma's. Both the girls are taller than their mother (and Jacqueline is only 9). Jacqueline's feet are so big they cannot get any children's shoes to fit her and she has women's 6's. I take 2½. They are both learning to play the piano, but Jacqueline is hopeless at it. However, she has joined the Brownies and gets on well at that. John helped me at the garden Saturday evening and on Sunday morning he cycled round to see some of the Yankee aerodromes.

On Monday morning I whitewashed the pantry. What a job! It runs under the stairs. To keep the dirt out of the newly-done scullery I pulled the door fairly close, and it clicked to and I had locked myself in. I yelled and hammered for about 10 minutes before the man next door came and let me out. They were just going off for a picnic. If they had got away I might have been locked in for an hour or more as Pa was ensconced in an armchair by the front-room and might have been there most of the morning. However, Harold came and let me out and I finished the job by lunchtime. I went to bed all the afternoon.

We also had a holiday on Tuesday and I spent the morning at the garden. Then the storms began but I managed to get a cycle ride in the evening with Flossie Clarke, who had had tea with me. We had a young lady from the Public Assistance Office to see whether Pa was poor enough to merit an Army Allowance from Jim!

---

[53] Leah's spelling of this word was inconsistent (a not uncommon feature of wartime writing).
[54] She said she was 4 feet 8½ inches tall (Diary, 31 July 1930). Jim was also short, around 5 feet 2 inches.
[55] See also below: 3 March 1944.

We had to answer questions about how much Jim had contributed to the household when he was a civilian, rent, rates etc.

I mentioned in March [the 22nd] about the Head of the Sales Department, Mr Garrard, marrying his typist. They were cycling in the country on Sunday when he dropped off his bike – dead. A dreadful shock for her, and all her dreams gone crash. She will be left very well off (perhaps) and she is still only 27.[56]

We had a long detailed letter from Jim. He seems to enjoy army life.

Monday, 21 June.
We had two more visits from the [Public] Assistance Board representative. I was at work both times so I have left a detailed letter for them to digest when she calls again today. The mother of one of the girls in the Office is a widow with all 3 sons (one a bachelor) in the Services and this one young daughter. They allow her 3s 6d per week as she has had to go out cleaning to make ends meet. I do not suppose therefore that we shall get much.

I have gathered 13 lb. peas to date and enough new potatoes to last all this week. It has been a nice weekend after all the rain. Roses are everywhere – in the hedges and gardens. We have some like great cabbages. Also the pale pink rambler has bloomed for the first time. I took a cutting from John's. It is called 'dawn blush' or some such name and is paler than Dorothy Perkins, Hiawatha etc. It is just like a wild rose.

Last Thursday night I had an S.O.S. from Jim's tenant for a plumber as a lot have closed down, but I finally enlisted the help of the firm of builders Jim used to work for [he was a bricklayer], so I hope it is all fixed up now.

Tuesday, 22 June.
I had a long letter from Jim last night. He still seems to be enjoying life, although he is beginning to look for letters more, when in the past on holidays he never cared whether he had letters or not. They have just had their 2nd dose of inoculation and vaccination and all his hut are 'more or less dicky'. They have all sorts of intelligence tests and he says he has the best record of the 'intake'. I suppose the 'intake' is all the raw recruits who joined with him. The officer has told him he is good enough for the Tank Corps but being Grade II bars him. Well Pa and I are both pleased he *is* barred from the Tanks. I do not think he would like to spend his days pounding and rattling about in one of those.

I went to the doctor about my rheumatism last Friday. He has given me medicine and liniment. I was talking to a girl at the Office who goes to a London Hospital once a month about her rheumatism. She has been going since last year and when I asked if there was any improvement she said 'Very little, but they told me not to expect *any* improvement until after taking certain pills for *a year*.' Perhaps I do not give my various remedies a long enough trial. But I should not like to take

---

[56] Henry James Garrard (b. 1885) left his widow, Kathleen née Rogers (b. 1915), the daughter of a local grocer, a total of £555 3s 8d in his will, certainly not a fortune, even at that time. It represented about two years of a labourer's wages – which may have seemed substantial to a person in Leah's modest financial position. Kathleen Garrard remarried in 1962. We are very grateful to Ann Stephenson for her research on these two people.

one thing for a year without [a] doctor in case it was doing me harm in some other direction. For instance potash is good for many things (including growths) and I used to take it regularly but I found it made my heart queer, and I read it was bad for the heart.

I am just thinking, Winnie. It is about time I heard from you. I received your last letter in January. It may be that my or your letters have been lost at sea.

Saturday, 26 June.
Nothing much to report. The King has got safely back from Africa.[57] To judge by the sound of all the planes we hear every day and night, they must be having hell in Germany.[58] The newspapers are full of it too. They certainly won't be in a hurry to start another war, I surmise. Aunt T. says Noble (Jessie's husband) [in Bomber Command] is tired out going over 'you know where' every night. That is how she puts it to evade the censor! Also to judge by the smiling pictures in the papers, we think Queen Bess has been enjoying herself with the King out of the way. She looks in her element.[59]

---

[57] The King's Private Secretary provided an inside account – in his diary for 25 June – of the King's return home: 'Rose at 5, and in the middle of a light breakfast got a message that the King's aeroplane [returning from Morocco] was an hour ahead of schedule, and would reach Northolt [airport] at six instead of seven.' He: 'dashed off as soon as possible, and arrived there, simultaneously, with Winston, to find the aeroplane had already landed, and the King and the others drinking coffee in the mess. They all looked well, though several of them, including HM, have had mild attacks of "Gippy Tummy". The whole trip has been a great success [it received lavish coverage in the press]. The PM drove back to Buckingham Palace with the King, and later brought the War Cabinet down to see him.' (Duff Hart-Davis, ed., *King's Counsellor: Abdication and War: The Diaries of Sir Alan Lascelles* [London, 2007; first published 2006], pp. 135–6). The King had left London for Algiers on 12 June, his first trip outside England since December 1940, and toured various strategic sites in the Mediterranean, including Malta, where he was rapturously received on 20 June. As his biographer has remarked: 'the fact that the trip had taken place at all was a harbinger of things to come. The Mediterranean was no longer an Axis sea; the King had crossed from North Africa to Malta twice in thirty-six hours in a cruiser escorted by four destroyers without seeing a hostile ship or aircraft.' (Sarah Bradford, *King George VI* [London: 1989], p. 357).
[58] Her surmise was unquestionably true. Some of the destruction and aftermath of the bombings in the summer of 1943 are described in Beck, 'Under the Bombs', pp. 61–79: pp. 71–2 and 78 in particular describe some of the hellish realities on the ground. Han Erich Nossack's *The End: Hamburg 1943* was written in November 1943, some three months after the crippling raids in July 1943, and conveyed a sense of the survivors' horrors, immediate and prolonged, which were well beyond those ever experienced in England: 'Rats and flies were the lords of the city. Insolent and fat, the rats disported themselves on the streets. But even more nauseating were the flies. They were large and fat and of a shimmering green; no one had ever seen flies like this. They wallowed in swarming clumps on the pavement, sat, copulating, on top of the ruined walls, warmed themselves, bloated and tired, on splinters of window glass. When they could no longer fly, they would crawl after us through the narrowest crevices, soiling everything, and their rustling and buzzing was the first thing one heard in the morning. They didn't stop until October.' (London and Chicago, 2004; first published 1948, translated by Joel Agee, p. 44).
[59] During the King's absence the Queen acted as Councillor of State and performed some of his public duties, probably enjoying the limelight. An admiring biographer wrote of one incident that was seen as testifying to her standing with the public, even without the presence of her husband: 'On the day on which it had been announced that the King was in

Monday, 28 June.

I worked like a nigger [offensive language now, in common usage then] Saturday evening, just gathering stuff and digging potatoes, from 6 to 9 p.m. and ¾ hour cycling. It took me an hour to pick 1 lb. blackcurrants, of which I made 2 lb. jam and stewed some. I sold 10 lb. potatoes for 1s. They were recently 4d lb. in the shops.

Yesterday I had tea in Flossie Clarke's garden and we sat there until 8.30. It was a good rest. They have a nice secluded garden. Had a letter from Jim saying they can have leave next Sunday or the following Sunday. They are to draw lots for the days next Wednesday.

Tuesday, 29 June.

I went to the garden last evening and noticed that all the countryside signposts have been put up again. The big trunk road signs have been up for a few months, such as to Leicester, Northampton, Luton, but the sort that say 'Biddenham – ½ mile' have reappeared. It looks as though invasion of Britain is entirely out of the question. I expect that if not already down, they are busy taking them all down all over the continent now.

Wednesday, 30 June.

We heard from the Army Paymaster that no allowance can be made for the support of Father while Jim is in the Army. So that is that.

Thursday, 1 July.

I called at [no. 16] Adelaide Square last evening, to tell [cousin] Sybil [Cuth-bertson] the broad beans are ready if she wants to come and get some, as she is fond of them (she is a vegetarian). Willie Forsyth had just turned up without warning from Liverpool. He is still on the sick list with his eye, but his Firm had asked him to take charge of a ship while in dock, as that is what he has been doing for the last 3 weeks. He talked about all the food he'd had on board, including oranges and grapefruit. Sybil and [cousin] Mabel [Forsyth][60] went on at him for

---

North Africa, Queen Elizabeth was in the East End of London. It was a most moving expe-rience. She was greeted with overwhelming enthusiasm. The cheering crowds brought the Royal car to a halt, and swarmed all over it.' (Dorothy Laird, *Queen Elizabeth the Queen Mother* [London, 1966], p. 224). Other signs were noted of her independence: 'On 22 June she held an investiture at Buckingham Palace. There were several hundred people, mostly servicemen and women, to be awarded their honours. The ceremony took much longer than usual because she spent more time than the King in talking to each of those being honoured.' (William Shawcross, *Queen Elizabeth, The Queen Mother* [Toronto, 2009], pp. 570–1). The King was well known for his reticence. This was the first time a queen had held an investi-ture since the reign of Victoria (*The Times*, 23 June 1943, p. 7). Leah may have been hinting at a certain disapproval of what she saw as the Queen's showiness – and, if so, this was an opinion shared by others. On 11 December 1936, just after the previous King's abdication, a London diarist, who commended the new King's 'reserve', went on to say that: 'The only possible snag is his wife who (now Queen Elizabeth) has shown an unfortunate tendency to play to the gallery in similar lines to Edward.' (Robin Woolven, ed., *The London Diary of Anthony Heap 1931–1945*, London Record Society [London, 2017], p. 168).
[60] They were both residents at 16 Adelaide Square.

not bringing even one fruit home. Sybil and her husband are going to the Tyne for a holiday during last week in July and are going to see Uncle A.

Monday, 5 July.
On Saturday was the English Folk Dance Festival and there was a party in the evening to which I went. It was an open-air affair in the grounds of the Girls' Modern School [Cardington Road]. It was very enjoyable, but very hot dancing until the sun got low. My rheumaticky leg played me up.[61]

Jim came home yesterday morning and stayed until after tea. It was all too short. He is not having a week's leave at the end of the first 6 weeks, but has to go straight on to another 10 weeks' course in dear knows what part of the country. I thought he looked thinner in spite of all the food he gets, but I was not surprised when he told about all the attempts they have had with inoculation and vaccination. He nearly fainted last Thursday when the smallpox began to work, but he would not go to the M.O. [Medical Officer] in case they stopped his leave today. His arm is still bad. The rose mallows are blooming. They are very beautiful; I have not seen them before.

Friday, 9 July.
Had a letter from Jim yesterday. He is going into Royal Signals training company next week but does not know what part of the country. He said he'd heard that Noble (cousin Jessie's husband) was shot into the sea but took to the dinghy and was rescued. He has 9 more flights to make and then he has a few months' rest on ground work.

Monday, 12 July.
Flossie Clarke [at 7 St Leonard's Avenue] and I had arranged that on Saturday we take our teas to the garden, park our bikes there and go for a walk up the hill alongside the wood and see where it led to, but although we had tea at the garden, it rained so a walk across fields was out of the question. I got my legs and feet wet and the rheumatism has been in full force all the weekend. I have been to the doctor for 3 weeks now – but no improvement. He is only giving me salicylate of soda which I had already been taking myself for 2 months (February-April) without benefit. He has also given me a liniment like furniture cream. I am using the 2nd bottle of that – so you may know that I am not stinting the rubbing.

I received another letter from Worthing asking me to go for a week. I will try and fix up a week in August. Father is well enough and willing to go to Luton while I am away.

The papers were full of news that the Allies had invaded Sicily. Not much comment at work.

---

[61] Folk dancing during the previous year's 'Holidays at Home' is noted in Stuart Antrobus, '"Holidays at Home" in Bedford during the Second World War', *Bedford Local History Magazine*, no. 100 (September/October 2017), pp. 41–50, which includes (Fig. 6) a photograph from the *Bedfordshire Times*, 31 July 1942, of a performance by members of the local branch of the English Folk Dance Society.

Tuesday, 13 July.
Someone counted 70 bombers going off this morning.

Friday, 16 July.
I have been at home 1½ days with a very feverish cold – the result of last Saturday's wetting. I sweated so much I thought the rheumatism would have been washed out of my system, but it is worse in my arm. Even my fingers are stiff.

Gerry Goodwin, the engineer who broke his foot last January, has now caught cerebral meningitis. Very few people get over that.

Monday, 19 July.
We never heard from Jim all last week. It seemed as if he had dropped into the void, as we knew he had moved from Bury St Edmunds. He had written last Thursday from Catterick Camp, but the letter only reached me today. You may have heard of Catterick; it was a famous camp in the 1914 war. He says it extends 10 miles by 4 miles; and they are much overcrowded and he has to sleep on the floor instead of in bunks. He had just had an interview, as follows: 'Sit down! Can you use a typewriter?' 'No sir.' 'Can you use a teleprinter?' 'No sir.' 'Have you all your fingers?' 'Yes sir.' 'Are they supple?' 'Not too bad.' 'You can be a telegraph-board operator.' So after half a life-time they are going to make him into something like you were Winnie. I am wondering if he means 'telephone board' as surely they always use the teleprinter nowadays. Perhaps he has to send telegrams outwards. He says the Signals have highest pay of any unit – but hardest worked. The worst news is that he does not get leave for 15 weeks!! Not until end of October. He may get a weekend (100 miles limit) and would then go to Sunderland. Catterick is in North Yorkshire.

Tuesday, 20 July.
Had a letter from Jim this morning from London!! They were rushed there on Saturday. He said they all cheered when told to pack for London and 'even the Scotsmen are hoping to have a pennyworth of Tube and go round Limehouse.' He is in Putney but not in proper billets. He is sleeping on the floorboards of an empty house at present, but 'hopes for a house with a bed and H. & C'. This (if it lasts) will alter the leave question and we may see him soon.

Friday, 23 July.
Twice this week I have seen an open lorry load of Italian prisoners going through the town at great speed. They have big round patches sewn to their coats between the shoulders. There was a soldier with a gun at the back of the lorry. I took it from their appearance they were Italian. They looked fairly young, and not unhappy. I expect they had been working in the fields.[62] About a fortnight ago, an Italian pris-

---

[62] Harvest labour was always at a premium and special efforts were often made to supply it. One source of labour was Italian POWs (*Bedfordshire Times*, 16 April 1943, p. 4). Italian POWs had helped to pick potatoes the previous year. They 'are being placed on various farms, to which they are transported each day' (*Bedfordshire Times*, 23 October 1942, p. 4). The importance of Italian labour-power to British wartime agriculture is highlighted in

oner working in the fields nearby [in Tilbrook, Huntingdonshire] cut off his guard's head with a billhook, took his rifle and ran off. He tried to shoot a number of people and was finally killed in a farmhouse bedroom himself. This was about 10 miles from Bedford. They said he had gone mad and become a 'killer'.[63]

The harvest is starting very early this year. Yesterday in a cleared field I saw a gleaner. Last autumn was the first time I had ever seen a gleaner (only read of them in the bible and elsewhere) and the fields were full of them. People are only allowed to keep a few hens and their food is rationed; they try to smuggle in a few extra and feed on kitchen scraps. Hence, the gleaning to get hen food.[64]

Heard from Jim again yesterday. I have sent off a parcel of things he asked for: shoes, bathing costume, pack of cards, maps and guide to London. I also sent soap, dates and apples, but have forgotten a dozen trouser buttons he asked for!!

Monday, 26 July.
Saw in morning paper that Mussolini has resigned. This is a very unexpected turn of events to me. I wonder if the people demanded it, or whether he is a coward.

It has been a fine summery weekend after a very cold, dull week, but there is nothing particular to report. I tried 12 shops for a white brassiere but there is not such a thing to be had – most shops have pink ones.

Wednesday, 28 July.
At 20 past 5 yesterday evening it was all round the Works that Italy had surrendered unconditionally. You should have heard all the talk up to 5.30 p.m. as to which countries would fall into our hands next, what we would do with the Italian fleet, repatriation of prisoners etc. The rumour was all over the town – supposed to be given out on the screens at the cinematographers – but it was all quashed by the 6 o'clock wireless.

Mrs Simmons did not turn up yesterday and Father went round to enquire.' A neighbour said she had gone away for a few days and had not had time to inform us.

Bob Moore and Kent Fedorowich, *The British Empire and Its Italian Prisoners of War, 1940–1947* (Basingstoke, 2002), chap. 2. Servicemen might also contribute to the harvest. In August 1943 a US airman was photographed helping with the harvest near Bletsoe: it appears that this was staged for propaganda purposes, to show Americans in a positive light (Smith, *Hertfordshire and Bedfordshire Airfields*, p. 272). US troops helping with the harvest were also reported in the *Bedfordshire Times*, 13 August 1943, p. 6.

[63] This highly exceptional incident of murder is discussed in Stephen Risby, *Prisoners of War in Bedfordshire* (Stroud, 2011), chap. 4, and reported in the *Bedford Record*, 13 July 1943, p. 1. While there were numerous speculations about the motives of the Italian, Antonio Amedeo, including his craving for a woman (Land Girls were nearby), none was clearly established and it was generally concluded that he had gone insane.

[64] A woman who worked in North Buckinghamshire in wartime, not far from Bedfordshire, recalled that: 'A few people kept tame rabbits and others chickens, but the food to feed them was getting scarce. At reaping time it was quite common to go gleaning for oats or wheat, a little extra.' (Doris White, *D for Doris, V for Victory* [Wolverton, Milton Keynes, 1981], p. 21).

Tuesday, 3 August.

One of the quietest Bank Holidays I have ever spent.[65] Saturday was sweltering. I spent the morning cleaning the house as Mrs Simmons had not been all the week. I took my tea to the garden. F. Clarke was to have brought hers and we were going to have it in the shade at the edge of the cornfield on the hill, but it was too hot for her to venture out. I sat in the shade of the garden hut but the sweat poured off me all the time. In the evening I had a bonfire and as all the stuff was very dry, after a hot week, it burnt well. While watering the tomatoes I noticed a storm brewing and hurried off home as I had no mac or coat, but I was caught in a terrific storm along the road. I had to shelter under trees; the lightning was streaking down left and right and seemed to go to earth in the road just in front of me, but I hoped that being at the edge of a small wood I would be safe enough from the lightning – not like being under a solitary tree. Sunday and Monday were much cooler and pleasanter. Father came to see the garden on Monday but it was a great effort for him to walk from bus stop.

Wednesday, 4 August.

We had a letter from Mrs Simmons last week saying she had to go away in a hurry, but would be back this week as usual. She did not turn up yesterday, however. Perhaps she decided not to travel at Bank Holiday. I do hope she does not leave us but it looks like the first signs. As my doctor is on holiday I went to see his deputy last night. He has prescribed iodine and some tablets for the rheumatism.

My friend Flora, who was expecting twins, had them last week but both dead. They were boys, each weighing 7 lb.

Monday, 9 August.

Nothing special to relate. Went to see Flora on Saturday afternoon. She herself is going on well and hopes to go home on Monday. Went to garden in the evening to gather beans etc. It rained all the time as I sat in the hut and shelled peas I had been drying. I have a jar of dried peas ready for the winter. There are some cucumbers nearly ready for gathering and I picked the first tomato. I had seen traces of a rabbit in the garden and on Saturday night I saw the rabbit itself – only a small one which scuttled off through the hedge – but I hope we are not going to be pestered with them.

Went to Adelaide Square on Sunday evening. Sybil and Billy [Cuthbertson, her husband] are on the Tyne for a holiday. Helen and her boy, Gordon, are staying for a holiday from Luton. Mabel was there, of course, and Willie Forsyth, who is fed up waiting for a ship. Helen's husband was there for the weekend and went back to Luton while I was there; her girl, Dylis, is having a camping holiday. She is a telephonist at the G.P.O. and she has been working one year.

---

[65] People were being discouraged from travelling far for pleasure (train transport for war purposes was to get priority) and 'Holidays at Home' were actively promoted. These recreations in Bedford were described in some detail in the *Bedford Record*, 27 July 1943, p. 1 and 3 August 1943, pp. 1–2. See also: Antrobus, '"Holidays at Home" in Bedford during the Second World War', note 61.

Friday, 13 August.

Cold as winter. To judge by the sound of planes this week Germany is still getting hell. It was bad enough for us getting all the bombing early in the war; what must it be like after being worn down with the restrictions and misery of nearly 4 years of war? I wonder if you have seen Churchill this week. I see by the papers he has been to Niagara Falls.[66] The girls (or women) at the lunch table go on about Mary Churchill, ATS, having so much leave to gad about, but I think that if her father wants her company surely he is entitled to it for all he does for the country.[67]

We had a little excitement in the Works [W.H. Allen & Sons Engineering] on Wednesday. They had just come back after a 9 days' holiday and the men in the Machine Shop had a sit down strike. I went and had a peep at them from a gantry leading from the Offices. All the machines were stopped and men standing or sitting about talking. If I had not been told, I should not have known it was a strike – it looked so much like some of the Offices working!! Especially the Drawing Office. I do not know the facts of the case – it is all very hush, hush – but there has been a reshuffle of all heads of departments and the Machine Shop objects to its new Head; also they say it affects the men's bonus. Other Shops struck in sympathy. They managed to get them to start work in the afternoon and there is to be a meeting about it today. Loud clamour of disgust by all those discussing it.

Tuesday, 17 August.

I have heard no more about the strike. On Saturday night we had one hour of the double summer time reduced [this hour was lost in the evening and gained in the morning]. It is a pity with so much to be done in the harvest fields and the holidays on too. They give us the extra hour daylight in the evenings early in April, when it is too cold to take advantage.

It is grand to see all the cornfields in our district at this time of the year. A good many of the fields are stacked and on Sunday afternoon I saw lumbering across Bromham Bridge (26 arches) a threshing machine plus gasoline tank, caravan etc. Later I saw it parked on the roadside nearer Bedford, so they must be going to thresh for all the smaller farms that have never grown corn before. I visited my friends' small-holding on Sunday evening. That is the friend who had twins. They have taken about an acre of an old apple orchard and have calves, pigs and hens.

---

[66] Churchill left Britain on 5 August and did not return until 19 September, after extensive travels and talks in both Canada and the North-East United States. His visit to Niagara Falls was not his first; he had been there in 1900 (Gilbert, *The Road to Victory: Winston S. Churchill 1941–1945*, p. 469). *Road to Victory*, chaps 28–30, recounts these weeks abroad. Leah's question to Winnie suggests that she lived somewhere in Southern Ontario, perhaps not too far from Niagara Falls (where she took a holiday in September 1944).

[67] The Prime Minister's daughter, Mary (born 1922, later Mary Soames), a member of the Auxiliary Territorial Service, sometimes accompanied her father on his overseas trips, and this was resented by many ordinary citizens, who were mostly living under significant constraints and routinely confronted with the well-publicised question, 'Is your journey *really* necessary?' Mary's privileged life did not sit well with these people (see for example our edition of *A Shop Assistant in Wartime: The Dewsbury Diary of Kathleen Hey, 1941– 1945*, Yorkshire Archaeological and History Society [Woodbridge, 2018], pp. 125–26). Mary's own account of her trip this month to Canada is found in Mary Soames, *A Daughter's Tale: The Memoir of Winston Churchill's Youngest Child* (New York, 2011), chap. 14.

He is a cobbler by trade and looks after the stock in his spare time! And they live 2–3 miles from the holding. He certainly won't ever get fat, especially as he has dug some of the ground and [is] growing vegs.

Jim seems to be having a good time in London going to shows and show-places. No sign of any leave yet. He is finished at 2 on Saturdays and Sundays but after crossing London and 50 miles to Bedford, he would have no time here.

The ban is placed on Worthing this week – i.e. no visitors allowed. My Aunt Sarah is trying to get a permit from police for me. I hope she is successful. I will go snap if I do not get a rest and change. I expect they are massing troops on that coast for some attack on the Continent.

I saw Sybil and she has seen Stella, who, she said, looked well but still in bed. Perhaps the latest operation has done the trick. Apparently Uncle A. is very anxious to get back South!!

Wednesday, 18 August.
John's birthday. He will be 39. It was announced yesterday that all Sicily was in Allied hands. According to an American journalist in this morning's paper, the Americans entered Messina 50 minutes before the British. We had an alert during the night – heard no bombs. I keep reading about raids and damage on South Coast towns (no names given). It is really a bit risky to go there for a holiday.

Friday, 3 September.
Fourth anniversary of outbreak of war. We are to have 2 minutes of silence at 11 a.m. on account of it being a day of prayer.[68]

You will notice the long break since my last entry. Well, I had my week's holiday at Worthing all right. On the journey I managed to go wrong on the underground when crossing London and found I was going through Whitechapel. I got out at the next station and managed to get to Victoria. We had to change at Brighton and the loudspeaker there was warning people to have identity cards and *permits* ready before exit. I wondered what it would be like at Worthing, 10 miles further along the coast, as I had no permit. However, Worthing was not a banned area. The sea air was grand, but it was well nigh impossible to see the sea! The coast is entirely lined with pill-boxes with just a few feet between and those spaces are filled with piles of barbed wire. The beach was prohibited and, in fact, I never saw one entry on to the beach. The whole area was filled with Canadian soldiers. All their tanks, lorries etc. were parked in the roads near the sea, under the trees in private estates etc. There were many regiments, but all Canadian. It struck me as funny to see 'Ottawa Highlanders' wearing tartan too. The girl who helps my aunt is engaged

[68] Details in the *Bedford Record*, 7 September 1943, p. 1. The printed chronicle by Herbert Edward Barker, *A Bedford Diary of Four War Years* (np, 1943), written in later 1943, concluded on this day, the fourth anniversary of the outbreak of war, with words of hope (p. 31) that were rare before later 1942: 'The war still continues it is true, but it is a happier England and a happier Bedford that continues to accept, without complaint, its many tribulations. It is with grateful hearts to God for deliverance in the past and with our eyes on the imminent future, that until the final victorious chapters can be written, this is THE END.' (We are grateful to Stuart Antrobus for sending us a copy of this source.)

to a Canadian, so is her sister, and the butcher's assistant is married to one and my Aunt says it is the same all over the place, so after the war there will be an influx of Sussex girls in Canada as there will be of Bedfordshire in the States.[69]

I had a nice restful holiday with lovely weather but nothing like a seaside or country holiday on account of movement being so restricted. There were no raids or warnings during the week. Father stayed at Luton. Twice we had the police at the house while I was there as the blackout was faulty. After the double summer time and going to bed in daylight, people have not got into the way of blacking out. As I was dropping off to sleep one night this week there was a loud rapping at the door. Pa had not blacked out his little window. Pa immediately put out the light and as there was no more knocking we did not go down. We do not know whether it was the police, ARP warden, or a neighbour. The blackout is a nuisance; it takes such a time to undo next morning.

Since being back at the Office I have been up to my eyes in work and the benefit of the rest has quite worn off.

Saturday, 4 September.
A letter from Sunderland was waiting for me last night. They had news on Wednesday that Noble (Jessie's husband) was missing after the big raid on Tuesday. Jessie is in great distress and they sat up all night waiting for more news.[70] Quite recently he was shot into the sea and rescued. Italy [was] invaded yesterday.

Wednesday, 8 September.
Yesterday was the 7th anniversary of my operation and the 6th anniversary of Pa going into hospital for 9 weeks. We are still alive and kicking. On Monday night, though, I had a near squeak. I was cycling over Bromham Bridge, a long bridge with 26 arches but very narrow. I was blinded by the setting sun. A car was coming towards me and a vehicle was behind me. I thought the driver behind me might not see me on account of level sunlight so I kept well in to the bridge wall. It was evident that the vehicle behind was trying to overtake me just as the car (a jeep) and I were about to pass. I was amazed to find that it was a *bus* overtaking and then I heard the grind of an impact. The vehicles drew apart and stopped and I dismounted. An American boy got off the jeep and he looked so crestfallen I asked

---

[69] C.P. Stacey and Barbara Wilson, *The Half-Million: Canadians in Britain, 1939–1946* (Toronto, 1987), chaps 5 and 6, tell some of the stories of these men. Of the roughly 500,000 Canadian troops posted to Britain during the Second World War, a great many were based in Sussex and Surrey. It was understandable that many of them established relationships with local women, romantic or opportunistic, transient or permanent. A significant percentage of the 45,000 war brides who travelled to Canada after the war, often with their children (p. 180), probably came from these two counties. Relationships with the locals were sometimes tense, frequently inflamed by the local press; but they improved over time and there is scant evidence of misdemeanors beyond the high spirits that might be expected of lonely young men far from home and often frustrated by inaction. Anglo-American weddings in Bedford-shire are reported in the *Bedford Record*, 25 May 1943, pp. 1 and 3, and in other issues of this paper throughout the year.

[70] Noble Hugill, aged 29, was a member of a Stirling bomber crew that left Mildenhall air base in Suffolk on 31 August 1943. It was shot down on its mission to Berlin.

if anyone was hurt. He said 'Hurt!! *You* might have been.' The bus was an army bus – empty – and the driver was a soldier. There was a nasty gash on the side of the bus where they had scraped past each other. As the driver seemed unhurt I was going to hurry off, as there was not much daylight left and I have no lights but they stopped me and took my name and address, as a witness I suppose. I did not realize my danger until afterwards. It certainly was a tight squeeze between the bridge wall and the bus and the bus was drawing to the wall as it passed me.

Great rejoicings next door; Bob Last walked in on Monday night unexpectedly for 9 days leave from Gibraltar. He is Joy's husband.[71]

Thursday, 9 September.
It was announced last night that an armistice had been made with Italy. This morning's paper said it was actually signed on 3rd September – the day we 'invaded' Italy. Everybody seems to be taking it very quietly (there are 2 flags on our Office buildings). All the excitement was when there was a false alarm about peace with Italy.

Your letter of 12 August received this morning. This is the first I have heard from you since last January. You do not seem to have heard from me either. *The Monarch of the Glen* must have gone to the bottom of the sea. Your letter seems to have been in the water. The flap was hanging loose and no sign of gum anywhere. The cutting about Roland was all stuck together and when I got it unstuck parts were unreadable, especially about young Irvin's gift for mechanical drawing (on the wall paper I gleaned). I got the gist of the cutting and it was very interesting. The wedding photo of Olive's sister was quite O.K. and they are a good-looking couple. The children's letters returned have evidently been in the water as all the letters (words) are running but *your letter is quite O.K.* The whole package felt slightly damp but no censor's mark anywhere. It is very mysterious. Perhaps the postman had an accident.

Tuesday, 14 September.
I took my tea to the garden on Saturday and dug the main-crop potatoes for ½ hour. Flossie Clarke and her sister came up and helped me a bit, then went off blackberrying.[72] They gave me some of their blackberries, took some of my garden

---

[71] One William Last, labourer, was householder at 101 Marlborough Road, some 100 yards up the road from the Aynsleys.

[72] Picking blackberries was a common activity in many parts of rural England in late August to October. It was remembered by one evacuee as a seasonal activity in south-west Bedfordshire (Michael Dundrow, *A Lasting Impression: One Boy's Wartime in the Country* [Dunstable, 1981], p. 151) and was mentioned in other wartime diaries: for example, Chris McCooey, ed., *Despatches from the Home Front: The War Diaries of Joan Strange 1939–1945* (Tunbridge Wells, 1994), pp. 72–3 (near Worthing, West Sussex); 'The Diary of Leonard Adamson 1941–1942', in Patricia and Robert Malcolmson, eds., *Warriors at Home 1940–1942: Three Surrey Diarists*, Surrey Record Society (Woking, 2012), p. 170; and Patricia and Robert Malcolmson, eds., *A Londoner in Lancashire 1941–1943: The Diary of Annie Beatrice Holness*, Record Society of Lancashire and Cheshire (Liverpool, 2016), pp. 29–30, 34, 44–5, 119 and 121. This was one of the many ways in wartime of achieving a degree of food self-sufficiency.

produce and then went home for their tea. When I was setting to work again after tea, I noticed a soldier talking to 2 other gardeners down the lane and behold it was Jim!! He had got back by 5 o'clock, had tea with Pa and dashed straight to the garden. He had no leave, but sneaked home for the weekend, the other men getting passes etc. for him and covering up (they hope). I hope he has not been missed by the authorities and suffering for it now. He came home specially to get the potatoes up – and cleared the ground, which is a great load off my mind. He went back at 8.10 on Sunday night. It was nice to see him again. He read your letter and the cuttings.

Although he was not expected (I'd had a letter on Friday saying he had no leave until October), luckily there was lots of food in the house. For breakfast he had fried sausage, potatoes and tomatoes, stewed blackberries, marmalade and bread, preceded by an apple; dinner cold roast lamb, runner beans (1s lb. in shops), potatoes and apple pie; [for] tea, tinned salmon, cucumber, tomatoes, lettuce, finished up stewed blackberries, lemon curd, chocolate cake and biscuits. Not bad for wartime fare? I told him we had used up [the] last jelly and asked him to try to get some in London. I managed to get some peanut butter at Boots the chemist this week: I have put it by for the winter. Jim goes to a Canadian Club, 'The Beaver', for snacks and gets peanut butter in the sandwiches. He says there is a woman there who makes hot pancakes, spreads marg thick on one, then another pancake, then hot syrup on the top. He likes them. What are they called? Our Canadian draughtsman has been left our Works for a year so I cannot ask him.[73]

Friday, 17 September.
Nothing much to report. There was an alert last night; some said they heard bombs dropped but I did not. Last night our planes were going over in dozens and at 3 a.m. I was wakened by their coming back. I have sold a ½ cwt. potatoes for 3s 6d. In shops they are 5 lb. for 6d. Sold 2 lb. tomatoes at 1s per lb. – 1s 4d in shops. Last week I sent box of tomatoes and 2 cucumbers to Aunt T. in Sunderland. The acknowledgement said they came in the nick of time as there was nothing for dinner so they had salad. I do not know what Aunt T. is trying to imply by that – whether there is a real dearth in Sunderland or whether she is exaggerating. I guess tomatoes would be scarce but 'nothing for dinner' sounds the limit.

---

[73] The Beaver Club, meant for 'other ranks', opened in February 1940 and was located in Spring Gardens, just off Trafalgar Square near Canada House, home of the Canadian High Commission. Although designed to serve Canadian troops, British, Australian and New Zealand troops also visited it. 'The Beaver Club offered a wide variety of services: a canteen featuring Canadian-style food, writing and reading rooms, games rooms, an Information Bureau where the servicemen could get all kinds of facts about London, including particulars of available accommodation, and assistance in planning leave throughout the country; checking [i.e., chequeing], banking facilities, showers and baths, and a barber shop. A large corps of voluntary women workers helped to staff the club.' From the beginning the Beaver Club proved enormously popular – particularly so, perhaps, because the Americans closed their facilities to non-Americans. Jim's enthusiasm for the food was echoed by a Canadian sergeant who wrote in 1945: 'Had supper at the Beaver Club, and what do you think it was? Waffles with real maple syrup and coffee with cream floating on top – boy, was it ever good!' (Stacey and Wilson, *The Half-Million*, pp. 102, 104, and 106).

You can get fruit and vegs where they grow. When Bedford had a glut of plums in August there were none in Worthing as they are not grown, but there were heaps of tomatoes while Bedford had none. Growers are not allowed to transport far. Of course nothing much is grown up North and they have big populations to snap it all up. Sent a box of tomatoes to my old friend Cissie in Sunderland.

Monday, 20 September.
A nice weekend. On Saturday afternoon I went blackberrying near the garden, and bottled some of them on Sunday. Bottling is a new art for me; I did some damsons last week, one jar a success but the other would not seal. I do them in ordinary jam jars but use vacuum snap closures and only boiling water (no syrup or tablets). Everybody else seems expert at the job.

There was a plane burning on the hill opposite the garden; it had crashed just before I arrived. It was too far off to know the extent of the damage. Heard from Jim; he had been to Zoo on Saturday afternoon, a ballet at the New Theatre (Sadler's Wells Corps) in the evening and was going to play tennis Sunday afternoon.

Wednesday, 22 September.
Had a short alert just after going to bed. I did not get up. This morning had a letter from Uncle A. enclosing yours of 11ᵗʰ July. Stella seems to be greatly improved and is putting on weight, which is something to be thankful for. The weather had been very cold since Sunday. I have donned my thick Harris tweed coat. I am afraid the tomatoes will not ripen and there are loads of green ones to come on.

Friday, 24 September.
On Wednesday night there was a long letter from Stella herself. She thinks she will be in the San[atorium] over Christmas. There was also a letter from my friend Cissie. She was very pleased with tomatoes. She has had 3 new ceilings put up, all the windows renewed and the main roof repaired, but the roof over the room that juts out the back has to be done. She is now waiting for decorators and her furniture to be repaired. I think I mentioned she was blitzed last May. It takes a long time to get put right again. We are all compelled to pay War Damage Insurance (Pa pays £1 1s 0d, Jim £3 6s 8d per annum) – only house owners – and people get all bomb damage made good. What does not seem right to me is that wealthy people who only rent their house do not have to pay anything but their furniture would be made good. I suppose I ought to be grateful we have suffered no bombing and not think about it, especially as I pay nothing myself!! It has turned milder again and I did not fetch all the green tomatoes from the garden last night, but I can see frost has blackened some of the bean vines. Sybil came up – she has a key to the garden and helps afternoons when she can. She is going to have a bit of garden for herself and I showed her where to start digging. She takes most of the beetroot and is going to pickle me some.

Monday, 27 September.
Nothing much to relate. A fine weekend and I had a good bonfire and got rid of all the rubbish. Next day I shovelled the ash round the fruit trees. I weeded in the north-east corner (see map) and planted snowdrops. I have had rose mallows in that

corner during the summer (a flower new to me) and they were very beautiful. I had some cos lettuce that had grown higher than my shoulder!! They were very fresh and green but useless for salad, so I staggered along to the mystery man with an armful for his fowls. He gave them a couple and said the rest were good enough to boil as cabbage. They certainly were better than his cabbage, which were riddled with caterpillars. I asked him his name; it is Hughes. They seem very poor people – slummy. The wife had told Sybil she used to be a typist in London earning £5 a week.[74] I wish you could see her. You rarely find such a dirty unkempt creature nowadays. She once said to me that the seats in London parks were so dirty she always spread newspaper before she sat on them! I smiled to myself. I think she is a bit missing in the upper regions, but she certainly is well spoken. I brought 20 lb. green tomatoes, only 2 lb. of which had slightly turned colour. There are tomatoes all round the house. I bottled some ripe ones.

Tuesday, 28 September.
It is very cold and wet. It was in the newspaper today that central heating was permitted in Scotland and the 6 most northern counties in England. It has turned cold earlier this year; last year the edict was 'no heating until 1st November' but it had to be relaxed in middle of October. We found our heating coming on in the middle of this afternoon in spite of the regulation against it. The girls in the work-shops could not work in the cold; it was bad enough in the offices. The coal output is less than ever and 7000 more miners have come out on strike (in Scotland).[75]

Friday, 1 October.
Ever since the heat has been on in the Offices it has turned warm and wet. I went up to the garden straight from work to get vegs for weekend. Frost has got the cucumbers since last Sunday but the tomatoes do not seem affected yet. I gathered 3 lb. just turned colour. I gathered runner beans, carrots, parsley and mint, also a little spinach, and then had to hurry home as it is dark about 7 o'clock. I think it is about the last time I shall get to the garden on a weeknight until next Spring. I shall miss it very much. I see they are advertising a B.B.C. Symphony concert at the Corn Exchange for next Wednesday [at 7 p.m.] so winter has fairly started.[76] I

---

74 Wartime brought many newcomers to gardening – and prompted various authorities on the subject to advise them.

75 The Government was now aggressively committed to restricting the domestic use of coal in order to maximise supplies for war-related activities. Firm limits were to be imposed on how much householders could buy. The Ministry of Fuel and Power put out repeated notices from later 1943 regarding strict regulations for consumption and calls for frugality. 'The time has now come', as one announcement put it, 'when a measure of hardship must be accepted in order that military operations may be pressed forward' (*Bedford Record*, 7 March 1944, p. 3). To make matters worse, coal output was declining. According to *The Times*, 18 September 1943, p. 5: 'In each week of the three summer months of this year the coal output in Scotland has been 25,000 tons lower than it was a year ago. The average output of each man is less. In all the coalfields together the output in August was 210,000 tons less each week than it was in August last year.'

76 *Bedfordshire Times*, 1 October 1943, p. 9. A notice in the *Bedfordshire Times*, 15 October 1943, p. 9, indicates that lunch-hour BBC concerts were to be held fortnightly on Fridays at 1.15 p.m.

went to another lecture last Tuesday night on 'Autumn on the Farm' by a member of the War Agricultural [Executive] Committee. It was very interesting and the discussion afterwards was very lively. It is hardly a subject to interest you Winnie, or any other city dweller, but nearly everyone here has some interest in 'the land'. As Tony next door (aged 3) said this week: 'The country is not very far away is it, Auntie Leah?' One thing the lecturer said that astonished me (and I hardly believe it) is that English farms are the most highly mechanized in the *world*. I wonder what Americans and our colonists would say to that statement [Leah was right to be sceptical]. He also said that all the sugar on the ration in this country is produced by ourselves from sugar beet. This is borne out by a man I spoke to yesterday and who had just come from a fortnight in Peterborough. He had never seen anything like the constant stream of vehicles loaded with beet arriving at the sugar beet factory there. All day long and every day they were arriving. It is their harvest time I suppose. It is a very expensive business producing the actual sugar.[77]

Monday, 4 October.
It has been a nice weekend. I took my tea to the garden as usual on Saturday. I weeded and shaped the flower beds in N.E. corner and started weeding the N. hedge. I find I like jobs that affect the shape and appearance of the garden better than I like dealing with the crops themselves. I suppose if it was not for the war I would never have thought of growing my own vegetables, but as you said in your last letter to Stella, home grown vegs taste *much* better than those from a shop. We even thought last winter that our own dried haricot beans tasted better than bought ones. They certainly did not require any soda to cook them soft. We have our own dried peas this year.

Flossie Clarke and her sister arrived, on their way home *from* blackberrying, for some potatoes, and we arranged to go to the pictures tonight straight from work. They had an American soldier staying with them last weekend and they *did* like him. Flossie has an old school friend in America and he is a relation of hers (or her husband). It was his first leave in 2 years, having just come from Ireland. The Clarkes are the sort to make anyone feel at home (although they are all females, the father being dead), and according to them this American had all the virtues a man could possibly have, so they must have had a nice weekend. At any rate, Flossie stayed away from work Friday, Saturday and Monday to entertain him, which is more than I would have done.

Just as they left and I was settling down to my tea, and book, Doff Simmonds arrived to leave her bike with me while she went blackberrying.

Father decided to go to Luton and stay a day or two, so on Sunday afternoon I took him to the bus. It was a good job I went with him as I had to stand a long time in a queue for him while he sat on a seat in the square. He could not have stood all that time and he would never have got a seat in the bus if he had been at the end of the queue. I went home, had an early tea, then off to the garden and did a lot of

---

[77] The production of sugar beet, which was subsidised, had increased by at least twenty-seven percent since the later 1930s. In 1944 the area of sugar beet reached the high total of 431,000 acres (Keith A. H. Murray, *Agriculture* [London, 1955], pp. 201, 206 and 238, a volume in the *History of the Second World War, United Kingdom Civil Series*, ed. W. K. Hancock).

work along the N. hedge and defined a path along it. There was an alert during the night but, as usual, I did not get up. I had some scurrying around this morning to leave the empty house ship-shape.

Wednesday, 6 October.
What a dreadful [ink] blot I have just made above [on part of the word 'scurrying']. I went to the pictures Monday evening, the first time for ages. It was *The Great Waltz* with Strauss music. It was fairly good.[78] I am afraid I am hard to please with films nowadays. I prefer a straight drama to something with music popped in, in season and out of season. When I got home after 9 p.m. I found Pa had not returned and I had to grope for the backdoor key in the barn, blackout [the house] in the darkness before I could light up. Everything was as I had left it at 8.10 a.m. Apparently there was another alert during the night but I never heard a thing.

Pa came home Tuesday teatime and was just having his tea when I got home. He would not commit himself as to whether he had a nice time or not. The talk and discussion at the Adult School was on 'Science and the Community'. I thought it very unsatisfactory. It was agreed that science meant *all* knowledge and then they debated as to whether we were better off with or without science. The trend of the debate was as to whether we were the better for wireless, explosives, modern chemistry etc., and when I pulled them up and asked if they still meant by science 'all knowledge including music and art' they all agreed 'yes'. So unless they specified which 'science' and the community they were talking about, I considered you could get no answer, as surely there could be no community without some sort of knowledge. The discussion was as nebulous as if it had been on 'Action and the Community'.

Saturday, 9 October.
There was quite a long alert on Thursday evening, but nothing worse at Bedford. London, however, had rather a bad raid, the worst for over a year. It was said to be a new experience for the American and Canadian troops stationed there.[79]

Last night on my way home from work I cycled to Goldington to collect rent for Jim as they [his tenants] had not been with it for 6 weeks. It is nearly 2 miles on the other side of the town. I went via the Embankment and Russell Park and I was struck with the autumn beauty. The Embankment gardens were full of bright autumn flowers and the trees had all their autumn tints. The wide level stretches of grass in Russell Park were deserted except for one American soldier sitting on a seat who seemed to be lost in a brown study. The river runs through, lined with pollard willows, and there are fine avenues of lime trees. It is not a scene you would find anywhere in the North of England. On the farther side of the river to the Embankment – called Mill Meadows – there is a military encampment. The men practice on the river with invasion barges. It has been there some time but it is so long since I was in this neighbourhood it was new to me.

It is a lovely day today and I feel peeved I cannot go to the garden. I am going to a party at 5 p.m. at Trixy's, so will do some arrears of shopping early in the

---

[78] This 1938 American film was based loosely on the life of Johann Strauss.
[79] London had been spared heavy raids since 10/11 May 1941.

afternoon. You might think I ought to be sick of the garden, but I never am. Now that the evenings are dark, it is the one thing I long for in the stuffy, drab offices – the weekend and the peace and freshness of the garden. 'Music while you work' has just struck up [on the radio] so I had better go and do some to the tune of it. It is not in the Offices but comes from the factory through the open windows.

Monday, 11 October.
I have had a heavy cold over the weekend; on Saturday I was in a fever, Sunday was one constant stream from my head, but this morning I feel better provided I can keep warm. I think a cold is not bad if it comes away through the nose. I made good use of that tin of lemon you sent 18 months ago.

In spite of what I felt like on Saturday I thoroughly enjoyed Trixy's party. Her spread was even bigger than last time and there were 10 to tea and 11 to supper. There were stewed pears, prunes, pineapple jelly with chunks of fruit in and raspberry jelly, jam, honey, homemade jam tarts, queen cakes, rock cakes, bought bakewell tarts and a big cake. Supper was the same plus sandwiches.

There were 5 people I had not met before, including a farmer, Evan Costin, who looks typically Welsh. His sister Dorothy was there too, whom I do know. What struck my fancy was that they were telling us about an Italian prisoner they have living with them to help on the farm, and no guard of any sort. They said he was a splendid worker, but neither knows the other's language. Evan is trying to learn Italian from a book. In the middle of the party Dorothy went off to the doctor's 2 miles away to fetch the prisoner's medicine!! She came back again. Apparently he suffers from sleeplessness. Then at 10.30 she said it was time they went home as she had to be up extra early to get the prisoner's breakfast (or something) as he was going to early mass at Ampthill!!![80] No wonder you see pictures of Italians wild with joy at being taken prisoners. War has some amazing phases.[81] Of course, there is the other case I mentioned on 23rd July. That poor Italian had gone mad. You can well expect madness and sleeplessness, if they get any knowledge of what is going on in their own country.

Wednesday, 13 October.
Jim says they are having all exams this week and if he gets through in good time he will be home on Thursday night. If not, it will be Friday morning. He says they were on the edge of the raid last week, but the A.A. [anti-aircraft] firing was

[80]   There was a POW camp at Ampthill, which would have included a chapel (Risby, *Prisoners of War in Bedfordshire*, pp. 23–5).
[81]   A London boy who had been evacuated to Totternoe in south-west Bedfordshire remembered vividly the Italian POWs who arrived in the village to work on a dredging project. He and his pals went to watch and mock them: 'We found a group of twenty or so friendly, darkly handsome young men in strange maroon coloured uniforms with green patches on their back, working with skill and precision, swinging axes, wielding picks and sawing timber to cheerful cries and snatches of song. There was nothing to laugh at there.' There were 'a couple of British guards leaning on their rifles and smoking – it was all so relaxed, so unusual and unexpected, so fascinating.' Restrictions were minimal, and the children socialised freely with the prisoners, to the extent that language barriers permitted (Dundrow, *A Lasting Impression*, p. 81). Such freedoms for Italian prisoners were commonplace.

nothing to write about. I think he means that the noise was not as bad as some people make out.

I was at another lecture by an American on 'America' last night. I thoroughly enjoyed it. The lecturer (Jackson) was from the American Red Cross Club (for American soldiers).[82] He seemed very well educated – had been to Harvard in fact – and I could well understand every word and phrase he used; quite unlike the last one, who was from Chicago and although he had been to college I had the greatest difficulty in understanding his speech. Mr Jackson was born in Colorado, educated in the East, lived somewhere else, and had been in the 48 states, so he was well qualified to tell us a bit about America – and he did: all about the industrial North, the 'solid' (?) South, the Eastern States that are most like the English, the vital middle West with its farm lands, how the miners live in the mountains, cowboys, the Red Indian question, the Negro problem, education, slums etc. He was a very charming man, and like a flapper I 'fell' for him. I meant to ask him what he meant by 'solid' South, which he kept saying, but I forgot when discussion time came. One thing that interested me (trust me to fasten on to anything agricultural) was that in the region they breed cattle, the cattle can live on nothing but buffalo grass and water all winter, but once the ground is ploughed buffalo grass will never grow again. His favourite topic was Red Indians.

Monday, 18 October.

On Saturday afternoon Jim went to a big Scout do in the town[83] and I tried my luck again at shopping. We both went folk dancing in the evening – but I think I am getting too old for that exercise; after 4 dances I was completely done up and would not dance any more. I arrived late and there were only 2 more dances when I stopped, so it did not look too badly.

What a bad year this has been for clothes moths. They are in all Jim's clothes and he spent Sunday afternoon running a hot iron over them, which he said killed the eggs. Even his hat was eaten and white flannels that were parcelled up. He had put naphthalene in all his pockets and trouser bottoms, and the only suit that escaped was one I put newspapers over. I wish I had done it to them all. My clothes have escaped but I have a very air-tight wardrobe and I *never* leave the door open. I killed a few moths daily all through the summer. It is unusual to find so many here.

Wednesday, 20 October.

The newspaper never came this morning and I was going to call at the shop to see about it, but a neighbour called out 'No papers this morning. They have bombed

82 The American Red Cross had a club on Bromham Road. Another for officers was soon to open at the junction of Goldington Road and Kimbolton Road: 'There will be sleeping accommodation for between two and three hundred officers, and the club will contain a restaurant and snack bar, lounge with radio, library, recreation hall, and other amenities.' (*Bedford Record*, 12 October 1943, p. 1). Its premises featured a large and impressive mural of the four-engine B-17 (reproduced in Lutt, *Bedfordshire at War*, p. 96).
83 This gathering was described in detail in the *Bedford Record*, 19 October 1943, p. 2, with a photo on p. 1. Hundreds attended. Jim's personal photograph album from the 1920s (held by his son, John Aynsley) is dominated by pictures of his attendance at summer Scouts' camps and other such gatherings. Scouting was at its heyday during the interwar years.

the line near Luton.' I have heard it was at Leagrave, which is on the same side of the town as John's house. Jim is going there tomorrow so we will get details. He has asked me to go to the theatre with him tonight to see one of those mystery shows – sort of Maskelyne and Devant affair.[84] He has not spent one evening at home since he came on leave and I reminded him he ought to give Pa one evening, so he is going to stay in on Saturday, his last evening.

Friday, 22 October.
Jim had a nice time at Luton yesterday. Three bombs only were dropped the other night and John's house was not affected in any way. Although I may not mention it, we have alerts every night lately and London has had bombs at different times.

Monday, 25 October.
Jim heard at the barber's on Saturday that bombs were dropped in centre of Luton on Friday evening, but I have heard no details. We had a long alert at the time and the 'All Clear' went just before I had a bath. I was glad because it is most weird hearing bombs drop around while you are in a bath. It happened with me once because I did not want to waste the hot water that was in the bath when the alert went. I read of a case where [a] bath containing [a] lady was blown into the street in London.
    Jim went back to London last night. He has another 9 weeks' training and hopes to get a leave just after Christmas. He has done a lot of digging in the garden but it has been a wet week.

Wednesday, 27 October.
We have had thick fog for 3 days. Some shiploads of repatriated prisoners have been coming in from Germany and some of the least injured or well-recovered have come to Bedford (Kempston Barracks) before being dispersed or drafted back to the army. Some people saw them unloading from the train early yesterday morning.[85] The lecture last night was on 'America in World Politics'. We will know a bit about America at this rate. The lecturer was a schoolmaster who has never been to America. He is from one of the London secondary schools evacuated to Bedford. Next week we are having Sir Adrian Boult speaking on 'Interpretation of Music'. He is a famous BBC Symphony conductor. As we are only 22 members in our Adult School we are trying to get as many friends as possible to swell the audience.

Monday, 1 November.
It has been a dreary wet weekend after a foggy week. The garden was saturated but I managed to transplant a few wallflower seedlings to fill in gaps along the side of the path. Also on Saturday afternoon I took a trowel to the wood to get

---

[84] 'A Magic Review' at the Royal County Theatre (*Bedford Record*, 16 October 1943, p. 8). Nevil Maskelyne and David Devant authored *Our Magic: The Art in Magic, The Theory in Magic, The Practice of Magic* (London, 1911).
[85] There was a 'Welcome Home' for some of these former POWs at the Toc H Club, Bromham Road. Later, they were taken to the cinema as a treat (*Bedford Record*, 26 October 1943, p. 1 and 2 November 1943, pp. 1 and 3).

some primrose and bluebell roots but I could not find a sign of one after ¼ hour's search; all had died completely back. There was an alert last night and paper says bombs fell on London.

Wednesday, 3 November.
Had a letter from Aunt Tiny. No news of Noble but 3 weeks ago they heard that the wireless operator on the same plane was a prisoner. They are dreading Xmas. Also some of Janet's birthday cakes arrived – made by Lily. Not tasted yet. There was a list of her presents, including £2 10s 6d of money. Some of it is for books. If that child buys any more books she will be smothered in them.

Father is very poorly; it is time he had a liver injection, but he will not answer when I talk about it. There was a very good lecture last night by Sir Adrian Boult. He spoke informally and there were a lot of questions asked. He seems to have conducted orchestras, both English and Foreign, all over the Continent.

Friday, 5 November.
At 9.15 last night I heard bombs fall which shook the window sharply. At the same time I could hear the plane, but the alert did not go until 5 minutes after. I learnt today that they fell at Wootton (about 5 miles away) near an airfield, and killed 2 cows.

Mrs Simmons left word yesterday that she was going to her husband and did not know when she would return. After doing some housework etc. it was 9.45 a.m. before I reached the office. I took the opportunity to tell them as Mrs S. is expecting a baby at Christmas, and my Father is so ailing, I must definitely try and get my release for half-time. They were quite sympathetic.

Monday, 8 November.
Your letter dated 2nd October, in which you say you have the worst cold for years, arrived this morning. You evidently had not received mine written in September as you do not mention it and ask me to write soon.

I am going to the dentist tonight – what I absolutely hate and dread.

Tuesday, 9 November.
The dentist stopped a tooth and completed the job last night, for which I was pleased as he usually spreads a job over 2 or 3 visits. At 7.25 this morning, while I was having breakfast, we had a visit from the police. Pa was showing a light from his bedroom. He said he knew him and would have to have a talk with him. I said 'Would you like to go up now?' and he said 'Good heavens, no!' The bobby said it wanted ½ hour to [the] finish of blackout but according to the newspaper it only wanted another 10 minutes and was fairly light when we were talking at the front door. When I went up and tackled Pa about it, he said he thought it was past blackout. Pa looked very ill when he got downstairs. What he must feel like, and why he puts up with it rather than have a liver injection, I don't know. It was 9.50 when I reached the Office. No word from Mrs Simmons.

Wednesday, 10 November.
I forgot to mention that Uncle Albert walked in unexpectedly on Friday evening. He was on a week's holiday and staying at Adelaide Square. He came again last

evening and will be on his way North now. He looks well and seems as happy as a sandboy [i.e., carefree], which shows Stella must be doing well.

Monday, 15 November.
It has been a wretched weekend: thunder, hail, ice, and rain and cold wind all yesterday. On Saturday I spent all the afternoon trying to get navy wool for gloves for a Christmas present for Janet. I only succeeded in getting yarn – 4 oz. one coupon. I am making some with pre-war red wool for Jacqueline. There is a pattern knitted in, which I am doing with a bluey grey. The 4 fingers are in one compartment and can be worn over ordinary gloves if it is very cold – what I would call mittens, but they don't here. Spending so much time looking for wool made me forget I wanted a door mat. I heard a shop had a stock of them, but they are always closed when I go by from work. I dare say they would have been sold out in any case. Another thing I have hunted for all this week – brown shoe polish. I have not succeeded in getting any yet. I went to a folk dance class on Saturday night – to make a bit of a change.

The bombs that fell on a dance hall last Sunday evening were at Putney where Jim is, but he has not mentioned it in his letters. There were 180 killed.[86] I found we had a lb. margarine spare so I have packed it to send to my aunt at Worthing, where I stayed in the summer. She will be glad of it to make her Christmas cake. We have had our bacon ration cancelled and in exchange we get 2 oz. margarine each. We were glad of it when Jim was at home, but now it accumulates. If I can get released from morning work I will do a little cake making. I also sent her ½ lb. chocolate out of my sweet ration.

Tuesday, 16 November.
Your letter dated 23rd October arrived this morning – it has only taken 3 weeks. You say *The Monarch of the Glen* must be in Davy Jones' Locker [i.e., at the bottom of the sea]. Well after what you said about somebody taking all the chocolates and things you sent the Raws, I think it might have been stolen. Jim will be interested to hear Stan was in the Signals.

We also had a letter from our Mrs Simmons saying she is not coming to work any more. Considering she is expecting at Christmas, I should say not, but I was leaving it to her to leave when she thought fit. She was a good worker, and got on well with Pa. I took the matter up at the Office about getting my release from morning work. I have a form to fill in for the Ministry of Labour and must obtain a doctor's certificate that Father is not fit to look after himself [see next entry]. Which reminds me that Pa actually let the doctor give him an injection of liver extract yesterday. He never told me until just on bedtime, remarking 'Did I mention I got punctured?' I thought he was talking about his bike but he meant a puncture in his arm!

---

86 On 7 November 1943 a dance hall in Putney High Street was bombed, killing eighty-one people and injuring at least 200 more. This serious raid appears, in passing, as wartime background in a 2018 work of fiction, Michael Ondaatje's *Warlight* (London, 2018), p. 21.

Tuesday, 23 November.

This diary is getting neglected. Last Wednesday I got a certificate from the doctor which stated that Father had pernicious anaemia and senile decay and was unable to look after himself. My release [from full-time employment] came from the Labour Exchange on Saturday afternoon (very quick work) and I start part-time work next week. I went to the garden both Saturday and Sunday and collected sprouts, carrots and beetroot, and worked at tidying up; also planted some cuttings of hawthorn to form hedge on south fence. Planted cuttings of gooseberry and blackcurrant. Pruned apples. Berlin had its worst raid of the war last night. Hitler's house destroyed.[87]

Had a letter from Jim. As I had enquired about the Putney dance hall raid, he said some of their company had to be treated after the 'incident'. He said no more, but he said he was at a Folkdance party at Morley College [in Lambeth, for adult education] on Saturday night and there was a raid on. All trains and buses were stopped and he had to stay in Waterloo station until the 'all clear'. He said nothing about being 'gated' [i.e., confined] for staying out after hours!!

Thursday, 25 November.

Had a letter from Sunderland last night. Jessie has had official notice that Noble was killed on 1st September in operations over Berlin. His burial place is not known, so they presume he was burnt.[88]

Monday, 29 November.

It has been a wretched damp weekend so on Saturday afternoon I went to do some Christmas shopping. There seems more toys about this year but very expensive. All I bought was some Xmas cards and a green suede belt, but I had a good look round. I had to go to the garden on Sunday afternoon because the woman who lives in the bungalow and has the imbecile child, Mrs Hughes, had asked me to bring some wool from the town. She has given the wool for somebody to knit socks for her child and the knitter was so long knitting them she asked me to call and get the wool and pattern book back for her!! This is the woman who looks like a very poor tramp. I expect the knitting woman thought she would never see the money for them. She let me have the wool back straight away. I have started the half-time arrangement today and would you believe it, those men have given me more work than ever. I have typed 21 letters this afternoon.

Had a letter from Jim and he expects to be home for Christmas. Also he took part in a concert and all the performers did so well they are to have extra 48 hours leave before Christmas so he might be home any time now.

---

[87] Some 764 RAF aircraft were dispatched to attack Berlin, of which thirty-two were lost. Aircrew casualties were 167 killed and twenty-five taken prisoners of war. On the night of 23/24 November 383 aircraft were sent to Berlin; twenty-six were lost, 123 men were killed and twenty-four taken prisoners. These details are from Martin Middlebrook, *The Berlin Raids: RAF Bomber Command Winter 1943–44* (London, 2000; first published 1988), pp. 112 and 118–19. Leah's remark about 'Hitler's house' was not just a rumour. Middlebrook (p. 142) reports that one consequence of the bombings of 22/23 November, 'the worst raid of the war for Berlin' (p. 141), was: 'the destruction of Hitler's private train in a railway siding. Hitler was not present in Berlin at this time; he was at his headquarters in East Prussia throughout the Battle of Berlin.'
[88] He was one of 225 airmen killed that night (Middlebrook, *Berlin Raids*, p. 78).

Thursday, 2 December.
Had an alert last night but I do not know of anything happening. I see by the paper that Roosevelt, Churchill and Chiang Kai-shek are in Cairo together [actually the previous week, to plan the war against Japan].

Saturday, 4 December.
With this half-time arrangement I do not go in at all on Saturdays. I cooked a nice dinner – baked lamb, potatoes, sage and onions, all in one dish, and macaroni pudding and stewed apricots, and we wished Jim would walk in to dinner but he is evidently not having his extra 48 hours this weekend. This week has been so wet, and yesterday I was so fagged out with a week of hard typing in the afternoons (I have been relieved of one man but I still have to type for 7 others. I have kicked up about the 7th as he is head of the switchgear test department, which is nothing to do with my own department, which is Engineering Design. I think I am going to be relieved of him too) that I determined I would not go near the garden, but it was such a lovely day I went after dinner. I did a bit of hedge trimming, collected sprouts and intended digging some carrots but the first one was such a wopper I said to myself 'that will last us a week.' It weighed more than 1½ lb. I have some carrots left in the ground like a large sandcastle in which most of them are stored. It is the best way to keep roots. I came away just as the sun had reached the horizon and the moon was coming over the trees on the other side. I passed an aircraft carrier, i.e. a motor trailer 60 ft. long, and on it was the remains of a plane; such tiny little bits – I guess the plane must have crashed with all its bombs on board and got blown to smithereens. We used to see a lot of damaged planes being transported on these carriers and once I saw an almost intact German plane complete with swastikas. Planes were very busy this afternoon and some were so high I could not see them, but could see the streaks of vapour coming from them. I gather there cannot be much of Berlin left this week.[89] Churchill and Roosevelt seem to have gone on and met Stalin in Tehran.[90]

Monday, 13 December.
I have just got back to the Office after being away since Wednesday. Father has had a bad turn and I had to get the doctor in. He lost the use of his legs. On Friday the doctor said he would rally if he took things calmly; whereupon Pa got up to dinner (after sleeping most of the morning till 12.30) and then went out on his bike in the bitter cold!! Of course he was worse again after that.

Jim has been home from Friday night to Sunday night. He is coming again on Friday until over Xmas (10 days) and then is moving elsewhere immediately. The only things he wanted for Xmas were a pocket mirror and torch. I got him a mirror

---

[89] The RAF conducted four major raids on Berlin in late November.
[90] Churchill arrived in Teheran on 27 November and stayed there until 2 December. This meeting, the first between the leaders of the three great Allied powers, is chronicled in Gilbert, *Road to Victory*, chap. 34: 'They represented, Churchill told the meeting, probably "the greatest concentration of worldly power that had ever been seen in the history of mankind".' (p. 570). The Big Three discussions focused on their strategic military plans for 1944 and, to a lesser extent, the political character of postwar Europe.

in case, the size of a playing card, and it cost 10s 6d! Daylight robbery.[91] Also I had to go to 4 shops before I could get bedsocks for Stella. She likes them like Wellington boots, but those I got only cover the feet. I had to give 2 of my precious clothing coupons for one pair.

Wednesday, 15 December.
Father seemed a little better last evening (after being worse with going out on Friday) so I went out to my usual Tuesday lecture. I had a Christmas letter and Postal Order for 20s from my Aunt at Worthing. She used always to send a parcel of things to eat but now she cannot get the luxurious sort of things she used to send. She used to send things like gooseberry jam, Passion Fruit preserve, guava jelly etc. I have started to type out this diary so that I will have a spare copy in case of accident, and I am reminded of lots of things that happened last Spring that I had forgotten entirely.

Wednesday, 22 December.
Your parcel arrived on Monday in nice time for Christmas. We had the butterscotch pudding today. It was lovely. The parcel had not been tampered with and every-thing was safe. The thing in it that I needed most at the moment was the cough sweets. I have not been able to get any during the last week or more (they are unrationed). I am sending some of the cake decorations to Lily as I have no icing of any sort. Sybil showed me a cake she had made and iced last week. The almond paste was made of soya bean flour and almond essence. I was not very enamoured with the bit of paste she let me taste. I remember making it of ground nuts and almond essence once.

Thursday, 23 December.
I never can get a minute at this diary, just when it might be more interesting being Christmas. The Americans have given a party to the children. It was held in their Red Cross club.[92] The elementary school in our street had a party on Tuesday: all the children were carrying their own cups. So there is some food to be had. On Sunday I tackled a sort of Christmas cake as the baker cannot let me have one. It is the first I have made for about 12 years and I hope it turns out all right. I forgot I no longer possessed a cake tin and had to borrow from Peggy next door. I found she had no fruit so I let her have ½ lb. sultanas, to be refunded when she can get some. She must be a bit slow as she has the same grocer as we do and she has not had any of the sultanas or dried apricots they have had lately.

[91] This sum represented around a seventh or an eighth of a semi-skilled working man's weekly wage. Many everyday manufactured items had become very hard to obtain.
[92] This was a season when the British and Americans exchanged hospitality. US servicemen gave gifts to local children and to hospitals to distribute as part of the 'American Bundles for Britain' scheme, and also held parties for poor children. Some Bedfordshire families invited Americans to their homes for Christmas dinner (*Bedford Record*, 21 December 1943, p. 1 and 28 December 1943, pp. 1–2).

Christmas Eve.

It has been a bright frosty day and I have not been to work all day as the factory closed this dinnertime and I shall not go back until Tuesday afternoon. This is as long as pre-war Xmas holiday. I got some beef from the butcher for dinner tomorrow. I have not set eyes on a bird of any description this season. The only drink I could buy was lemon barley water. The man who sold it to me said 'It will be a nice Christmas drink if you mix a bottle of rum with it.' All the wine shops are labelled 'No wines or spirits.' The chrysanthemums on the market square (the cheapest place to buy anything) are 10s a bunch. I am using the jasmine out of our own garden.

Talking about the market reminds me that the children [her nieces] sent me a bundle of elastic. Lily said in her letter 'We found a shop with elastic last Thursday.' Well I never knew it was scarce because last time I was at the market I noticed a stall full of elastic. I am mentioning this to let you know that while a thing might be scarce in one town there is plenty in another.

Jim stayed at Luton last night. All the family are going to Lily's mother today to stay over Christmas. They go every year.

Mabel Forsyth [cousin, at 16 Adelaide Square] was operated on last Friday for a rupture. While she is in hospital they are going to do her varicose veins. She has them very bad. Father seems to be going on nicely at present.

Sunday, 26 December.

We have had a very pleasant quiet Christmas. It has been very calm and still with no sound of aeroplanes, and the church bells first thing Christmas morning (before it was light) were the loveliest I've heard. They say Halcyon Days are about Christmas time – well these have been Halcyon Days.[93] We had our tinned chicken for supper and all enjoyed it. Jim is going back after tea today.

Wednesday, 29 December.

I had a belated Christmas present arrive this morning, from my friend Celia in Sunderland. The one that had her home shattered last May. They had put most of the house right but not the back room (their kitchen-living room) and they arrived to do this on the Sunday before Xmas! They stripped the roof, put new beams in and re-slated it. She said the noise was like having a shipyard over her head. What a mush in the house for Xmas! Also a letter from Jim. He expects to be moved to Thirsk in Yorkshire, so may get to Sunderland.

Friday, 31 December.

New Year's Eve. Nothing is made of New Year here. The shops will be open as usual tomorrow. The Navy has been shining this week; the [battleship] *Scharnhorst* and 3 destroyers sunk [the former in the Arctic, the latter in the Bay of Biscay].

*   *   *   *

93 Halcyon days once referred to calm weather around the time of the winter solstice.

1944

Monday, 3 January.

I went to Mabel in hospital yesterday afternoon. She has had both operations (rupture and veins) and is going on well. Sybil and Helen were there too and I went to tea with them. Helen's little boy, Gordon, was staying at the house. He is 9 years old and had made the mince pies we ate. They were really nice pies and it was when I was complimenting Sybil that she said Gordon had made them. He carefully weighed all the stuff out first. His mother says he makes a very good Yorkshire pudding! It is the first time I have had pies made by a small boy. He has got the sweetest face I have ever seen on a boy – too sweet for a boy – but he is a very nice boy for all that. Jacqueline and he were playmates for years but I think they are growing out of each other. She'd be more of a boy than he. Helen lives close to John and Lily, and says Jacqueline is growing a lot quieter and Janet is a regular Aynsley.

Wednesday, 5 January.

I heard two terrific thumps at 7.45 this morning. I expected to hear the syrens go, but it was two Fortresses crashed near Bedford.

Monday, 10 January.

I have kept this diary a year now so you will have a fairly good idea of how we are living (in Bedford) in wartime. This weekend I have been turned out of my little office that I shared with Mr Townsend. Since I have been on part-time I have not done his work and now they have given him a typist all to himself so naturally she should be in the room, and I am out in the Design Department among a dozen others. Everybody thinks this is the best and that I must have been bored to tears in the little room, but I preferred the seclusion.

The new typist is a married woman bombed out from Kent. She has a son 16½ who has just been apprenticed in our firm. She is looking for a house and has just come from Bourne End, Bletsoe!! There are not more than 6 houses in that hamlet and I am wondering whether she has anything to do with the people who bought Uncle Albert's house. I shall ask her a few questions when I get to know her.

The Folk Dance Club had its annual party on Saturday and I thoroughly enjoyed it. It was held from 4 p.m. to 8 p.m. on account of the country people's buses. No buses run after 9 p.m. and cars are not allowed for pleasure [since mid-1942]. Of course, a good many cycle nowadays.

Jim has been at Thirsk in Yorkshire, nearly a fortnight. He is stationed in the workhouse.

Wednesday, 12 January.
Adult School Christmas party last night. About a dozen of us are arranging to go to the Ballet Rambert at the end of the month [27–29 January at the Bedford Town Hall].

Friday, 14 January.
Father has made up his mind to go to Luton this weekend. It is a bit risky for him at this time of the year, but I could not alter his intention.

Monday, 17 January.
Father went to Luton yesterday and I am wondering how he got on because it was freezing cold and inclined to be foggy. He had not returned during this morning. Being alone in the house I attempted to make some ginger nuts, but they did not turn out like the proper North country ginger nuts with the treacle oozing out of them. They are more like ginger snaps, which I am not very fond of, but I do like the nuts my Aunt Tiny sometimes sends.

We have been troubled with petty thieving; last week we had milk stolen from the doorstep and the week before money taken from the bag we put out for the baker (one of the neighbours saw some children do this). You may think us very careless leaving things outside, but all the years we have lived here we have had no trouble like that except for an evacuee boy who took some clean laundry left on the doorstep. Bedford was supposed to be a very honest town and the chief magistrate or judge used often to be given a new pair of gloves because there were no [criminal] cases at court. I remember seeing what looked like my bike in front of the butcher's. I reported it at home and Mother said 'Goodness, I borrowed it yesterday to go shopping, forgot about it, and walked home!' So she went after it post haste. I am afraid the character of the place has changed with so many strangers living here.[1]

Tuesday, 25 January.
Your New Year card arrived yesterday (posted 5/12/43). It had been opened by the censor. Also a newsy letter from your Father written on Christmas Day. It amuses us all the paper he uses, as we have to be very careful. We are not allowed to use full sheets in the Office but must type on both sides of small sheets of letter heading. Envelopes get used over and over again with fresh labels, but we must use new envelopes to send abroad so I have a special packet for sending to Canada.

We have had terribly high winds this weekend and the trellis in the back garden has broken down. I am wondering what has blown away since Saturday at the other

---

[1] A few months later a letter from a housewife concerning evacuees stated the opinion that: 'Bedford has already much more than its safe quota of juveniles' (*Bedfordshire Times*, 28 July 1944, p. 7). These outsiders included evacuees, official and private, from cities threatened with bombing (mainly London), munitions workers, men and women in uniform and employees of the BBC. The sudden arrival of many 'strangers' was, if not universal throughout wartime Britain, certainly very common, including in relatively remote regions: for example, Patricia and Robert Malcolmson, *Wartime Cumbria, 1939–1945: Aspects of Life and Work*, Cumberland and Westmorland Antiquarian and Archaeological Society (Carlisle, 2017), especially chaps 1, 2 and 5.

garden as it is very exposed to wind. I planted shallots on Saturday, but had a friend to tea on Sunday so did not get to the garden.

Tuesday, 1 February.
On Saturday night I went to the Ballet Rambert at the Town Hall. It is the first ballet I have seen for 7 years or more. It was enjoyable but 'wartimish' and I have certainly seen better. The only music was from 2 pianos, instead of an orchestra, and the corps was so small we had to have musical interludes while they were changing costumes.[2]

It was a nice dry weekend and I planted a row of broad beans. The wind had not caused much damage at the garden. I am reading a book by an American called *Magic Gardens* [1939]. She is very enthusiastic on herb gardens, and I think I will start a patch.[3] I already have mint, sage, parsley, rosemary and lavender, but there are at least 20 others. The idea is to brush past them, or tread on them, while walking about the garden and causing them to release their scents. I was once in the herb garden at Hampton Court and it certainly had a heavenly smell.

I heard from Stella recently. She gets to all meals and goes [on] walks; also she had a week at home just after Xmas. This is an improvement on this time last year. Jim is at York for a fortnight.

Monday, 7 February.
Now that a year of this diary has gone on and shown you how the war affects us, there does not seem to be much point in carrying on with it, but it might be interesting when it comes to recording the end of the war so I will carry on a bit longer, but it strikes me that in the meantime it will be just a repetition of last year's doings.[4]

---

[2] The Rambert Dance Company was started in London in 1926 by Marie Rambert, using the name Ballet Rambert from 1935. During the war, according to its website, it: 'became a full time touring company and ... did a great deal of valuable work appearing in a range of venues including factory canteens as well as theatres, and in this way made its own contribution to the war effort.' The *Bedford Record*, 1 February 1944, p. 3, noted that: 'the only available stage was the very inadequate Town Hall and they deserve great credit for venturing to produce their fresh and charming *scenes de ballet* with such a dreary background. The *Bar aux Folies Bergères* ... painted for us a delightful picture of Paris in its gayer days.' The *Bedfordshire Times*, 4 February 1944, p. 5, was also critical of the venue for the ballet: 'the miniature Town Hall, with its creaking, tiny stage and its impossible back-stage and dressing-room facilities. Had not the Corn Exchange – the only other hall in the town – been solidly booked for dances, canteens, and concerts, they could have pirouetted on more spacious boards, but with an equally dusty and unkempt background. That their production had the freshness and charm it achieved was a greater triumph in view of the attendant difficulties.' There was no orchestra; the music was provided by two pianos. 'The audiences, which packed the hall for all six performances, would have been larger if the whole of the balcony could have been used; but the very hard seats and the layers of dust which covered them meant that to stimulate the mind by the rarely-seen Ballet meant at least a minor mortification of the body.' The Ballet's visit was made possible by the Council for the Encouragement of Music and the Arts. Serious cultural offerings of this sort were vastly popular during wartime in many parts of the country.
[3] The author was Rosetta E. Clarkson; the subtitle is *A modern chronicle of herbs and savory seeds ... Illustrated from the old herbals etc.*
[4] As it turned out, her fears were largely unrealised. There were to be new happenings and events – along with established activities and routines – until at least the end of 1945. From that time repetitions were more marked.

I had a letter last week from my friend in Sunderland. She has had whooping cough! And she is 43. She mentioned that she had managed to get a lb. of dried apricots, which she was saving until the summer as they get so little fruit, and that they have just had their first onions for months. As we had 5 [ration] points left, and plenty of prunes in the house, I got her ½ lb. (3 points) and also filled a cereal carton with onions and sent her them. In our ration books we each have 20 points to use each month for all dried fruits, tinned fish, meat, fruit, all cereals except oatmeal, biscuits, syrup etc. You can use them all on one sort of food if you like, or have bits of each. But a person living alone could never have a tin of the best salmon as that is 24 points and you cannot use any points out of their proper months. Father and I have 40 a month between us and [this is] ample as we now use very little tinned fish or meat.[5] We use most of them on dried fruit when we can get it. Tinned fruit is never seen nowadays. You have to give them for dried peas and beans (as well as tinned) but we use our own homegrown that I dried. The month ended on Saturday and a fresh period for all rationing begins today. Pa dashed out first thing to get his sweets!!

It was a lovely weekend for the garden and I spent several hours [there]. The newspaper said to get all parsnips out of the ground so I dug up ours. They were tremendous; one weighed 3½ lb., which I gave to Mrs Hughes, and one weighed 4 lb., which I gave to next door. The reason why I was so generous was because those big ones are too much for Pa and I. An ordinary one lasts us a couple of meals. I also dug up all the rest of the carrots, and prepared ground for sowing peas and parsnips. Saturday night I went to the folk dance club. When I got home at teatime Sunday John was there but was just on point of leaving as he had no lamps and had to cycle back to Luton (20 miles), which he reckoned would take 1½ hours. I remember the time when he did it in an hour. He is going to try and get me a 14 inch zipp as he hears they have some in Luton.

Wednesday, 9 February.
The pound per head of oranges, so much talked about in the newspapers, have arrived in our district.[6] I saw a long queue for them at a shop in the town yesterday. Father went for some this morning, complete with ration books, but although the oranges were in the shop they were not serving them until this afternoon. I told him not to stand if there was a queue. The shopkeepers seem to delight in queues. These are the oranges from Spain that had bombs among them.[7] Bombs

---

5   Government advertising enthusiastically promoted the virtues of carrots and potatoes.
6   This distribution of oranges was at the rate of one pound for each ration book, whatever the person's age, and 'Oranges must be sold only against ration books' (*The Times*, 4 February 1944, p. 2). Many adults would have been consuming their first orange in three or more years.
7   This incident of sabotage was reported in *The Times* the previous month (15 January 1944, p. 2): 'Time bombs placed in ships coming here with oranges from Spain have hampered a plan of the Ministry of Food for making available to all adults as well as children 1 lb. of oranges a head every four weeks from early in January to March or April. The first orange ship from Spain was on her way here when there was an explosion at sea which destroyed some 200 or 300 cases each containing 60 lb. of oranges, and damaged many others.' Fortunately, there were no personal injuries: 'On the arrival of another ship immediate search was made among her load of oranges, and another time bomb was found. A further ship is due

have been discovered this week in a shipload of onions.[8]

Thursday, 10 February.
Father stood in the orange queue yesterday afternoon and got *one orange*. We had royalty in Queen's Park yesterday. The Duchess of Gloucester visited Allen's Engineering Works and the Duke visited the Observation Station. The newspaper did not say in which district of Bedford but the only Observation Station I know of is just outside Queen's Park on the way to my garden. It is for plotting the positions of aircraft.[9]

Wednesday, 16 February.
At 10.20 last night I heard a plane crash. I thought it was in the fields beyond the next street, but apparently it was as far away as Cranfield Aerodrome [some 7 miles south-west]. The noise shook our windows and the glow lit up the sky. It was evidently bomb-laden. They say the biggest raid ever was on Berlin last night. *I* did not hear many planes going over.[10] There was a fairly big raid on London at the weekend, most of the damage being by incendiaries.

Friday, 18 February.
Was at a concert at the Boys' Modern School in aid of the Red Cross Prisoners of War Fund last night – mostly (I believe) B.B.C. artists.[11] There were a lot of old-fashioned songs such as the Rosary, Indian Love Lyrics etc. and I really enjoyed them. It took me

---

and a careful examination of her cargo will be necessary. These precautions have inevitably delayed distribution of the oranges, and apart from those destroyed, others will probably be lost owing to the delays caused by the need for examination of every case arriving. Precautions to prevent outrages of this kind are taken at the ports where the oranges are put aboard, and it is possible that the bombs were put in the cases in the orange groves.'
[8]   *The Times*, 7 February 1944, p. 2, wrote reassuringly about the discovery of a bomb in a crate of onions found on a ship from Spain: 'It is quite certain that the intention of the enemy in placing these bombs on board was to sink the ships; they are not aimed at the civil population of this country. It is most unlikely that any further bombs have escaped discovery in the search which was made, but if anyone in possession of a crate of oranges or onions finds anything suspicious among the contents he should get in touch at once with the local police, and not attempt to handle the suspected object himself.' Having described the appearance of these bombs, the article then 'emphasised that individual oranges and onions are in any event perfectly safe to handle.'
[9]   A photo in the *Bedford Record*, 15 February 1944, p. 1, showed the Duchess inspecting the Women's Land Army. The *Bedfordshire Times*, 11 February 1944, p. 6, reported that she visited a WLA hostel at Copley and printed a detailed account (p. 7) of her four hours in Bedford. The day's events also included visits to a hospital, nursing detachments and day nurseries. The Duke's visit was to the Royal Observer Corps Centre. For security reasons, royal tours were rarely announced in advance.
[10]   Almost all of the planes involved took off from bases in eastern England. According to Middlebrook, *Berlin Raids*, p. 263, 891 aircraft were dispatched, of which forty-three were lost; 265 airmen died and fifty-four were taken prisoner of war. 'It was the heaviest raid of the war on Berlin; the 2,643 tons of bombs estimated to have been dropped in the area were greater than the tonnage which had caused the Hamburg firestorm [in July 1943]. Among the bomb loads were no less than 470 4,000-pounders and fifteen 8,000-pounders. But a substantial part of the effort was wasted' because so many bombs fell in open country or lightly-occupied neighbourhoods (pp. 268–9).
[11]   This was, according to the *Bedford Record*, 22 February 1944, p. 3, a 'pleasant concert of lighter music', the backbone of which was the BBC Theatre Chorus.

back to my youth, before wireless, when we used to perform at our friends' houses for our amusement. A Bedford prisoner, escaped from Northern Italy, appealed for funds for the Red Cross.[12] It has been trying to snow all day, but it does not lie.

I tried to make carrot jam on Wednesday night but it was not a success. I boiled it for 1¼ hours but it did not set and I dare not waste any more fuel (gas), which they are always appealing to us to save. It tasted just like sweet boiled carrot. I had put in a stick of cinnamon, some orange skin, and finally I added a teaspoon of the lemon juice you sent, which all made it smell delicious. I will put it in tarts and puddings with a few sultanas or other dried fruit.

Tuesday, 22 February.
It has been a cold cheerless weekend. Snow has fallen every day for a week but melts before it has made a covering. They keep bombing London again, and the people have taken to sleeping in the Underground railway stations again. It must be cold and cheerless in those places this weather. We get warnings nearly every night lately but nothing worse happens.[13] Father is not very well – is sick but will not give his inside[s] a rest so as to get over it. Jim does not seem so comfortable at Thirsk now; a very cold draughty mess-room, dirty food, and no warm place to sit in after meals. Some of the trouble will mend when the summer comes; but I suspect he has had an unusually comfortable time, for the Army, up to the present. He goes into York every Monday evening for Folk Dancing and while they were on special duties in York for a fortnight he had a grand time; saw *Yeoman of the Guard* and the *Mikado* [by Gilbert and Sullivan] and had a musical evening at an Army captain's house where he sang two solos himself. At another house he visits he met a woman who has crossed the Atlantic 19 times and been to Geneva 6, so he seems to have made some interesting friends at York. Trust Jim for that; he'll never be bored, nor dissipated.

Friday, 25 February.
Last night London was raided for the 5th night in succession. The [anti-aircraft] guns of the outer defences of London are heard in Bedford. I thought at first they were bombs falling in quick succession. The flashes of the shells exploding in the sky can be seen from our street. They look like a perpetual firework display in the South. Of course all this is not 50 miles away, the Northern outer defences being about St Albans, perhaps 20 miles north of London.

Monday, 28 February.
No warnings Friday, Saturday and Sunday nights and apparently not much enemy activity over the country. Planted peas and spinach over the weekend but I doubt

---

[12] 'In the interval, Lieut. Panton, a Bedford man who escaped from an Italian prisoner-of-war camp, gave an account of his experiences with special reference to the welcoming comforts sent out by the Red Cross' (Ibid.).
[13] Germany resumed serious bombing of Greater London in later January 1944. These 'Steinbock raids' (also known as the little blitz or baby blitz) continued on and off until later March, with a final major raid on the night of 18/19 April (Ramsey, *The Blitz Then and Now, vol. 3*, pp. 318–55 and 363–4; Maureen Hill and James Alexander, *The Blitz on Britain* [Croxley Green, 2010], pp. 238–9). Some 1,500 Londoners were killed in these raids (Gavin Mortimer, *The Blitz: An Illustrated History* [Oxford, 2010], pp. 160 and 163).

they'll not move much in this cold weather. However, March and April will soon rush by and I have only Saturday and Sunday afternoons to plant in. It will take me an afternoon to get the onions in, as you have to rake and trample the ground 3 times to get it right and the soil must not be at all sticky.

Wednesday, 1 March.
It is a year since Aunt Bella died. Willie Forsyth came home on leave last week. I do not know whether I have mentioned it, but he is back to sea. His eye still troubles him and he went to the specialist as soon as he got home. He has to have the lashes plucked out as soon as they come through. A man in the Office has warned me that oranges will be for sale tomorrow. He knows because his wife works at the wholesale greengrocers who distribute them. Everybody's wife has to work somewhere, unless they have a young family to look after.[14] I wonder if we will be lucky enough to get any oranges this allocation?

Thursday, 2 March.
Got 2 lb. oranges this morning: 7 oranges for 1s 6½d. A lot of shops have them and no queues for them.

Friday, 3 March.
While typing out this diary I notice what a lot I had to say about rheumatism. I have not been nearly so bad this winter. I still feel it, but it does not make me feel ill. Perhaps being on part-time work and not so hard-pressed at home has something to do with it. I have felt fairly well all winter in spite of the bad epidemic of flu there has been.[15]

Last night I went to see Flossie Clarke and found she has been at home all the week with a cold. She read the following out to me and asked me what I was reminded of.

> A rainbow on a hill – a summer shower
> Of silver drops, a honeysuckle flower.
> A winding lane, between the sweet wild roses
> A burst of sunshine as the June day closes.
> A grey old church and organ music pealing
> A day into my memory for ever stealing.

---

[14] Leah's impression about women working was broadly correct, though some women with no dependent children did not work much, or at all, outside the home (they had been granted exemptions) and the work done varied greatly and included many part-time jobs and volunteering, such as with the Women's Voluntary Services. It is probably true that by 1943 almost all women in Bedford in their twenties, thirties and forties had been interviewed at the Labour Exchange to determine how they could best contribute to the war effort, given their personal circumstances, and whether or not they should be required to take up employment beyond the work they were already doing. Also, many women took up paid jobs because they needed the money, others from motives of patriotism.

[15] The monthly reports from late 1943/early 1944 submitted to headquarters by WVS Organisers around the country testify to the extent of influenza during these months (Royal Voluntary Service Archive & Heritage Collection, Devizes, Wiltshire).

As soon as she uttered the second line I said 'The bike ride on Whit Tuesday evening' and when she got to the end I realized she had composed it herself. What different impressions 2 people can get on the same event. My only memory was the terrific downpour that came on just as she was gathering the honeysuckle. But it was the first time she had been [on] that rise, whereas I had been several times. It was all just as she said, however. What it must be to have a poetic mind.

Wednesday, 8 March.
Saturday was bitterly cold, but I went to garden and sowed 3 rows of onions. I noticed some rhubarb had pushed through the ground so I put an old bucket over it to try and force it. I went folk-dancing at night and got my blood warmed up a bit; when I came out it was snowing. Although there was a thin covering of snow on the ground Sunday morning, the day got out beautiful and spring-like and I planted 4 more rows of onions. There was a letter from Jim Monday morning. He said 'By [the time] this reaches you I shall be on my way to Sunderland.' This was written on Friday. I guess he was on his way *back* on Monday as he only had 48 hours leave.

I turned his wardrobe out on Monday. I don't think it has been done for years as I never had the time. The moths had been busy. I made some bags of fine net and am putting rosemary in, as I read recently it keeps them away. We certainly have plenty of rosemary and it might as well be used. I am reading a good book on China, *My Country and My People* [1936; revised 1939] by Lin Yutang, a Chinaman educated in America [and best-selling author]. Chinese fascinate me.

Wednesday, 15 March.
Last Thursday afternoon as soon as I got into the Office I was told 'to go and look after the Chief Engineer (Mr Russell Taylor) until further notice.' It appeared his typist is ill, also Miss Barber, the General Manager's secretary, is ill, and the Executive Department is in a muck-up. Mrs Cantie, a new woman for whom I had to move out of Mr Townsend's office, is to look after my Department. I have been floundering in papers, catalogues and journals ever since. I never thought the Chief's office could have got in such a muddle. It looks a little straighter by this afternoon.

I hope I don't get this job permanently. I have not got the true secretary's personality – there is too much fetching and carrying and running around – and I am much too old to change [she was 42]. Why, he cannot answer the telephone on his desk, if I am near, until I have picked up the receiver and handed it to him, and then he hands it back to me when he has finished speaking. His arms are a bit longer than mine, seeing he is 6 feet 2 inches, to put it on the stand. Mr Russell Taylor is deaf – and Scotch. He has some invisible apparatus that helps him to hear, which he runs off a battery normally, but to save his battery he plugs himself in and looks like an enormous dog on a chain in the office. One is apt to trip over the flex [i.e., insulated wire]. Whenever he wants to go out he has to unplug himself. I get many a silent laugh.

There was a bad raid on London last night. The General Manager, Mr Fleming, also Scotch, was going up to London today but St Pancras station has been bombed and four trains were cancelled this morning, so he cancelled his engagement. This information is not in the news; they never tell us details, but important people seem to know everything.[16] The newspaper was an hour late this morning so I wondered if the railway had been hit.

On Sunday night I saw a wonderful sight. At about 8 p.m. there was the loudest drone of planes I've ever heard. I went outside and the sky was covered with the red and green lamps of planes flying very low. Some were dropping flares. We presumed they were Fortresses [B-17s] just returning from a daylight raid, as it is rare to see lights on planes in formation. The flares are landing signals.

The weather was much better last weekend and I planted lettuce, radish, parsley, nasturtiums, and haws to try and get hawthorns in the hedge.

Saturday, 18 March.
Last Thursday one of our London representatives was in the Office. He lives at East Molesey [Surrey, near Hampton Court] and he told us what a bad time they had in Tuesday night's raid. His uncle, who was away from home that night, had an incendiary go right through the house to the ground floor and burnt everything, including a valuable library of 1000 books, many of them first editions. On account of his uncle and aunt being away from home no-one knew the bomb was there until it was too late.

Had a letter from Jim yesterday saying he is coming for 7 days leave on Tuesday. Also we got our 2nd allocation of oranges – 1 lb. each.

Aunt Tiny, Jessie and the baby were going to Worthing at Easter, as a sort of distraction when they lost Noble, but Aunt T. has so got the wind up because they have started bombing London again, they have decided to stay at home. Apart from the bombing, I am glad they are not going, because the journey would have been terrible for them. It is about 350 miles, and there is the crossing of London and changing at Newcastle. If they were lucky enough to get seats (and I have seen women with babies stand for hours) they would have had to stay put as the corridors are crammed with people and luggage, and with a young baby you need to be able to move about a bit.[17]

Thursday, 23 March.
Sunday afternoon was too nice for work so I went to the woods to look for primroses. As I was climbing the hill two children attached themselves to me. The huge 13 foot high hedge at the side of the path, that used to be covered with blackberries, sloes etc., was razed to the ground and not even bundles of firewood left about. The

---

[16] The authorities, as always, did not wish to disclose to the enemy the extent and character of the damage done by raids. If 'important people' were more in the know, this may have been partly because most of them had telephones (unlike households of Leah's social class) and thus could readily pass information along; and many of them would have travelled and had connections with people well beyond their own localities, which was bound to make them better informed.

[17] Overcrowded trains were by now the norm and frequently remarked on, though few travellers wrote about what must have been a common and troubling deficiency – i.e., inadequate toilet facilities. Overcrowding is touched upon in Michael Williams, *Steaming to Victory: How Britain's Railways Won the War* (London, 2014), pp. 62 and 64.

children told me the Italian prisoners had been at work on it. There were not many flowers out but I dug some roots and planted them in my garden.

Jim came home Tuesday night – been on the journey since 9 a.m. and the distance not 200 miles. He planted half my early seed potatoes yesterday, and went round visiting friends at night. Today he has gone to John and Lily's and will stay the night.

You know how I usually lament that Father refuses to have an injection when he ought; well Sunday was the first time I broached the subject since he has gone off colour lately, and he went on Tuesday and had an injection. Things *are* looking up. This is better than waiting until he is reduced to the point of helplessness.

I am getting more used and reconciled to this new job. It is really a *very* light job compared with my usual one. Also they now consent to have windows open. I really could not stand the atmosphere when I first started. The Engineering Department, on the top floor, was open to every wind that blew (a bit too airy for me at times) and it got the sun all day, and it felt very oppressive in this ground floor stuffy room. It appears the usual typist would never let them have a window open. Well, I have 'learned 'em different'.

The typist has had a miscarriage. This is the second she has had while in the office. She was away 6 weeks last time. One of the girls, who married an American last August, is going to have a baby in June. Unheard of state of affairs in peacetime but we are used to anything nowadays. By the way the typist who is ill is married. Her husband is in my department (The Engineering, or Design, Department).[18]

Sunday, 26 March.
Yesterday and today have been perfect Spring days. The daffodils, red primroses, purple crocus and blue scyllas [i.e., scillas] are out in the back garden. I was sitting out in the deck chair this afternoon. In other people's gardens the almond trees and Forsythias are in blossom and children go by with bundles of primroses – so Spring is in full swing. At the other garden the broad beans are through the ground *but we do want rain.*

I don't think Jim is enjoying his leave so much this time. Nearly all the friends he calls to see are away from home at the time. I must say how we all enjoyed the chocolate pudding the other day which you sent at Xmas. I opened the 2 lb. jam jar of damson I bottled myself and we had them in a pie today. They kept the 6 months quite well. Also I opened a large tin labelled 'prunes'. I remember grumbling at Father when he bought them a long time ago, as we can usually get plenty of dried prunes. But I was surprised to find the tin full of large blue plums, very sweet. If I'd known what was in [it], they would probably have got used up long ago. So we have had a little variety in food this week. Jim says they do not get enough greens in the army so we have had plenty of them as there are lots to go at in the garden still.

---

[18] Before the war it was fairly unusual for a married woman to work outside the home. Indeed, many organisations refused to employ married women – and they were virtually non-existent in engineering works.

Thursday, 30 March.

Jim had lovely weather for his leave, and it rained last night so the seeds ought to be sprouting now. We are working until 6.30 at the Office today as it is Stock-taking. I am not stock-taking, but we have to work overtime just the same. Also the full-timers have to start at 8 a.m. I was asked this afternoon to look out [for] all the personal possessions of Mr Russell Taylor's secretary. So I asked if she was not coming back any more. I was told 'I am afraid not' but nothing was said as to whether I remain in his Office, or not. I cannot make up my mind whether I would like the position permanently or not. There is certainly much less typing – but a bit more running about. A parcel arrived from Worthing this morning – some home-made fudge, a beret shaped hat, a brooch and a bunch of heather flowers for hat or coat. The hat is just the thing I want for cycling and my old one is very shabby.

I spring-cleaned the pantry under the stairs (where I locked myself in last Whitsun) and Mrs Simmons is coming on Monday to help with Pa's bedroom. She brought her new baby round this morning. He is a lovely little thing. As she cannot get a bath [tub] for him she has to bath him in a bucket!!

Father had a second injection this week and is going on nicely now.

Thursday, 6 April.

Well, this *has* been a week. On Sunday morning I cycled to Goldington for the rent [for the property Jim owned] and got soaked. As usual, they were not up when I called at 11.30 a.m. I heard a man's voice and discovered Mr Monteith (whom I have not yet seen) was home on leave from Italy (16 days). On Monday morning there was a huge patch of wet on Jim's ceiling; on Tuesday morning there was a large pool on his floor. It happened some men were mending a neighbour's roof and while their tackle was so near I got them to do ours yesterday. This was smart work as I had put in an order at a builder's to do a leak above my bedroom last November and they have not turned up yet. These men did all the loose slates so we are now all O.K. I hope. I have been trying since early January to get the trellis re-erected, but I suppose that it is not urgent enough work. These men who did the roof would not do the neighbour's ceiling which fell down last autumn, as they are not allowed to do indoor repairs!! Shortage of materials perhaps.

I have been informed that I am permanent secretary to the Chief Engineer, and when I took the opportunity to ask for a rise I was told it was impossible to give me one as I was a part-timer. I pointed out that married women who had not typed for years were being set on at only 3s a week less than my wage, and that surely after 9 years with the firm I was more useful to them. Miss Barber said that after 2 months to get into it they were quite as good! Can you beat it? And they have made me the secretary of the second most important man in the firm! Today Miss B. came and asked if I would join the pensions scheme they are starting. I said as I was only taking home 26s 4d a week I could not possibly afford to pay into a pensions scheme. Let her put that into her pipe and smoke it. My actual wage is 33s 6d but income tax and insurance are deducted every week. Of course I only put in 20 hours a week, but I do more work than some who do the full 44. Apparently no account is taken of that, and they know you cannot leave to get another job because the Ministry of Labour won't let you, as the firm is doing Government work. Can you wonder at strikes? I forgot to mention that in the course of the argument I suggested I wrote to the managing director. She is his secretary, and she said she would speak to him but held out no hope.[19]

Thursday, 13 April.

We had really nice weather at Easter. I did not go anywhere special. On Saturday I tried to bury an old bath-tin round the mint bed to keep the mint from spreading everywhere. It was very hot and I think I overtaxed myself, so I just rested around on Easter Sunday. A friend gave us 4 new laid eggs, which were very acceptable. On the Monday a friend and I walked by the wood and across fields to the village of Stagsden and gathered primroses on the way back. I got the map out and laid down my leather gloves and promptly forgot all about them. Luckily we decided to return by the same route and an hour later I noticed them lying on the grass. It was a bit of luck as there were plenty of people in the wood.[20]

I forgot to mention that my Aunt at Worthing sent us for Easter some home-made fudge, a navy hat, a posy of heather flowers and a brooch.[21] The fudge was very nice and I sent Jim's share on to him (along with his swim suit which he asked for) and the hat, beret shaped, was just the thing I wanted.

It is just as well that my Aunt at Sunderland cancelled her visit to Worthing because just before Easter all the coast from the Wash to well up the Bristol Channel was banned to visitors. We do not know what this portends but everybody thinks it has to do with the invasion of the Continent.

Jim does not like Huddersfield, says it is smoke blackened[22] and always raining, but they have good swimming baths and a good billet which has been fitted up for Auxiliary Territorial Service (girls) and much more convenient than men usually get.

Monday, 17 April.

Nothing special to relate. Mr J.R.T. has gone to Glasgow so I have some time to scribble. I have spring-cleaned his desk while he is out of the way, and as I filled a waste paper basket from it I am expecting the band to play when he gets back and begins to miss bits of paper. On account of the shortage of coal, night work has

---

[19] It seems that the weekly wage of an experienced and full-time secretary in Bedford was around £3 10s, before deductions. Since Leah's job was defined as 'essential' to the war effort, given that she worked for a company that supplied munitions, she could not take a job elsewhere without official approval, so she had little choice but to accept the conditions imposed by her current employer.

[20] She was probably referring to Hanger Wood, south-west of Bromham.

[21] In fact she had reported these gifts on 30 March.

[22] Annie Schofield, a housewife in her mid-forties from the Bradford area of West York-shire alluded to this regional fact of life when she remarked on 8 February 1942 that: 'the soap ration seems to me scarcely enough for us people up in the Northern industrial areas, especially us who do our own washing. ... [I]n houses like those in this district, with floors and surrounds to be scrubbed every week, and paint which ought to be washed every month, I'm sure it is not enough. Take curtains alone. Lots of people in the country need only wash curtains once a year – many only twice. But here they must be washed about every six weeks.' (Mass Observation Archive, Diarist no. 5423). While coal was burned almost every-where, its use was especially noticeable in densely-populated industrial West Yorkshire.

had to stop. This will reduce production, but I expect the workmen are not sorry as nightshift is very inconvenient for most families.

I probably have not mentioned that the 'Music While You Work', which they have in the factory, is controlled from the office I am now in, and it is my job to switch it on at 3 p.m. but I am constantly forgetting it.[23]

It has been a dull showery weekend, just right for the garden. I planted 2 rows of potatoes and some salsify. I do not know what salsify is like nor how it is used but I like to try new things. The rhubarb is coming along and I have had 2 tarts, but I must say that after Father had eaten a piece of the first one he said 'What is there in this tart beside grated carrot?'!! Flossie Clarke came to tea yesterday. Today I have spring-cleaned stairs and passage.

Wednesday, 19 April.
Primrose Day: Father's birthday. He is 74. This morning's paper said that yesterday 1,750 Fortresses (which only operate in daylight) were over Germany. During last night planes droned from sunset till morning, so the R.A.F. must have followed up the Americans. The Germans must have had a cheerful 24 hours. I wrote to you, Winnie, on Monday as I think your last letter (promised in January) must have got lost in transit.

Tuesday, 25 April.
I have fixed my holiday for last fortnight in August so as to be well out of the way of the invasion – if it ever takes place. All travel will be stopped when that takes place. The people who have arranged to go away for holidays are quite worried in case the invasion of the Continent takes place just at the same time. I think it is best not to make arrangements these days – but if you have set your mind on a change it must be worrying, as it was for me when they put a ban on some places (but would not divulge where) just when I wanted to go to Worthing last summer. Father and I have arranged to go to Luton next Sunday and he will stay overnight.

When I arrived at the garden on Saturday I found a man and his wife digging the ground opposite the gate. The talked broad Scotch and said they had bought all the strip along the quarry for £200 and were going to live on it in their caravan which they have at Kempston. As none of the strip is wide enough to build a decent house on, they have been robbed to pay £200 for it.

Thursday, 27 April.
I feel rheumatism worse lately. I think the more I exert myself over spring-cleaning and gardening the worse it gets, because I feel it less in the winter when I am less active although it is the time of the year you ought to feel it more. It is a perfectly lovely day today and after I finished housework this morning I sat in the garden

---

[23] 'Music While Your Work', launched in June 1940, was intended to help relieve the monotony of much factory labour and thus boost workers' morale and efficiency. Over time it came to enjoy a wider following and in April/May 1944 was one of the ten most popular programmes on the BBC's Forces service (Asa Briggs, *The History of Broadcasting in the United Kingdom, Volume III: The War of Words* [Oxford, 1970], pp. 200, 521, and 537).

knitting without hat or coat. The purple aubretia and golden alyssum make the garden look very bright. I am meeting Sybil at the other garden tonight.

The man I work for now is a major in the Home Guard, and to judge by odd whispers I overhear, there is something in the wind about 'sabotage' and 'Irish'. At any rate all the Home Guard have to go on real guard until further notice and I have typed the Order for one Company to look after 4 bridges and the railway lines between. Of course, I am supposed to keep this information entirely to myself, but you will not read of it until it has all blown over. They are saying the I.R.A. is still active and I think we are afraid of them 'putting a spoke in our wheel' when the Invasion is on the move [i.e., the opening of a Second Front in Europe]. All travel to or from Ireland is stopped. The men in the Home Guard do not know it is the Irish they are to guard against. They have only been told 'Saboteurs'.[24]

Monday, 1 May.
A perfect May Day; that is to say for us, but I suspect somewhere on the Continent does not think so. The noise of planes has been incessant. In bed this morning I thought the invasion had surely begun. I looked out at 7 a.m. to see if I could see troop-carrying gliders but they all seemed [to be] squadrons of bombers surrounded by fighters. As the sun was at a low angle they all shone silver underneath and looked very impressive. Some lots were returning and as they were all moving north or south it seems that France is getting it – which I don't like.

Father and I went to Luton yesterday and he has not returned yet. We had a very nice time and they all seem well. Jacqueline's head seems emptier than ever but she beats Janet at swimming. I had not seen them for over a year and wondered how grown-up they might have turned, but I was pleased they are both 'little girls' in spite of being taller than their mother. Lily had a superb tea – no signs of wartime fare. I have been spring-cleaning the living room this morning. It is much easier with Pa out of the way, as I did not bother to cook a proper mid-day meal for myself.

Wednesday, 3 May.
Very high wind last night and today. The carpenter promised to come and do the trellis today but had not turned up when I left home this afternoon. Was at a lecture on *Hamlet* last night by a man called Garrett, a schoolmaster and a member of the Dramatic Society. It was very interesting.

---

[24] It is unsurprising that extra security precautions were being taken during these weeks leading up to D-Day. Eire, a neutral nation during the war, was widely seen as harbouring Nazi-sympathizers. It was suspect as a source of Fifth Columnists and a potential base of hostile action, or at least intelligence-gathering, against the United Kingdom. Eire was cut off from the UK at this time to prevent details about the planned Normandy landings from falling into enemy hands: Germany had diplomatic relations with Eire and employed agents there. Given these fears, in mid-March 1944: 'Britain suspended all travel between its shores and Eire's ports as well as all cross-border traffic. Aer Lingus flights to Britain were halted, and Irish travellers were forbidden from using British or American civil flights out of Eire. More restrictions followed on telephone calls and the importing of British newspapers.' (Ian S. Wood, *Britain, Ireland and the Second World War* [Edinburgh, 2010], pp. 64–5). As for the I.R.A., it was actually very weak at this time.

Thursday, 4 May.

The carpenter came and lowered the trellis yesterday; 4 months to get that job done, and now it is not complete but it is safe from falling and it is a good thing to get all the ropes and props that were keeping it up out of the way. I went to the doctor last night on account of rheumatism but found *he* had just taken ill and was in bed, so I will wait until he is about again. I woke a few times in the night chewing something gritty, and this morning I found either tooth or old stopping has come away, so I made an appointment with the dentist. At the Office men are at work scraping black paint off the glass roofs and places where shutters could not be fitted. This looks as though they expected the war to be over next winter.

Tuesday, 9 May.

There was a very sharp frost during Saturday night and all 6 rows of early potatoes are blackened. Some men tell me they will recover, and some say they are done for. I must wait and see. Also some nasturtium plants in the back garden were killed. The rain we had on Friday has saved the onions and they look fine. There is a lot of blossom on the two espalier apples but what with frost, hail and high wind I am dubious about their setting for fruit. There are a lot of young gooseberries but *they* all look diseased. However, there is a glut of rhubarb. It was lovely at the garden both Saturday and Sunday evenings; the birds were singing beautifully and there is a robin redbreast [that] follows around wherever you disturb the earth.

I finished spring-cleaning yesterday – which is a relief.

Monday, 15 May.

I received your letter of 24/4/44 this morning. I wrote you on 17/4/44 so our letters crossed. I am sorry to hear about the trouble you and Olive have had. It is a pity Olive lost her baby, but I think it would be a bit awkward for you to start all over again.[25] I should certainly not want it for myself, although I often would like to lay hands on the kids round the doors and see if I could bring them up better than their mothers can. They all seem such good material spoilt by wrong treatment. It is sometimes quieter to me to have Tony in our house than in his own next door. It is not Tony who makes the noise but his family chiding him – nag, nag, nag – and as he knows it is only noise he takes no notice. The woman on the other side has two boys and she nearly weeps at the burden of them. She says the doctor says she would be much better if she could get away from them. They are really quite nice little boys, nearly 7 and 8, never ill, and no trouble at all, but she is a woman without a ha'porth [halfpennyworth] of sense [and thus a foolish person] and I'd like to dip her in a tank of water when she starts that sort of talk. She was *so* relieved when they both started school.

I went to the dentist this morning and had two teeth drilled. Then I popped into Sybil who lives next door and found her with a crippled hand. She put her finger out of joint when cutting the fins off a fish!! The doctor set it and sent her to have it X-rayed. Two hours after coming from the hospital she attempted to peel some

---

25 Since Winnie's life in Canada is undocumented, the news to which Leah was responding cannot be established. It did, however, prompt her to disclose her views on mothering and the behaviour of her neighbours.

potatoes and put it out again. She said she never felt so awful in all her life as going to the doctor again and telling him.

Last week the weather got so hot that I got into a summer frock on Saturday afternoon, but by teatime there was a thunderstorm and it rained all the evening, severe frost last night and bitter-north-east wind today.

I went to a friend's to tea yesterday. I have known her 12 years and although she has often been to our house I have never had a meal in her house before and felt rather intrigued that it had happened at last. I began to wonder whether there was a skeleton in the cupboard, or whether they had sworn a vow never to give folk a meal.

There was an alert during the night and 14 enemy planes were brought down over the country, but I do not know where the raids were.

Friday, 19 May.
Been a very cold wet week, but the rain will have done a lot of good as there has been a long drought over the southern half of the country. On Tuesday I bought a score of Brussels plants (4 inches) and planted them but did not go to the garden yesterday as it was too cold. We had a letter from Jim with his address omitted and no clue why except that he says he will write again soon. He must be on the move, but why he could not mention it I do not know. I have started to crochet some green silk toilet mats for Lily. I have not done this sort of crocheting for years, but you do not have to give coupons for the silk, as you do for wool, and therefore it is all the craze at present. I have ordered tomato plants for tonight but I do not think I'll collect them as it is much too cold for them.

Tuesday, 23 May.
The weekend was as cold as winter. On Sunday I went to see an old friend in the country. She will be 88 next August and still keeps house for her son. I usually enjoy the cycle ride there but it was too wintry so I went by bus. The hedges were white with hawthorn, but we were glad to sit around the fire and talk – she talked, I listened. Jim is now at Whetstone, North London.

Thursday, 1 June.
I thought I would never set pen to this diary, and even now I am doing it on an evening I usually go to the garden. Last weekend was Whitsun and was glorious summer weather. On Saturday afternoon Flossie Clarke and I set off on our bikes for Ickwell Bury, the home of Wells the brewers[26] about 7 miles away [to the south-east], where they were giving a folk dance party on the lawn. We were told they would provide drinks and we were to bring our own food. It was such a hot afternoon we took our time and ate half our tea under a tree on a hilltop. We were just feeling nice and comfortable when Flossie asked what was the big conical thing hanging just above our heads. It was bees swarming! We picked up our traps

---

[26] Charles Wells Brewery was founded in Bedford in 1876. The Wells' residence was The Old House, dating from the late fourteenth century.

and scooted. We told a farm hand about it and he said he would see about getting them collected, but the swarm was still hanging on our return journey.

Mrs Wells gave us tea *and* eats. It was very hot and we shirked as many dances as we dare and explored the gardens. These are very extensive – one walled garden leading into another, and a lake with swans on and a peacock that spread his tail for us. The gardens were not too well kept – no labour I suppose – but there was a long vista of peonies and a tree with roses as yellow as buttercups! A very sweet scent. Mrs Wells has another house in the same village with a smaller but most exquisite garden. It[27] is at present a convalescent home for men in the forces, and some of the men in their blue suits were looking on at the dancing. It was a most lovely summer day with all the hawthorn and horse chestnuts in bloom, buttercups in the fields, birds singing and cuckoos calling. On the way back we stopped on the same hill (well away from the bees) and ate the remains of our tea. It was very peaceful, and cooler, and we wished we were camping out instead of having to go back into the town.

Whit Monday was very hot and I slipped up to the garden in the morning to start a bonfire while it was somewhat cool. It was lovely and cool in the shadow of the high hedge at the east end, where I had the fire, but sweltering elsewhere. I took my tea in the afternoon to the garden, and read and fed the fire occasionally. I got well sunburnt, though I kept in the shade as much as possible. I planted out tomatoes on Tuesday and it has rained today so they will be well settled in. My back has been worse lately and I was at the doctor's last night. He has changed the medicine. Father was sick as soon as I got home tonight so I stayed away from the garden and did some ironing and wrote up this diary. Last week I went to cinema and saw *Jane Eyre*.[28] I get less and less smitten with pictures every time I go, and it will be a long time before I go again.[29] The worst part was we had to stand for an hour (and paid 2s 3d) and arrived in the middle of the picture, which always spoils it for me. I have just started the third exercise book for this diary.

Our apple tree, instead of being covered with apples this year, is infested with hairy caterpillars. One fell on my book as I was reading and another was crawling up my bare leg. I dare not go near the tree now.

Saturday, 3 June.

It is a year today since Jim joined up. We had a letter saying he would probably be going to Luton today as they only give 24 hour passes for a radius of 25 miles. It has been nice and fresh today and I did quite a bit of work at the garden. The grass on the *lawn*! is as high as hay, but I cannot keep up with trimming the paths and

27 At this point the entry for this date is continued in a new volume (Z1606/5), number 3 (her numbering). At the end of volume two she compiled two pages entitled 'Books I have enjoyed this year [1944]', adding four books read in 1945. These books and her comments on them are found in the appendix, 'Some Books Read by Leah Aynsley'.
28 At the Plaza Cinema, the Embankment. Starring Orson Welles and Joan Fontaine, 1943.
29 Women's attachment to the cinema varied enormously. In contrast to Leah, an infrequent film-goer, Madge Martin, wife of an Oxford vicar and a couple of years older than Leah, commonly went to over a hundred films a year and saw some of them more than once (Patricia and Robert Malcolmson, eds, *A Vicar's Wife in Oxford 1938–1943: The Diary of Madge Martin*, Oxfordshire Record Society [Woodbridge, 2018]).

edges of plots, so the plot must go. There was a nasty accident in Cambridgeshire yesterday. An ammunition wagon blew up – 500 homes demolished. Everything connected with the station was blown clean away. Some men who saw the wagon alight gave their lives in detaching it from the rest of the train, which was all loaded with bombs. Cambridgeshire is not far from Bedfordshire but we are not told exactly where it happened. People want to know how the wagon got set alight.[30] I am writing this at 10.30 p.m. by daylight – double summer time.

Tuesday, 6 June.
Yesterday the news was that the Allies had entered Rome. Today as I was sweeping the front a carpenter working nearby said 'They've started.' As I looked puzzled he said 'The invasion has started.' He said he'd heard it on the 8 o'clock news and that they had attacked Le Havre in France. I wish you could see all the roses to be seen from our window, deep cream ones. They grow from next door and the dividing fence which comes close to the house (not the famous trellis which divides the gardens) is a bank of roses – not ramblers but individual tea roses. We have two bowls of them in the house. I have never met such a strong growing climber. Every year it has tried to grow round the living room window and I usually keep cutting it back, but this year I let it. I shall cut it back as soon as it ceases blooming.

Friday, 9 June.
Things were very quiet here on the day of the invasion of France.[31] People were eager for news, of course, and as I was arriving home at tea-time I found people of an engineering firm near home coming away from the church in our street [All Saints, at Iddesleigh Road]. As it was a very hot evening I went to the Adult School and heard an interesting talk on The Ballet.

I received your letter (May) yesterday. Your Father is wonderful – 76 and going to business every day. I have a book out of the library on Rheumatism. It says some

---

[30] This accident happened early in the morning on 2 June at the station in Soham, Cambridgeshire, when a fire developed on the leading wagon of a heavy ammunition train and some of its cargo exploded, killing the train's fireman and the Soham signalman. *The Times*, 3 June 1944, p. 2, reported that: 'The station buildings were wrecked and houses nearby were so severely damaged that the occupants were made homeless. Scarcely a building in the town escaped some damage, and houses over a mile from the scene had their windows shattered.' A permanent memorial to the accident was unveiled in June 2007.
[31] 'As we go about our daily occasions in peaceful town and village', editorialised the *Bedfordshire Times*, 9 June 1944, p. 7, 'our thoughts will be constantly with the men who are engaged in that bitter and bloody struggle across the Channel.' In the next issue of the *Bedford Record*, Tuesday, 13 June 1944, all of page one was devoted to coverage of the 'Salute the Soldier' campaign, which, it was said, was 'stimulated by our men's deed on the other side of the English Channel and fresh victories in Italy.'
The *Times'* editorial also remarked on the prevalence of recent spring festivities: 'These past weeks have been times of high carnival in the villages, with bands and banners, music-making and dancing, athletic meetings and gymkhanas, and the crowning of May Queens. In the countryside, at any rate, the people have not lost the art of making their own amusements; and the trick of linking gaiety to the solemn purpose in view is no bad sign after nearly five years of anxiety and peril.'

people are susceptible to the oxalic acid in rhubarb, spinach and strawberries, so I am keeping off rhubarb and spinach.

Monday, 12 June.
There has been no more stir over the invasion of France. There have been an unusual number of Lockheed Lightnings [P-38s] racing about and that's about all. These are planes with double bodies [i.e., twin booms] and they certainly go very fast. This is Salute the Soldier week in Bedford – target £600,000.[32] I went into the town on Saturday afternoon to buy a frock and the town was packed as there was going to be a special parade at 5.30 p.m. I was glad to get the frock and dash home again. I had been to three shops last Monday morning for a frock. One said they expected some 'Junior Miss' sizes in at the weekend, and a Junior Miss I bought. I look like Alice in Wonderland in it if people don't look too closely at my hair! [She was very small.] It is a new size, copied from the Americans I suppose, but it fits me without alteration and I only had to give 5 coupons instead of the usual 7 for a woman's frock. It is blue plaid, and the material is something like the cashmeres I used to wear in the days of my youth, a bit heavy but we do not often get it very hot.

Heard from Jim on Saturday and he has moved from Whetstone to Hendon. He is so secretive he did not mention the fact, but I just saw it from his address. You have a relative there, I believe. Made 8 lb. rhubarb and ginger jam this morning.

Tuesday, 20 June.
There is quite a bit to relate since I last made an entry. First of all, Londoners are having a new worry – what they called pilotless aircraft [aka doodlebugs, flying bombs and V-1 missiles] but it is really a bomb with engine and wings attached. Jim says they sound like a little motor bike coming along, and when the chugging stops (because fuel is exhausted) it drops to earth and explodes. He says they like to shoot them down in the air and then there is not so much blast on the ground. Jim nipped home for a few hours on Sunday (with only a London Area pass) and said he'd heard 4 or 5 of them that morning. Londoners are spending a good deal of their time in shelters I am told, as they keep sending these things over any old time.[33]

I had a letter from Jim Saturday tea-time saying how difficult it was to get home, and if he did not get home he would be sending a parcel of unwanted articles home (soft shoes etc.). That was all I had to go on, but I stayed at home on Sunday instead of accepting an invitation to a village 7 miles out of Bedford, and a good job too as Jim rolled in about 2.30 p.m. and stayed until 8 o'clock. He says all proper leave is stopped and hints he might be going abroad soon, but I have my doubts as he mentioned how far back they had slipped in training during the

---

[32] *Bedford Record*, 13 June 1944, pp. 1–2; also 20 June 1944, pp. 1 and 3.
[33] These cruise missiles caused havoc, mainly in the south-east, during the summer of 1944. Details of the raids and their impact are found in Ramsey, *The Blitz Then and Now, vol. 3*, pp. 376–443; Mortimer, *The Blitz*, pp. 163–71; Hill and Alexander, *The Blitz*, pp. 242–8; and Patricia and Robert Malcolmson, *Women at the Ready: The Remarkable Story of the Women's Voluntary Services on the Home Front* (London, 2013), chap. 8.

6 months up North. All the enthusiasm Jim had for the army originally seems to have worn very thin, and he keeps talking of things he is going to do after the war. It must be weary for all the men who have been in it nearly 5 years.

Yesterday morning I bottled 2 2 lb. jam jars of my home-grown gooseberries. I tested them for vacuum this morning and they seem to be O.K. The advantage of bottling is you do not require sugar until you actually cook the fruit, and can use your saved up sugar for jam.[34]

Thursday, 22 June.
I had a letter from Lily yesterday saying that they were coming to Bedford tomorrow (Friday) for a day on the river [the Great Ouse] and would call and see us! This will be the first visit that she and the children have paid us for 2 years and she makes it a day I have to go to work. She says that John does not like to risk travelling on a Saturday or Sunday these times. She also said that they had had 2 of those aerial bombs the previous night. Whatever next! Fancy aiming the things all the way from France and hitting a smallish town like Luton. I can understand them aiming at a place the size of London and hitting; but hitting Luton is a bit weird.[35] One fell at Stopsley [north-east Luton], the district where my friend Maud lives. We shall hear a bit more tomorrow.

Father had a day at Cambridge yesterday visiting an old friend of his who is a cripple. He had a very nice time and stood the double journey in one day very well. Cambridge is 25 miles away. He said he passed lots of aerodromes and works on the bus journey.[36]

Friday, 23 June.
The Family arrived at about 11.30 a.m. on their way to the river. They are coming back to tea about 6 p.m. The girls looked lank and limp and as though a holiday by the sea would do them good. They had been standing in the train, which had perhaps exhausted them. One of our Company's representatives from London said they have been having a nerve-racking time. Up to Wednesday night the Germans had been sending those flying bombs over at the rate of one per minute; yesterday there was one about every 5 minutes. None of the children are going to school. London is evidently getting another packet. He says they watch the thing coming along and breathe again when it gets beyond them.

Tuesday, 27 June.
I went to a folk-dance party on Saturday evening on the Castle Mound. This is a hillock on private grounds overlooking the Embankment on which used to be Bedford Castle, but now there is on top only a lawn like a bowling green surrounded by tall trees. Being a hot day, it was lovely and cool dancing in the shade of the

---

[34] 'Gooseberries, packed with goodness, were strongly recommended [by the Government], while strawberries were cast into outer darkness as they took up so much space to cultivate' (Willes, *Gardens of the British Working Class*, p. 285).
[35] Since the accuracy of these missiles was poor, it is probable that Luton was struck unintentionally.
[36] There was also at this time a direct train service between Bedford and Cambridge.

trees. I hurried home early in case Jim had come, but he arrived for breakfast at 10 a.m. on Sunday and stayed till 8 p.m.

As I was cycling through the town to the folk dance, with a cool clean frock on, and saw all the Service people in their hot uniforms mouching listlessly about the main streets. I felt it was not fair that such as I should be going to enjoy ourselves in beautiful surroundings, while there is so much misery about, and when at the dance I heard that Londoners are flocking into Bedford on account of the raids, and cannot find places to stay at. Yesterday I heard on very good authority that St Cuthbert's Church hall is full of evacuees.[37] Mrs Cantie, the typist who came from Bourn End, was going to have a week's holiday in London, but her sister wrote and said on no account must she come to London as they are in shelters all day.

Jim does not say much. He had gone to Morley College on the Saturday evening and found it cancelled on account of pilotless planes, so he walked round the city near St Paul's Cathedral. I said 'There were no raids, then, if you were walking about.' He said one pilotless plane came over while he was exploring. He never mentions anything like that unless you dig it out of him.

Thursday, 29 June.
While I was in the doctor's last night there was a woman who had just come from North London. She said that between 12 and 3 p.m. ten pilotless planes had dropped in her district. Buildings were crashing down, wardens digging the people out, doctors racing about. She said we in Bedford have no idea there is a war on. I notice the newspapers never mention raids on London – they all refer to Southern England.

On Monday morning I made some gooseberry and rhubarb jam into which I popped a few strawberries left over from some that Ralph Sage had given to Jim on Sunday.

Friday, 30 June.
I went up to garden last night to gather a stock of stuff for weekend. I had the first picking of blackcurrants. I do not know whether I have mentioned it before, but the garden is over-run with moles this summer. They burrow near the surface and push the plants out of the ground. At present the tomatoes and cucumbers are being pushed out and the poor things never get a chance to take hold. I have bought a

---

[37] The report from the organiser of Bedford's Women's Voluntary Services for this month (written in early July) detailed the work of the Centre's WVS in receiving these evacuees. On 18 June: 'a hall was opened to house evacuees from London. Only three adults and four children slept there that night, and 12 altogether on June 19th. When the numbers reached 71, another hall was opened, a school hall. Each night the number has increased, the climax being on Saturday, July 1st when 126 souls were sheltered. The first hall has been manned night and day by WVS and the second hall at night. The school took over in the day time. The response of the WVS members to this emergency has been most gratifying. We also called in the Red Cross nurses to keep a constant rota to look after sick children. Many suffered from diarrhoea and some went to hospital. The British Restaurants have undertaken the burden of feeding with extra help from us on Sundays, as the BRs are usually closed on Sundays. The Billeting Officer has appealed to us to help find accommodation now that billeting orders have been issued.' (Royal Voluntary Services Archive & Heritage Collection, Devizes, Wiltshire. We are indebted to Matthew McMurray for his help with these sources.)

mole-trap (1s 6d) but don't know what to do with it. You are supposed to find their permanent runs and set the trap in, but that is a bit beyond me. I am hoping Mr Chambers, one of my neighbours, will be able to do something about it.

I had a letter from Stella this morning. She is still in the San[atorium].[38] Says she has to see the surgeon about having a bone scraped. I think she is as well in the San. until she is completely cured, seeing there is no woman at home to look after her.

Monday, 3 July.

This has been a very wet weekend; gardeners ought to be satisfied now. Jim came home Saturday evening on a London Area pass and stayed till Sunday evening. I asked him about P-planes. He said he heard the engines of one in his dreams on Friday night, but it went a mile further on and hit Colindale Hospital [he was in Hendon, to the south], and that is all he would say about them. I see by the newspaper that they were very active during Saturday night and Sunday morning, so it was well for Jim he was here.

We had a letter from Aunt Tiny. She, Jessie and the baby [Valerie] are all at Bristol. When she put off her visit to Worthing at Easter on account of travelling and raids on London she said she was going to 'stay put' until after the war. However, they had a good journey to Bristol and they certainly needed something to help them over the loss of Noble. Made 4½ lb. blackcurrant jam this evening.

Wednesday, 5 July.

Mr Bates, the draughtsman who works in the same office as I do, was very much put out yesterday; first because the hotel where he expected to spend a week's holiday soon has written to say all bookings are cancelled as they have been commandeered by the Government, and second, his sister in Dulwich went for a holiday on Saturday and on Sunday morning they had a message from the police to say they were bombed out, so they are coming to Mr Bates' as soon as holiday is up. He already has an evacuee and a niece living with him and they have only a 4-roomed bungalow.

Mr Russell Taylor, the Chief, is spending his holiday at present at Harrold, only 7 miles away, as he has to be on call, being a major in the Home Guard. It has poured most of the time since he went on Saturday. As he has two young children it will be a bit of a trial, cooped up in the heart of the country. I found the first mole in a trap last night.

Friday, 7 July.

The King, Queen and Princess Elizabeth were in Bedford yesterday, only we knew nothing about it until they'd gone. Apparently they went to an American aerodrome to christen a Fortress 'York Rose'.[39] I caught another mole. They are evacuating

---

38   Treatment for tuberculosis (still a common disease) usually lasted more than six months (Sheila Ferguson and Hilde Fitzgerald, *Studies in the Social Services* [London, 1954], p. 256, a volume in the *History of the Second World War, United Kingdom Civil Series*, ed. by W. K. Hancock).

39   Such royal visits were not announced in advance. This official naming of a B-17 *Rose of York* occurred at the US airfield in Thurleigh. According to Smith, *Hertfordshire and Bedfordshire Airfields*, p. 229: 'The original name, *Princess Elizabeth*, was rejected by the [USAAF] Eight's chiefs on the grounds that it would provide too much propaganda material for the

Londoners to Manchester, Lake District and even Newcastle.[40]

Thursday, 13 July.
Nothing much to report. After Jim saying he would not be home last weekend he turned up at 10 a.m. for breakfast on Sunday. Of course we were pleased to see him. That is 4 Sundays in succession he has been home. The weather continues to be wet and miserable. I fear we will have no summer. The P[ilotless]-planes are still arriving. I had a letter from Worthing asking if I would risk having a holiday there. I think it would be unwise to travel in that direction.

Thursday, 3 August.
This is the longest I have let this diary go yet. I have been so busy. The P[ilotless]-planes are as frequent as ever. Jim said that last Sunday he went round the Tower of London at 2.30 and just before then one dropped in the river and caused a dust and he got a bit as a souvenir.

The Sunday previous the Queen was in Bedford again, and I knew nothing about it until the next day. She was visiting the American clubs in Bedford and there was a picture in the local paper of her and Mr Harold Jackson. He showed her round and introduced her about. Now let me tell you, that this is the Yank that lectured at the Adult School and for whom I had a crush – ahem! (See entry for October 13th, 1943.)[41] To revert to P[ilotless]-planes, the place is full of evacuees and I daresay will get fuller still as Churchill said in his speech that the Germans have worse projectiles to send over London.[42]

German should the aircraft be shot down.' A photo on p. 228 shows the eighteen-year-old Princess this day (6 July) at Thurleigh, holding a bouquet of flowers, and with her other hand securing her hat against the wind. The Duchess of Kent had visited Bedford the previous month, on 19 June, to open an exhibition of handicrafts made by members of H.M.'s Forces (*Bedfordshire Times*, 23 June 1944, p. 5).

The famous orchestra leader and trombonist, Glenn Miller, was playing in Bedford this month with his Army Band, including at least one performance with the 'sweetheart of the Forces', Vera Lynn (*Bedford Record*, 11 July, p. 4; 18 July, p. 1; and 25 July, p. 3). Leah, whose artistic tastes were fairly traditional, never mentioned either.

[40] Cities well outside the south-east were now thought to be much less vulnerable than in previous years to German attack – and pilotless planes did not have the range to hit these places. The evacuations to the far north-west are discussed in our *Wartime Cumbria* (2017), chap. 7, and those to various other counties in our *Women at the Ready: The Remarkable Story of the Women's Voluntary Services on the Home Front* (2013), chap. 8. For Bedford, see below, note 42.

[41] The Queen visited two American Red Cross Clubs, at one of which (the officer's club) she was introduced by Harold Jackson, its Director (*Bedford Record*, 25 July 1944, p. 1), who was known to Leah from his October talk. Leah's remark about him is an unusual disclosure of intimate emotion. Normally she kept such feelings to herself. At the Bromham Road Club music was provided by Capt. Glenn Miller's US Army Band. Press coverage was, as to be expected, effusive (*Bedfordshire Times*, 28 July 1944, pp. 5, 6 and 7).

[42] 'As long ago as February 22nd', Churchill said on 2 August, 'I warned the House that Hitler was preparing to attack this country by new methods, and it is quite possible that attempts will be made with long-range rockets containing a heavier explosive charge than the flying bomb, and intended to produce a great deal more mischief. London, we may expect, will be the primary target on account of the probable inaccuracy of the rocket weapon. We therefore advise the classes for whom evacuation facilities have been provided by the

A friend of my Mother's, Mrs Leedham, who lives on the Tees, recommended me to try some herbs for rheumatism from a firm in Southampton. I wrote and described my symptoms and a fortnight's supply arrived yesterday – 15 s worth. We will see how I get on with this lot. I have been going to the doctor's for a couple of months this summer, and although his medicine helped a little it seemed to affect my heart. At any rate I felt pretty rotten generally. The doctor seems to be too busy to give proper attention. The hour's evening surgery sometimes lasts three hours.

When Jim was home a week gone Sunday, he said they might not be going abroad so soon. They might even give him a week's leave. He asked me to buy him a watch as he could not get [one] at the shops in the shopping hours. I went to the best jeweller's in the town and they had nothing but secondhand pocket watches, all gold but one silvery one, rather a turnip, which I bought for £7 7s 0d [i.e., a guinea]. The cheapest gold one was £25.[43]

Saturday, 12 August.
4 p.m. and I have just arrived at the garden complete with tea. It is a scorching afternoon but I am under the tiny bit of shade of the Bramley Seedling apple tree. My fortnight's holiday begins today and it is the first time for about 20 years that I have not gone away for a holiday.

Jim came home last Sunday night for 48 hours, which he says is embarkation leave. I had arranged to go into the country on the Monday (Bank Holiday) with 2 friends so Jim came too. We had a lovely time. We cycled to Newton Blossomville [now in the borough of Milton Keynes] and had lunch by the riverside. Except for a couple of anglers upstream we had the place to ourselves. Except for planes going over occasionally there was not a sign of war. The [Great Ouse] river was lined both sides with water lilies, and beautiful dragon flies were skimming about. A family of swans came by and the parents were actually uprooting the water lily buds, squashing them up a bit and then giving them to the young ones to eat!

Government, and others with no war duties here who can make their own arrangements, to take the opportunity of leaving the capital in a timely, orderly and gradual manner. It is by no means certain that the enemy has solved the difficult technical problems connected with the aiming of the rockets, but none the less I do not wish to minimize the ordeal to which we may be subjected, except to say that I am sure it is not one we shall not be able to bear.' (James, ed., *Winston S. Churchill: His Complete Speeches*, vol. 7, p. 6979). See also: 14 and 15 November 1944. These rockets started to hit Britain on 8 September.

As for the refugees from the pilotless planes, many from London did arrive in Bedford during July, and their needs and the challenges of accommodating them were fully reported in the press. People from Greater London, mainly mothers and children, were flooding into town; the need for housing was acute; and the billeting authorities were kept very busy (*Bedford Record*, 11 July 1944, p. 1; *Bedfordshire Times*, 14 July 1944, p. 7). The hardships and sufferings of the evacuees received a lot of press attention – and there were questions as to whether Bedford was doing enough for these distressed people (*Bedfordshire Times*, 21 July 1944, pp. 7–8). The acute shortage of housing in the town and the problems of homelessness had been publicly acknowledged before this new emergency (*Bedford Record*, 23 May 1944, p. 2 and 4 July 1944, p. 2).

[43] These very high prices reflected the cessation or near cessation of the manufacture of many consumer goods considered inessential, along with the collapse of many imports, especially from the Continent.

About 4 o'clock we got on our bikes and went to The Three Cranes at Turvey and had tea. This is a lovely old inn and so clean and we decided we'd like to spend a weekend there next year [see Illustration 7]. We got home about 9 p.m. and we had had a thoroughly lovely day in the sunshine (I took care to keep in the shade of trees when sitting about). Jim went back Tuesday night and we have not heard of him since.

The country looks lovely at present. Everywhere the harvest is being got in, but whether it is a good harvest like last year, or not, I have not heard, but some corn we were walking through the other Sunday, right on a hill top, looked very large and full.

So far, those herbs I started 10 days ago have not improved the rheumatism. In fact I think it's worse.

Monday, 14 August.
We have been having scorching summer weather lately. This is the first day of my holiday. I went to see Mrs Simmons this morning to see if she could do some housework for me this week and next so that I could make more of a holiday. She says her baby boy is getting a handful but she will come along Thursday and Friday afternoons and see what she can do.

Next door had a little evacuee arrive from London. Not what they call an 'official' evacuee, but the son of a distant relative who have asked them to take him in.[44] Flossie Clarke came to tea and then we cycled to Bromham, and then walked through the cornfields to Stevington. The fields are all on a hill, and it was glorious.

Wednesday, 16 August.
Yesterday Flossie and I took the two small boys next door to Hardlefoot Woodlands. This is a riverside haunt and tea gardens and these are the boys whose mother thinks they are too much for her and never takes them anywhere. We had a picnic lunch on a high grassy place with a wide view over the river. The boys were mad to go on the river and gave us no peace until we got at the landing stage in the wood, waiting our turn for a boat to come in. Flossie and I had deck chairs and the boys wanted them too, but I knew they would not sit in them. They never had deck chairs in their lives before and believe me they did everything but sit in them. They carried them all over the place and when I found Donald tangled up in 6 deck chairs which he'd made into a lorry I had to put my foot down and make them sit in them properly. It was tea time before we could get a boat so I asked them whether they would rather have tea or a boat. They plumped for a boat, so

---

[44] According to the *Bedford Record*, 15 August 1944, p. 1, many official evacuees still lacked billets and were forced to sleep in Rest Centres, which were intended only for short-term emergency shelter: 'Trying to sleep every night for several weeks in a large crowded hall, with dozens of other adults and children, queueing for three meals a day at restaurants, drifting round the town during the intervening hours with no anchorage and trying to keep the children out of mischief in the meantime – this is not a very attractive prospect, even if the alternative is dodging flying bombs.' The Rest Centre at St Cuthbert's Hall became a lodging house for those without a billet: 'Sometimes there are as many as 80 people in the hall at once.' Toilet facilities were limited and rows erupted over the drying of clothes, a practical problem in congested spaces.

we took them out in a punt and ate up all the remains of lunch for tea. They were a bit of a handful on the boat, but I think it was because Flossie and I were a bit nervous and fussy. As she remarked, 'We wouldn't mind our own children falling in the river but we don't want to drown anyone else's.' She made me laugh, but it was exactly my sentiment. If we'd had a man that could have dived in after them, I shouldn't have worried in the least by what they were doing – things like catching at the reeds and making the boat swing right round into the banks, hanging right over the side, and walking out to the tip of the punt. After I had reprimanded them half a dozen times I said 'Oh the joys of parenthood!' and it was then she made the remark quoted above. I must say they were pretty good all day, and we got home without any mishaps.

Today, my bike being at the repairers, I came to the garden by bus. I was 1½ hours in getting here – the buses going by chock full. I would not be without my bike for anything. Travelling by bus or train is so difficult these days. We had our first letter from Jim yesterday afternoon, Tuesday. I had begun to think he really had gone Abroad, not hearing for a week, but his letter was dated Friday so it must have got held up. We invaded the South of France yesterday.

Sunday, 20 August.
Last Thursday Flossie and I had a grand day on the heath at Woburn Sands. We took the train to Woburn Sands, about 12 miles from Bedford. There is about ¾ miles from the station to the centre of the little town and then about the same on the other side up rather a steep road to the heath, which is all pine woods with bracken and heather in the clearings. At the top of the steep road various roads branched across the heath, but some were closed by the War Department. We took the way to the right and reached Bow Brickhill Church [now in Milton Keynes] standing on the very edge of the heath, whence there was a grand view of the surrounding country and its village far below. We found a heathery spot with a good view and ate our sandwiches and rested for a couple of hours. Very few people passed by, but a jeep containing an American soldier and girl went towards Bow Brickhill and had to return as there is no way out for vehicles.

The heath belongs to the Duke of Bedford and before the war the old duke had an army of keepers who soon dropped on you if you were picnicing. Either the present duke, who is a pacifist, is not so particular, or else all the keepers have been called up for the war effort, but we went in all the forbidden places without let or hindrance, and never saw one keeper.[45]

We descended the hill to the village of Bow Brickhill to find tea. The inn was shut up and the sign 'No Beer' in the window and nobody else supplied tea. The climb back to the heath was very stiff and we longed for a cup of tea, but rather than walk all the way back to Woburn Sands we decided to do as we did on Tuesday – eat the remains of our lunch and do without tea. Flossie had half a sauce bottle of cold tea and milk, and I had a small bottle of water which I carried in case I wanted an aspirin, and what with plums, apples and tomatoes we managed to

---

45 The twelfth Duke of Bedford (1888–1953), an evangelical Christian, was a prominent fascist sympathiser and admirer of Hitler. His defeatist views were well known locally and disapproved of (Barker, *A Bedford Diary of the War Years*, pp. 28–9).

quench our thirst, and found another spot with a grand view to laze in. We slowly made our way back to the station, armed with bunches of heather, and reckoned we'd had 10 hours in the open air.

After 3 weeks of fine weather it broke yesterday and rained in torrents.

I have started to recover my eiderdown. I used a grey satin coat lining which has made the inner border, and Friday afternoon and Saturday morning I combed the town for suitable material to finish the job, but there is an absolute dearth of blue silky material. At last I found some with Wedgwood blue [back]ground and white and black flowers that shade into gray – a very cheap art silk only 2s 4d per yard, 1½ coupons per yard. I would have liked a richer looking quality, but the gray satin border sets it off and it is going to look nice. It will be a very cheap renovation.

Jim returned his bank book on Thursday, which he said he would do just before going Abroad.

Wednesday, 23 August.

The news from the front is good – the Allies will soon be in Paris. The Germans must realize they have lost the war.

Yesterday morning I took Father to Luton and left him there for a few days, and had a nice day at John's myself. Lily had a cupboard full of fruit she had bottled. She gave me some Victoria plums from her mother's tree and I have bottled them tonight. There are two railway lines from Bedford that I have never been on during the 23 years we have lived here. One goes to Northampton and today I determined to have a trip there. It was a nice little ride of about 20 miles through countryside, passing no works or factories of any sort, not even in leaving Bedford. The only stations were Turvey (where we had tea on August Monday), Olney, the town where the poet William Cowper [1731–1800] lived, and Piddington.[46] Northampton is a better shopping centre than Bedford or Luton. It was market day. The square is twice the size of Bedford's and the booths were well spaced out. I had for me an orgy of shopping and got a long sleeved overall that fit me for only 6s 11d and 4 coupons. I tried at a Jew's stall on the market for 2 ply navy wool. They had not any just then but I got a nice dull shade of green in 3 ply and they said they would bring some navy to Bedford market soon. It is very difficult to get wool in ordinary shops, but trust the Jews to find some.[47] I had tea at a very nice place and 2 Jewesses came to my table. To judge from scraps I hear, they were evacuees from London. By the way, on the Northampton station a notice was chalked up that as the water supply had failed no more evacuees could be accommodated. The failure is owing to the drought there has been this year.

Sunday, 27 August.

I spent an hour Friday morning mending a puncture. I took my tea to the garden and on the way the tyre went flat again, so I walked home and spent the rest of the afternoon mending another puncture. Saturday morning the tyre was flat again, so I must take it to my usual man, at the other side of Bedford, as it may need a new

---

46 She must have meant Podington.
47 Leah's opinion that Jews were exceptionally savvy – and perhaps cunning – on commercial matters was commonplace in England in the 1930s and 1940s.

tube. The only patches on are the two I put on last week, but perhaps the rubber has suddenly perished.

Father came home from Luton on Friday, and I went there yesterday afternoon to see my friend Maud and had a very pleasant visit. Today 3 men of the New and Latter House of Israel arrived from Hitchin, complete with beards, long hair and their own herb tea. Some friend of my Father had given them our address. Seeing 3 of them together was a bit overpowering. They kept their caps on all the time they had tea. They are young conscientious objectors and are tree-felling at Hitchin instead of on combative service.[48]

Saturday, 2 September.
What an afternoon we have had. It is years since I saw such rain, and a high north wind that drove it nearly horizontal. The yard that I went on my hands and knees to scrub on Thursday morning was covered with gravel, as were the window sills, which must have got washed out of the mortar between the bricks. I am wondering what the damage will be up at the garden.

We have had two letters from Jim this week, and gather that he is in Brittany, near where I spent a holiday in 1937, but the censor cut the bit out of his letter that gave the clue.

I started back at the Office last Monday after my holiday, and all I heard was about the shortcomings of the typist who had done my work the second week, and of the wartime conscripted typists in general, so I spoke up on my own behalf and said I didn't think we should be paid the same wages and asked if I could have a rise. It was rather an unusual request the first day back after a holiday, but I thought it was a good opportunity to strike up. Mr Russell Taylor said he would speak to Mr Fleming.

A box of heather arrived from Stella last Monday, and a note saying that she was going through another operation.

Tuesday, 5 September.
All the talk now is how soon will the war end; Brussels is now in the Allies' hands and we have entered Holland.[49] The vexed question is blackout – will the worn-out [material for] blackout need to be renewed now that darker evenings are coming? Our black paper blinds are all rags and patches.

We have all got the house decorating craze. During my holiday I painted the front lobby and yesterday the inside of the bay window – all with paint we have had in the house for years. It is very difficult to get hold of nowadays. I expect we all want to get freshened up for Peace. In spite of the newspapers saying there have been no fly-bombs over the country since Friday, we had an alert during the night and they say fly-bombs fell somewhere near – but I heard no bumps.

---

[48]   This was a millenarian religious group, perhaps better spoken of as a cult. Leah's parents had belonged to this sect – and perhaps her father still did. For Leah's comments on the sect see below: 28 September 1945, note 49.

[49]   Many of the reasons for the Nazi regime's ability to continue the war for another eight months are provided in Ian Kershaw, *The End: The Defiance and Destructions of Hitler's Germany, 1944–1945* (London, 2011).

Friday, 8 September.

The most cheering news yesterday was that 'Blackout' finishes on 17th September (the day double summer time ends). You have no idea what that means to us. Bedford has had 'starlights' for a few winters. Very few towns had that. It at least helped to prevent you from walking into lamp posts. Neither Luton nor Sunderland had that amenity.[50] We all think the war will be over by Xmas. Aunt Tiny has even got as far as proposing to make us a flying visit. She must be feeling chirpy.

Thursday, 14 September.

I got your card from the General Brock Hotel [in Niagara Falls, Ontario] on the 12th September. You do seem to be enjoying your holiday. I never realised that you have not had a holiday the last few years. I thought you just didn't bother to mention it, and there have I been grumbling because I did not go anywhere this year and I've never missed having a holiday for about 20 years. I hope you had a jolly good time because you deserve it.

We get letters regularly from Jim and at last he has received one of ours. He seems to be in Brittany, where I stayed for a holiday once, and seems to be faring very well – had chicken once and gets crushed pineapple or grapefruit juice before breakfast. Brittany is well behind the front lines.

I have arranged to have my bedroom distempered (wallpaper unprocurable). The decorator suggested 'blue – a nice peacock blue'! I said 'pale cream, or leave the walls as they are.' Then came the heavy rains next day and the roof leaked again. I went to the builders who did it in the Spring and told them the decorator was coming in 6 weeks. Their men turned up the very next morning. I *was* surprised; the war must be nearing an end.

Sunday, 17 September.

Double summer time ended today and of course it was dark an hour earlier this evening. A friend and I took a bus ride to Kempston and then a walk across fields, quite strange ground to me. We passed lots of Italians (erstwhile prisoners); there must have been a camp somewhere near [perhaps Stagsden]. They wear a uniform of a chocolate brown battledress, without the big spots on their backs nowadays. It was dark when we got back to town and we were looking forward to seeing the effect of the withdrawal of blackout, but there was very little difference; being Sunday the businesses were all shut up and street lighting is not altered yet.

I heard today that soon all the Americans will be leaving us,[51] some to go home and some to go East to fight the Japs. I also heard yesterday that at Chimney Corner

---

50 The arrival of the 'dim-out' was universally welcomed. 'Another glimmer of the lamp of freedom will be reflected on Sunday from behind the curtains of hundreds of homesteads', declared the *Bedfordshire Times* on 15 September 1944, p. 7, 'when, for the first time for over five years, patched and renovated black-out equipment will be laid aside with relief.' The writer remarked on 'dispelling the blanket of gloom that has settled over our towns and villages and hamlets during the nights of five winters'. This month's modestly increased lighting was, said the *Bedford Record*, 19 September 1944, p. 1, 'a little foretaste of the exultant radiance that will return with peace.' Improvements in Bedford's street lighting were introduced in the following weeks.

51 Numerous Anglo-Americans weddings were reported in the press this autumn.

[on Ampthill Road] they filled 1,000 bombs on Friday 'for the Japs'. I got this last item from a funny woman who works there. Her name is Aggie and she spends a lot of time at Thistley Green [Bromham]. She is very thickset and strong – wears trousers – and she has dug a good bit of my garden. She is going to do all my digging!!

Saturday, 23 September.
Nothing to relate except Sybil's husband is very ill with an ulcer and she has to feed him every 2 hours with milk food, so she cannot get up to the garden and has commissioned me to collect her produce and someone will call at our house for it.

Sunday, 24 September.
A gale sprang up during the night that made a terrible racket and also we had a siren at 5 a.m. The siren started off with the 'all clear' signal for 2 minutes and then went on to the up and down wail. I thought rain must have got into the works and it would never stop, but it did at the end of another 2 minutes. Once such a thing happened. Can you imagine a ship's siren almost at your bedroom window, rising very high and loud and then dying down and then without stopping rising – over and over again. I thought I would go crazy and so did everybody else nearby. It only kept on ½ hour but it felt like hours in the dead of night. There has been a very high wind all day. Pa has just been out to post a letter and says it is strange to see the church all lit up. During the week I at least expected to see pubs lit up, but were in inky darkness – no beer I suppose. The alleviation of the blackout has made very little difference as yet and I am still glad of a torch.

Sunday, 8 October.
This diary is now sadly neglected; it is a fortnight since I made the last entry. Jim's letters come regularly and I think he has got everything we have sent him. He has even answered a letter I wrote him last Sunday – so the post is pretty slick.
    My friend Trixy had one of her parties yesterday. She had invited an Italian prisoner who works on the Costins' farm, but he did not turn up, which is perhaps as well because one of her married sisters is dead nuts against them and had not been told he was coming, and if she had turned up unexpectedly there might have been trouble. Although I myself had no objections to meeting him, I would not for the world have told Jim about it as it seems to me that sort of thing would make a fighting man feel fed up.[52] Coming home through the town there were some bright arc lamps at certain points, which was a pleasant change.

---

[52] The press reported occasional complaints about the Italians in the county. It was said by one man there was a lack of oversight over these POWs and that they enjoyed an excessive personal freedom (*Bedfordshire Times*, 6 August 1943, p. 6). In Harrold they were accused of 'utterly uncouth' behaviour and aimlessly wandering the streets (*Bedfordshire Times*, 11 August 1944, p. 7). Certainly, the authorities did not consider the Italians to be much of a threat, and many of them enjoyed a high degree of independence. Local people's views of them were diverse, some positive, others suspicious or even hostile. These mixed feelings nationwide in 1943–44 are summarised in Webster, *Mixing It: Diversity in World War Two Britain*, p. 77. 'On the whole', concludes one authoritative book on the subject, 'the public response to the prisoners was a positive one' (Moore and Fedorowich, *The British Empire and Its Italian Prisoners of War, 1940–1947*, p. 163), though as they also point out: 'Some

They are spreading around some of the German prisoners and I hear some are working on the land. My friend Aggie the 'digger' is strong against all prisoners and keen on her bomb filling. She thinks the war won't be over yet a while. She was telling me this afternoon some things that go on in the R.O.F. [Royal Ordnance Factory at Elstow.] Of how the T.N.T. affects the health. There is a plentiful supply of milk but the younger ones won't drink it, so the T.N.T. makes them ill and they have 'to go off the powder' as she calls direct contact with the gunpowder. The 'contacts' can have a bath every day on the premises, but the other workers are only allowed one per week. Some of them get a skin rash, which can be cured by having a green substance painted on, but if they neglect this and the T.N.T. gets into the blood stream, these also 'go off the powder'. Aggie, of course, keeps all the rules and regulations and never ails a thing, and was digging this afternoon to get her dinner down, and goes on duty tonight.

I have had my eyes examined and am to wear spectacles for reading. I have been looking around to see what style I favour. I look dreadfully severe in any style.

I am afraid Stella has had another serious operation. It was not a small one as she had hoped. Billy Cuthbertson is go[ing] on nicely now but must stay in bed a full month.

Wednesday, 11 October.
The night before last I was awakened by a syren. A little later I heard a plane thug-thugging along and as it had an unusual sound I thought it must be a fly-bomb. This was confirmed when I saw a flash through the window and then the engine suddenly stopped. The apprehension waiting for the explosion was more than weird. I pulled the bedclothes over my head in case the windows blew in, and then the bang occurred but it was some way outside the town. Rumour says a few different places, but most say at Thurleigh [4½ miles to the north] where there is a Yank aerodrome. The newspaper said 'open field in Southern England', so not much harm can be done.

Saturday, 14 October.
I found that the first fly-bomb fell at Brook Farm, exactly between Thurleigh and Ravensden, about 6 miles from our house. It fell in a ploughed field so very little damage was done by the blast. I was awakened on Thursday night by the syren at midnight. I thought I heard the machine and thought I heard an explosion and certainly saw some flashes, but it fell further away at Henlow, perhaps 9 miles to south of

---

young women were able to get closer to the prisoners than the authorities (or their parents) would have liked' (p. 164–5).

The POWs' appeal to young women was a concern for some older people wherever Italians were based (Risby, *Prisoners of War in Bedfordshire*, pp. 61–2), and this was hardly surprising when so many young Englishmen were absent in uniform and unavailable. An evacuee in Totternhoe in the south-west of the county claimed that the local girls: 'fraternised with the prisoners as young men, feeling an instinctive attraction to the Latin race, and Aud and Betty and Joan carried on long conversations at a very slow pace with much gesticulating and repetition and fits of giggling. They came to know most of the Italians well, their names and something about them, and looked for their favourites each time we came down.' (Dundrow, *A Lasting Impression*, p. 82).

Bedford. Last night at 9. 50 again we had the syren and although I heard no engine it seemed as though our window was coming in at the explosion and the curtains blew inwards. The milk girl said it fell near Haynes, about 5 miles to south of Bedford. It must have struck something hard and made more blast than when it fell in ploughed field. I shall hear details on Monday as one or two folk at the Office live there.

After a week of bad weather it was lovely at the garden this afternoon. I planted some spring cabbage plants given me by one of the foremen at the Works, and then along came Mrs Thomson (the Scotchwoman at the caravan) with some curly greens plants – so I shall be supplied with greens next Spring. I have one more load of potatoes, and then they will be all home. I shall have about 2 cwt. [hundred-weight] from 21 lb. seed.

Saturday, 21 October.
It has been an appalling week since last Sunday – rain, rain, rain. I went to dentist last Monday evening and called in at Sybil's for a few minutes. There was Uncle Albert sitting having a meal. He had just arrived from the North for a week's holiday. He spent the evening with us on Thursday. He seemed to think Stella was going on well since her last operation; but I well remember how hopeful he was on his last holiday and expected her home for good at Christmas. Billy Cuthbertson is as ill as ever after being 5 weeks in bed. The doctor now wants him to go to hospital to be X-rayed. Nothing had been arranged up to Thursday, the doctor having been too busy. Doctors here are terribly overworked, and hospitals under-staffed.

Wednesday, 25 October.
I went to doctor's this morning. He says I am 'very much under the weather' and gave me a prescription for one pint of tonic. I only had one of the usual ½ pint medicine bottles and the chemist had not a bottle in the place, so on my suggestion he made up half the prescription and will do the other half when I empty the bottle. Pa is using one of our bottles and I have some rheumatism medicine in another but there is a great shortage of bottles. I often wonder what happens when a patient does not possess a bottle, because chemists will never sell you one.

We have had two letters from Jim describing his visit to Paris. Also he sent a pen for Jacqueline with an address at Versailles on the wrapping tape so we conclude he is stationed near Paris. His address has SHAEF (Supreme Headquarters [Allied Expeditionary Force]) in it. I thought that was because all letters would go there for clearing purposes, but someone says he is probably attached to Headquarters, and if that is the case I presume he will be always behind the lines – which is a blessing.

Friday, 27 October.
Had 2 teeth stopped at dentist's this morning. I may not have mentioned it, but I have ordered the first pair of specs I have ever had in my life. For the close type of work I do and all the reading I get through; I suppose I have done well seeing I am nearly 43.

Monday, 30 October.
I did not go to the garden on Saturday, but instead made another search for short stories or other suitable book for Jim. I tried Hockcliffe's [86 and 88 High Street] second hand bookshop this time, but there was nothing. The only thing they showed

me was a huge volume of ghost stories, but as Jim asked for something small that he could easily carry about, it was no use. I browsed round the rest of the shop and noticed most of the books left in stock were religious books – showing there was not much demand for same. One was called *The Destination of our Fallen Heroes*.[53]

At night I went to a Folk Dance party, the first dancing I have done since the Festival in June.

A week ago, when I opened my bedroom door in the morning, I noticed a strong smell of burning, and went to Father's room. There was a large hole in the carpet and the floor boards were so charred they could be scraped away like dust. Also his pillow was badly burnt and the feathers flowing out, pyjamas just a handful of charred ashes, and tweed coat half burnt. It appears (after a good deal of questioning) that he'd had a candle on the bed which had set a light to the pillow. He'd wet his pyjamas and thrown them on the floor but they must have caught fire and he had not noticed. As he was dropping asleep again he smelt burning and noticed the pyjamas on fire on the floor. He put his tweed coat over to stamp out the flames – and that was that. I have been trying to persuade him to have an electric light if we can manage it but he will not consent as yet, in spite of the fact that tonight when I got home I found there was only candlelight. He had broken the mantle,[54] broken the new one he put on, then broken the one out of the front room he put on after that. As all the shops were shut it was lucky there was still one in my bedroom gas to fall back on. Can you imagine anything so archaic? All I can get out of Father is 'Think how much worse off they are on the Continent'.

Thursday, 2 November.
Father has paid 2 visits to the doctor and has had medicine, but he says the doctor never mentioned an injection, and of course Pa himself would not. He is gradually getting worse all the time and had a queer attack at breakfast time; it seemed as though it might have been his heart. (Mrs Cocklan died 31st October aged 86.)

Friday, 3 November.
Had a letter from Jim. He is moving to Belgium and talks about seeing Brussels.

Wednesday, 8 November.
Monday night the weather was awful – howling wind and rain lashing down for hours on end. I thought to myself it was a good job there was no syren or bombs dropping on such a night. Father had another attack about 9.30 p.m. and I got him to bed and had the doctor to him the next morning. I threatened to leave home if he would not have an injection, and he submitted. But far from no bombs dropping that night, about the very time Pa collapsed Luton had a V-2 bomb [a ballistic missile]. I hear it dropped on Commer Cars' new canteen and as that is on John's side of the town I was glad to hear from Lily last night that their house was undamaged, but that John had been on rescue work from 10 p.m. to 6 a.m. Lily called it

---

[53] No book with this title is held in the British Library. Perhaps the book she saw was from 1915, *Our Fallen Heroes and their Destiny*, by Robert P. Downes.
[54] A gas mantle, according to the *Oxford English Dictionary*, was a 'fragile lacelike covering fixed over a gas jet to give an incandescent light when heated.'

a rocket bomb, and I am told they fall so rapidly from the stratosphere that there is no warning. This afternoon I am told at the Office that it is officially stated that the affair is *not* due to enemy action but was a gas explosion. There have been a few such explosions in London lately, and I am wondering whether the official statement is just to keep the Country from getting panicky. When I hear more I will set it down [see next diary entry]. They say that, unlike the fly-bombs, the V-2 goes deep into the ground.[55]

Wednesday, 15 November.
By last weekend the newspapers had divulged that V-2 rocket bombs were coming over and gave some pictures of the destruction they wrought, and that it had been kept secret (?) so as not to let the enemy know. Apparently they have been coming during the last two months, and up to the Luton one it was certainly a secret from me.

We had a cold snap last week and there was the merest spink of light in our gas fire, in spite of just having the pipes blown. So I had the Gas Company see to it and two of them came yesterday. Apparently the fire was in a very bad state and they had to take it back to the Works to have joints sealed. They got it put right by 5 p.m. Also the decorator came to do my room on Thursday but I told him it would have to be postponed while Father was ill. I have waited 10 weeks for him and now have to postpone having him.

[55] Leah's scepticism was entirely warranted. The first V2 missile hit London on 8 September 1944. However, for over two months the Government did not acknowledge this new German weapon, and sometimes encouraged the fiction that the explosions were caused by gas leaks. Churchill tried to justify this lack of openness in a speech in the House of Commons on 10 November – two days after an announcement on German radio of the rocket attacks: 'The reason for this silence was that any announcement might have given information useful to the enemy, and we were confirmed in this course by the fact that, until two days ago, the enemy had made no mention of this weapon in his communiqués.' The Prime Minister's words this day tended to downplay the peril of and damage done by the new weapon (James, ed., *Winston S. Churchill: His Complete Speeches*, vol. 7, p. 7030). The V2 raids are analysed and described in detail in Ramsey, *The Blitz Then and Now, vol. 3*, pp. 444–543; see also Mortimer, *The Blitz*, pp. 171–85 and Hill and Alexander, *The Blitz*, pp. 248–55.
    The V2 attack on Luton on 6 November killed nineteen people and injured almost 200 more. An apprentice (Jack Morrison) working at an instruments factory near the site of the explosion wrote about his experiences that day. Around 9.45 in the morning: 'I had just finished a snack when there was a crash which seemed to turn my ears inside out. Then I saw out of the corner of my eye the glass roof falling in and clouds of dust swirling down. Some of the girls dived under the bench but most people stood spellbound for a minute, wondering what it was. Then everyone dashed for the shelters and made for the door. ... Glass was everywhere [outside], doors were hanging loosely on their hinges, people were rushing everywhere. Never before have I ever seen so much confusion. Someone dashed past us and said "Commer Cars" and we knew. I dashed on the roof and when I looked over towards Commer Cars works adjoining ours the whole place was down and dust covered it. Houses were down, debris in the road, cars overturned, windows out, it was horrible. ... There was no warning, no aircraft, definitely no flying bomb, no whistle, just an immense crash and almost a whole engineering works in rubble and dust. Everyone is of the opinion it was a V2, in other words a rocket. I am just listening to the news bulletins to see what they say. Will they admit it was a rocket or will they try to make out it was a flying bomb?' (Ramsey, *The Blitz Then and Now, vol. 3*, p. 483).

Thursday, 16 November.

I went this morning and collected my first pair of spectacles. They have dark brown frames. I wanted rimless but was told they are not to be had at present. I only had to pay 9s 6d; the remainder being paid by National Insurance.

The war moves slowly at present; the main news being as to whether Hitler has gone mad, has had an operation on his throat for tumour, or is merely lying low because of unpopularity.

Thursday, 23 November.

Father had another injection this morning. He went to the doctor himself and told me he did not need an injection, nor was he going to have any more medicine but just going to tell the doctor he was better (which he wasn't by any means). I marvelled he was able to get as far as the doctor's, but it was useless my asking the doctor to call as Pa had vowed he would not have another injection. I don't know what sort of pantomime they had in the surgery as Pa is exceedingly slow in undressing and he was wearing a *cardigan and long-sleeved vest under* his flannel shirt.

Last night I was at a Bernard Shaw play, *Candida*. It was very amusing; his plays always are.[56]

Wednesday, 29 November.

There has been a very bad underground explosion at Burton on Trent. It was an ammunition store. Goebbels has just given out that one of their V-2 bombs has caused it, and that is what I myself thought was the cause. The crater it made is ½ mile across and the explosion was 90 feet deep and all the country around devastated. There were two explosions, some distance from each other, which might rather point to sabotage. Of course, an investigation is to be held, but it seems to me that every clue will be blown away.[57] Father is improving.

Monday, 4 December.

We had John pay us a visit over the weekend. He came on Saturday and stayed to on Sunday. While he was here we moved the furniture from my bedroom to Jim's and sent a card to the decorator to say he could start on the room when he liked. I thought I'd sleep in Jim's room until the job was over, even if until after Christmas, but Mr Markham was on the doorstep at 9.30 a.m., so we are getting a move on. John brought our Christmas presents 'Not to be opened until 25th December.' They are all keeping well and John was none the worse for his night out on rescue work. He cycled the 20 miles to and from Luton. I posted Jim's Xmas parcel this morning and smuggled in a fruit cake I'd made without declaring it on the outside (eatables are prohibited). I therefore hope it reaches him safely.

56   This play was a production by the Council for the Encouragement of Music and the Arts (CEMA), with Walter Hudd's company, at the Royal County Theatre (*Bedford Record*, 21 November 1944, p. 8).

57   This accident occurred on 27 November at an underground RAF munitions storage depot in Fauld, Staffordshire. The massive explosion caused widespread property damage and killed around seventy people.

Tuesday, 5 December.

The man finished my room at lunch-time today, but I am not pleased with it. I said 'pale cream', but he has done walls and ceiling a deep golden yellow, almost orange. He says it will dry lighter, but I have my doubts that it will ever be cream. It certainly gives a very sunshiny effect, but it is very blotchy and badly distempered. I have now the unpleasant task of cleaning up after him and replacing the furniture. While the bedstead was in pieces I made a third attempt to get the mattress repaired, but was told at the shop 'Impossible. No man. No material. Don't blame us; blame Mr Walton.' I have forgotten who Mr Walton is but he is Minister of something and decides on how many clothing coupons we have etc.[58] I then tried to purchase some wire to do it myself, without any success.

Saturday, 16 December.

Well, I got all the house nicely cleaned up and thought everything was nice for Christmas, when the newly distempered ceiling came down at 5 a.m. when I was in bed. That is to say, a good square yard of ceiling came down just at the side of the bed and covered the easy chair and the rug. The shock and dirt was bad enough as it was, but I was very thankful if did not land just on me. I got 3 pails of plaster up. I blame the decorator. He took off the old paper and said he had no more to recover the cracks. I offered him some, but he thought it would be safe enough without. The builders are coming in after Christmas and then the decorator will have to come again. Meanwhile I am sleeping in Jim's bed amid stacks of furniture from my room. It is nothing to having one's house bombed, but all the shifting of furniture has taken the strength out of me and the doctor says I must keep on with the medicine.

This war drags on; the papers have had most to say about our fighting the Greeks. Germany will be pleased.[59]

---

[58] The man spoken of was businessman Frederick Marquis, later Lord Woolton, Minister of Food until 1943 and previously an adviser to the Board of Trade on rationing policies (Julie Summers, *Fashion on the Ration: Style in the Second World War* [London, 2015], p. 70). Given his wartime prominence, it is striking that Leah had forgotten his very public responsibilities; perhaps this was a consequence of her not having a wireless. Oliver Lyttelton, later Viscount Chandos, a former President of the Board of Trade, thought highly of Woolton, as did many others: 'In his dealings with the public he had a sure touch: his training and experience, first as a social worker and then as the head of Lewis's, had kept his finger on the pulse of ordinary people. He had, too, the grasp of the obvious which is necessary in dealing with mass opinion and mass psychology, and he had a warm and sympathetic knowledge of the tribulations and struggles of the poorest classes.' (*The Memoirs of Lord Chandos* [London, 1962], pp. 299–300). Woolton's avuncular style helped to reassure ordinary citizens that he was striving to do his best for them in difficult times.

[59] While the German invaders of Greece had now departed, their withdrawal was succeeded by a civil war that pitted royalists and anti-communists against communist-led rebels, many of them veterans of the fierce resistance against the occupying Germans. The British were actively involved in support of the monarchy and were seen in some circles as determined to revive their imperial powers in the Eastern Mediterranean. Others accepted the need to rescue a broken Greek economy, restore law and order, and set up a genuinely democratic political authority, which Churchill declared to be his objective. The merits or demerits of British policy in Greece were matters of vigorous debate at home (David Brewer, *Greece, the Decade of War: Occupation, Resistance and Civil War* [London, 2016], pp. 191–6;

I made a Christmas cake last Sunday and am going to try and ice it tomorrow; with soya flour and almond essence and 1 lb. icing sugar I got in lieu of granulated and some of those decorations you sent last year. We all get extra marg and sugar this month, and I got a small pudding and 1 lb. mincemeat as we are well away, but there is no bird of any sort to be had, unless you rear your own. It is amusing to hear various neighbourhood ducks quacking and cocks crowing; then after Christmas, silence.

Sunday, 17 December.
I iced my cake this morning. I put on the red sweets you sent, like the small holly berries, and it looks quite cheerful.

I went along to Adelaide Square this afternoon to see how they are getting on. Billy [Cuthbertson] was out of hospital, and also, since I last spoke [with] or heard from any of them, Mabel [Forsyth] has been in and out of hospital; had her womb removed. She seemed well when last I saw her but took ill and was in hospital within a few days. Just as Billy was going into hospital Sybil put her finger out of joint again, so they are a trio of invalids. Mabel was in hospital a year ago with rupture and various veins.

Monday, 18 December.
I was wakened at about 4.30 this morning by an explosion. Shortly afterwards the sirens went. Heard later that a flying bomb fell in a Brussels sprouts field between Silsoe and Clophill, which lies midway between Luton and Bedford.

Thursday, 21 December.
No news from Jim this week, but that may be through disorganization of post due to Xmas. Flossie Clarke came to tea on Monday specially because Father wanted her to play the piano to him, but she'd no sooner started than he was sick and had to rest in the other room. Today he went to doctor's for an injection (instead of letting the doctor come to him) and the result was he had to go to bed when he got back and couldn't look at any dinner.

Friday, 22 December.
There was a letter from Jim last night addressed from a hospital. They have put him in there because of a touch of indigestion, so he says. I don't think he has ever had such a thing in his life before. Well, all the family have been in hospital now. What I did not like to see in the paper was that the Germans have advanced 35 miles into Belgium.[60]

What a list of illness there is among my relations: Father, Stella still in bed, Aunt Tiny been in bed nearly a month with bronchitis (the first time I've known her be really ill), Billy Cuthbertson just out of hospital and not yet back to work, Sybil

---

pp. 197–204 discuss developments during the following several weeks). Whether Germany cared much about these divisions among their foes is a moot point.
[60] This 'Battle of the Bulge', which began on 16 December, was the last major German offensive on the Western Front. A surprise attack through the Ardennes Forest pushed the Allies back and temporarily undermined public optimism.

with her useless finger, Mabel just had a serious operation, Aunt Sarah feeling her arthritis extra bad, me having medicine for anaemianess [a made-up word] since beginning of October, and now Jim in hospital. I hope you are all O.K. in Canada.

We had another week of rain and fog – in fact we have had months of it. It was so different a year ago; bright and clear, Jim home on leave for Christmas, a perfectly happy Christmas. I suppose, however, I've lots to be thankful for.

Jim was pleased with Christmas parcel and says the booklets are very popular in the ward. They are a book of drinking songs and a book of sea chanties that I thought might amuse him. They are rather coarsely illustrated, which I suppose is the attraction. I wish now I'd also sent a book of love songs that were on the same counter, but I thought Jim might not approve (of the illustrations).

Saturday, 23 December.
A postcard arrived this morning saying that Janet and John were cycling through to lunch on a tandem, and they arrived about 1 o'clock. Janet has passed a music exam with honours. They left at about 3.30 as they wanted to get home in daylight and the journey takes them about 2 hours.

The mother of the evacuee next door came and took him home for Xmas. She said they'd had a fly-bomb so close last night that the blast killed some rabbits in their backyard.

Sunday, 24 December.
A very uneventful Xmas Eve but during last night there was an alert and the window shook several times during it and also while the 'All Clear' was sounding. The sun came out this afternoon and I walked to Trixy with a gift for her. She was not at home but her Aunt (nearly 90) said Trix intended calling at our house this evening but she never turned up. After I left Kingsbrook Road I called at Adelaide Square and they begged me to stay to tea but I had told Father I would be home for tea and refused to stop. However, I found Pa half way through a rough and ready tea when I got home before 5 o'clock so I might as well have had tea with Sybil and company, especially as Trix never turned up. Sybil put her finger out of joint again last Thursday for the 4th time since August. They are talking of going to the orthopedic hospital at Oxford about it.

Thursday, 28 December.
This is said to have been the coldest Xmas for 54 years. Xmas Day was dark and foggy but Boxing Day was clear and all the trees and bushes were clothed with frozen fog, and the place looked like Fairyland and has not thawed yet. This will be a common sight in Canada but it is rare for hoar frost to remain 3 whole days here. I love this cold weather and feel I want no more tonic for the time being.

I went up to the garden on Boxing Day morning and gathered some frozen sprouts and dug up frozen carrots. There are an old couple who have been bombed out of their home in London and are living in a tiny cabin about 6 feet x 10 feet. I asked the man to do some digging of my garden and I found he had done it. He went over all Aggie's digging and said he took 17 hours and asked for 17s. One shilling an hour is very little for a man, but I think 17 hours was a very long time, and besides, he dug up my bulb plot so I might have lost all the bulbs as he says there were none in it. However, I am quite satisfied and I said he could use carrots and parsnips.

I went out to tea in the evening and just as I was getting ready Trixy arrived and offered to come back later on and give Father a game of chess, which was very kind of her. Had a letter from Jim on 27th. He has a gastric ulcer.

*   *   *   *

1 Aynsley family, 1935 (courtesy of John Aynsley)
Left to right: John Aynsley (Leah's brother) holding his daughter Jacqueline;
Jim Aynsley (Leah's brother); Leah Aynsley; Lily Aynsley (John Aynsley's wife)
with Janet Aynsley (her daughter) in front.

2 Leah and Jim Aynsley, 1940 (courtesy of John Aynsley)
Left to right: Janet Aynsley; Leah Aynsley; Jacqueline Aynsley; Jim Aynsley.

3 Leah and Jim Aynsley at the Bromham allotment, undated (courtesy of John Aynsley)
Left to right: Unknown; Jim Aynsley; Leah Aynsley.

4 [EPW035884] Housing at Queen's Park and the Queen's Engineering Works, Bedford, 1931 (© Historic England) Iddesleigh Road runs left to right, second road from the bottom. The Queen's Engineering Works (W. H. Allens) can be seen on the far right.

5   Bridgeman's Fish Shop, c. 1930s (courtesy of BARS)

Leah visited Bridgeman's fish shop (66 Iddesleigh Road) on 6 June 1945 hoping, unsuccessfully as it turned out, to purchase skate for her brother.

6   St Paul's Square, Bedford, c. 1940 (courtesy of BARS)
The Corn Exchange can be seen on the right. This was one of the venues used by the BBC
Symphony Orchestra throughout the war. Leah attended a number of BBC concerts.

7   The Three Cranes Hotel, Turvey, c.1950 (courtesy of the Francis Frith Collection)
Leah enjoyed cycling and on 12 August 1944 visited this 'lovely old inn'
with her brother Jim for tea.

8   Honey Hill Road street party, 1945 (courtesy of BARS, Beds County Press Collection) Leah mentions the preparations for a street party for VJ day on 15 August 1945 which included the burning of an effigy. Honey Hill Road's party, only a short distance away from Leah's home (see 18 August 1945), appears to be a more restrained affair.

9 Princess Elizabeth's visit to Bedford, 1946 (courtesy of BARS, Beds County Press Collection)
This visit, on 14 Februrary, was favourably reported in the local press. It was witnessed by Leah who
commented on the retroussé nose of the Princess and her likeness to her grandmother, Queen Mary.

1945

Monday, 1 January.
On reaching home on Friday night I found a telegram saying Jim was in Salford Royal Hospital near Manchester. I was pleased to know he was [in] England, but that was all the information we had and it was a bit worrying. At the same time there was a note from the tenant asking for a plumber to attend to a burst in the bathroom and making the usual stipulation: before 9.30 a.m. or Saturday mornings. I just wrote back and said she must find her own plumber as it was bad enough to get one at all without restricting them to those hours, and I would pay for the repair. On Saturday morning there was a letter from Jim saying a bit about the journey home. He is on a milk diet but during the journey (which seems to have taken the best part of a week) he had to take what he could get and felt none the worse for it. It seems most of his possessions have been left Abroad and his only money is Belgian. He had to owe someone a penny for a morning paper, and an old gentleman had come round and offered them writing paper and a stamped envelope, so he took some to write home.

There was a thaw Saturday morning but by teatime it was freezing again and still holds. A friend of Jim's sent us some apples for Xmas so on Saturday afternoon I returned the cloth bags they were in as bags are very precious. You have to provide your own paper when shopping.[1] We had the Barretts to tea on Sunday and this morning I took up stair carpet etc. and went to see about getting ceiling repaired as Jim may get home when he is better and want his own room.

The news is that during Friday night there was an earthquake felt from Manchester to Darlington. No damage was done but people thought it was the effect of some new German weapon.[2]

---

[1] 'Acute shortage of paper bags', according to an assistant in a grocery shop in Dewsbury, West Yorkshire, writing in her diary on 14 November 1944: 'Our paper dealer informs us we must not use our ration of sugar bags for other purposes than weighing up bulk sugar but does not say what we are to use for wrapping sweets, peas, rice, soap flakes or dried fruit.' Things were no better some four months later (10 March 1945). The shop had no greaseproof paper for fats and bacon: 'In the end we had to take proper bags and split them for wrapping, a dear and unsatisfactory substitute. People will not bring a bag back. We are now getting to the point when we refuse to wrap peas, soap flakes and biscuits at all.' (Malcolmson, *A Shop Assistant in Wartime: The Dewsbury Diary of Kathleen Hey, 1941–1945*, pp. 168 and 181–2). Paper was a controlled and rationed resource, and supplies of paper had been reduced from early in the war (E.L. Hargreaves and M.M. Gowing, *Civil Industry and Trade* [London, 1952], p. 92, a volume in the *History of the Second World War, United Kingdom Civil Series*, ed. by W. K. Hancock). They were now scarcer than ever on the home front.
[2] This earthquake occurred early in the morning of 30 December and 'Buildings in Manchester were violently shaken.' (*The Times*, 30 December 1944, p. 4). Tremors were

Wednesday, 3 January.

The men are coming next Monday to put a new ceiling in my bedroom. We are in a muddle, and there will be a mess. I hope we get straight before there is a likelihood of Jim coming home. We had a letter from Jim written on Xmas Day in Belgium. Therefore his journey home was not so long as I thought; he said that he was sent home the day after his last letter (which up to that moment was his letter dated 21st December). He reached England 4 days before his last letter from Belgium.

Monday, 8 January.

The men arrived this morning and took the remains of my ceiling down. They left the door open part of the time and [I] think dirt has got into all the other rooms. I feel ill at the thought of the work ahead.

Mrs Metcalfe, of Wilden, an old Sunderland woman we have known almost since we came to Bedford, died last Friday. She was 88 and was in St Peter's Hospital with pleurisy. Many are the pleasant summer afternoons I have spent in her cottage and garden in the country [four miles north-east of the centre of Bedford]. I went once this summer but, her husband now dead, the garden was a wilderness and the arbour he used to sit in was almost dropped to pieces.

Either Tuesday or Wednesday evening I heard a pilotless-plane and some people saw it (fire comes out of the tail) and although the thud was loud enough to make me pop right off my seat, it dropped as far away as Husborne Crawley, about 9–10 miles away [near Woburn Abbey]. We had 2 alerts that evening.

Thursday, 11 January.

The boss has gone to Scotland on business. I do not envy him travelling this weather, snow lying around. I have got some of the rooms cleaned up a bit, but with snow on the roof the new ceiling is not drying very well so may have to wait some time before it can be decorated. I have had some awful nights with neuralgia and now it has turned to toothache so I must have out the tooth that was stopped last October.

The last letter from Jim says definitely he has a duodenal ulcer. That is what Sybil's husband and John have and seem to be everlasting, although John's is not nearly as bad as Billy Cuthbertson's. It is unimaginable Jim not being able to eat anything and everything offered to him. People here with such complaints get extra rations of some foods. John gets 2 pints milk per day against the legal ration of 2 pints a week (and one egg per day). Our egg ration varies, sometimes one per month and never more than 2 per week. You must produce a doctor's certificate for special rations.

---

widely felt, as far north as Carlisle and as far south as Cromer in Norfolk. Buildings: 'more than 200 miles apart were shaken, but no damage was caused, and there were no casualties. In several Yorkshire towns and cities people were thrown out of bed, and large numbers, suspecting enemy activity, sought refuge in air-raid shelters.' (*The Times,* 1 January 1945, p. 8). Since there had been German V-1 attacks on parts of the North of England as recently as Christmas Eve (Ramsey, *The Blitz Then and Now, vol. 3,* pp. 498–505), seeking shelter this night was understandable.

Monday, 15 January.
I had the tooth out on Saturday afternoon. Now a hard bump has come in the jaw and I have a fat face. The dentist said the tooth seemed to have nothing wrong with it barring the small stopping he put in last October. The decorator looked in on Saturday and said we must wait another week for ceiling to dry. Snow has got all away. I went this morning and placed the rent collecting in the hands of an agent. Also collected the deeds of Jim's house, the mortgage now being paid off, and deposited them at solicitor's.

Friday, 26 January.
I have been very busy since my last entry, and also we are having bitter weather. First of all I must mention that your very pretty Xmas card (red and silver) arrived on 23rd January and olives arrived 24th. I see yours was posted on 1st December. Next day I was dusting and noticed the note on back of yours hoping parcel has arrived O.K. I am afraid it has not.

Well, last Saturday was the annual Folkdance party (4–8 p.m.) and I went off to it in a blinding snowstorm. I thought the weather would have thinned the ranks but the room was crowded when I arrived at 4.15. Later on somebody had persuaded a Scot to play bagpipes for some of the dances, and he arrived complete with kilt and a bag piper. First he played a schottische [a lively dance akin to a Highland fling] and I had the heartiest laugh I've had for months. I only looked on and I'm glad I did. He kept piping on and on and far too fast until the dancers looked worn out and in pain and when someone remarked to me 'He seems to have more puff than they have' I began to laugh and couldn't stop. It looked more like folk on a treadmill than dancing for pleasure. When at last he stopped and the folk got over the shock, the reaction made them all laugh fit to kill themselves. The Scot himself looked most puzzled and hurt.

Next day was cold and sunny and I walked through Biddenham, where the quaint roofs, thatched and otherwise, were covered with snow, and across snowy fields to the river. The river and the bare willows and poplars looked sepia against the snow. Boys were tobogganing on Honey Hills and I stood and watched them a while. It seemed a most dangerous run to me as, unless they took a skillful turn at the bottom, they were liable to shoot straight into the river. Since then we have had more snow, fog, frozen fog, and now the river is frozen right across. This only happens in very severe weather for us. Manchester, where Jim is, had 27 degrees of frost last weekend. At the foot of our stairs where the thermometer stands, is 34 degrees – 2 above freezing.[3]

---

[3]   The *Bedford Record*, 30 January 1945, p. 1, provided details on these conditions (the weather was now being reported in pre-war style): 'One of the coldest spells experienced in Bedford for a number of years [it had also been very cold five years before] has meant hilarious enjoyment for the energetic, severe handicaps for those engaged in manual labour, and shivers for everybody, since the thermometer began to fall again on 19th January. One of the coldest nights came on Thursday [the 25th], when 16 degrees of frost were registered. Many townsfolk who rose early on Friday morning expecting a hot cup of tea for their breakfast were highly disappointed when they found both their milk supply and water-pipes frozen. Bedford's plumbers have been in constant demand, and have found it difficult to cope with their numerous orders.'

However, my room is re-decorated and the house put straight, and just waiting for Jim to come home. He has got his discharge and as long as he is strong enough to travel he can come home. My neuralgia is gone and I am feeling stronger, but rheumatism is active.

Thursday, 1 February.
All last week I noticed Father kept kicking up mats and there seemed something wrong with his feet. On Sunday he had 3 falls and I find he is losing the use of his legs. He would not sit still and kept trying to get around. One of his falls was in the larder under the stairs and the man next door had to lift him out. Next day he had 2 falls, but since then, by carefully holding on to furniture, I have not seen him fall since. The doctor gave him an injection on Tuesday and says his legs may get better – but I have my doubts. He burnt another pair of pyjamas to cinders on Sunday. I stayed at home Monday and Tuesday but went to work yesterday.

The hard frost lasted over the weekend and on Tuesday morning we woke to a fresh covering of snow of at least 6 inches. It had drifted at the back door to nearly a foot. But the thaw set in that same day, and next day there was very little snow left – but what a mess.[4]

Tuesday, 6 February.
When I got home on Thursday I found a letter from Jim saying he might be home that night or Friday. He arrived Friday night. I also found that evening that Father's crown was bleeding and that he had another fall, so I stayed at home Friday afternoon. I reckon Jim has come in the nick of time. Father is failing fast. He fell halfway down the stairs on Sunday morning, so without any more argument we got his bed downstairs. The doctor gave him another injection this morning. The Russians are pushing on well towards Berlin, and I am wondering if Uncle A's dream will come true yet – war to last 5½ years – which means it ought to finish in a month.[5] The snowdrops he sent from Simonburn [Northumberland] are blooming in the garden and they do look nice.

Thursday, 15 February.
Not many entries just at present. All my spare time at the Office is devoted to trying to catch up in typing out this diary, because when Jim is well enough to work I shall have to be at home all the time on account of Father, and I won't have a typewriter

---

[4]   A heavy fall of snow (some eight inches) on the night of 29/30 January was followed by a sudden thaw: 'With the thaw came streams of water from burst pipes, caused in a good many home by insufficient lagging. Plumbers in the town were inundated with orders, a large number of which have still to be completed, and householders are having to devise ways and means of checking the flow until the workmen arrive. Some serious cases have been reported where extensive damage was caused before the burst pipes were discovered.' (*Bedford Record*, 6 February 1945, p. 1; also *Bedfordshire Times*, 2 February 1945, p. 6).
[5]   During the war there was constant speculation as to how long it would last, and people routinely heard and shared prognostications, which were all over the map. Most of them turned out to be wrong. During the months since the spring of 1944, when victory seemed more or less assured, most predictions were overly optimistic – including this one (though it was not too far off).

to use then. Jim is going on nicely. Father is fairly well in himself but his legs are practically useless. He keeps trying to get about the room and often falls so he must always be watched.

Monday, 19 February.
This is the anniversary of my Mother's death 17 years ago.[6] Yesterday was a warm spring-like day, which probably accounted for Father being restless. He persisted in trying to get around, and kept falling and upsetting things. It was like having a mischievous baby in the house. Many days like that and I will be completely worn out.

Thursday, 22 February.
With the doctor giving Father 4 injections in 4 weeks the latter is full of beans but legs no better. We keep having one accident after another. I was awakened in the middle of the night before last by a loud crash. When I got downstairs I found Jim carrying Father from the living room to the room he sleeps in. He had pulled half the things off the chiffonier;[7] a beautiful biscuit bowl was smashed to atoms and the biscuits scattered, the teapot stand broken, and 2 ornaments including a glass vase given me at least 35 years ago. I was very sorry about the biscuit bowl as it was very uncommon and beautiful. All this because Pa had fancied a biscuit in the middle of the night.

Monday, 26 February.
John came to tea yesterday. He brought Father a huge egg out of their rations, some elderberry wine and a reading bracket [frame to hold a book]. He took back an old blue Japanese dressing gown that I have given to Jacqueline. Mabel called later in the evening with 3 eggs. I planted a row of broad beans on Saturday and a row of shallots the previous Saturday. Jim did some gardening last week and says he will be fit to start work in a fortnight. So today I told Miss Barber I would be leaving soon to look after Father all day. It seemed to be a shock to her and she said she did not think she could replace me in a fortnight. Mr J.R. Taylor is still away with flu.

Tuesday, 27 February.
Yesterday afternoon Father managed to pull the whole sideboard over. It is a pretty mahogany chiffonier you may remember, with wood spirals supporting an upper shelf. All the upper part was broken away, the things came out of the cupboard (including a dish of stewed apple), dishes were broken and everything in an abominable mess. It took Jim an hour to clean the place up. The sideboard lodged against the dining table; otherwise Father may have been pinned beneath it. It shook Jim's nerves and he feels he'd like to get away somewhere for a bit of rest. Father's only comment when I came home was 'Worse things happen at sea'!! It so happens that an invitation came this morning for Jim and I to go to Worthing if John and

---

6   Leah's mother, Mary, according to her death certificate, died at home of cancer, aged 59. Her husband was present at her death, and perhaps Leah as well, who was then aged 26. Her mother had been ill for some time.
7   A moveable low cupboard with a sideboard top.

Lily will take Father. Of course it is out of the question. It appears Aunt Tiny from Sunderland is going to Worthing to stay with my Cousin Belle. Apparently Jessie (who lost her husband Noble a year last September) is going to marry again and Aunt T. does not agree and is going to live on her own in 2 rooms somewhere and is very upset. She asked if she could come and give me a hand with Father for a fortnight, but as she is the sort that likes people to wait on her I had to put her off, as I have as much as I can manage. Our troops are within 10 miles of Cologne.

Thursday, 1 March.
I gave my official notice of leaving yesterday. I leave a week tomorrow. Our troops are within 7 miles of Cologne.

Monday, 5 March.
During Saturday night and again during Sunday evening we had alerts and the Germans actually sent planes over a wide area of England. This is the first time they have sent piloted planes for about a year.[8] I hope we do not have to return to 'Blackout'. Jim has been busy at the garden every morning last week and on Saturday afternoon. On Saturday I had a bonfire in back garden, then washed Pa's hair, and went to a Folkdance party in evening. It was crowded. I went to garden Sunday afternoon and planted spinach. Also trimmed minute lavender hedges and weeded corner where the primroses grow. I counted 22 flower buds on the daffodils, so there will be some colour soon. This is the sort of gardening I like – Jim doing the heavy work and I pottering among the flowers and herbs.

Wednesday, 7 March.
In this morning's paper I see that the Allies have taken Cologne on one side of the Rhine. It is a mere shell and Mr Bates said they have had no water in that city for 3 months. I am gradually taking home all my personal possessions from the Office, rather a mournful proceeding. I wrote Olive last week.

Saturday, 10 March.
Well, I left the Office altogether yesterday. I was presented by friends among the staff with a beautifully illuminated testimonial with 131 signatures wishing me well, and £7 10s 0d in the form of 10 savings certificates. Very nice of them. It was harrowing to the feelings bidding goodbye to them and there were lots I missed whom I would have liked to see. Jim has gone off to Luton for the weekend, armed

---

8   According to Ramsey, *The Blitz Then and Now, vol. 3*, p. 528, in March 1945: 'Attacks by manned aircraft were carried out on the nights of 3/4th and 4/5th, the first involving about 70 aircraft, the biggest force to operate over the country since May 15/16, 1944. Activity lasted 3½ hours and 75 incidents were reported, widely scattered over Northumberland, Suffolk, Derbyshire, Oxfordshire, Yorkshire and Lincolnshire. The last two counties were most affected, with 24 incidents in each, and the worst incident occurred in Ipswich, where nine people were killed. Elsewhere, machine-gunning, anti-personnel bombs, cannon fire, HEs and incendiaries were all reported. The next night, when only 10 enemy aircraft operated, six crossed the coast and there were two incidents in Lincolnshire and a third in Suffolk. Total civilian casualties for the week were 169 killed, 461 seriously injured and 65 missing.'

with 2 eggs and 1½ pints [of] milk. I spent this afternoon working in back garden and planted sweet peas and sweet williams. I shall be tied to the house a lot this summer so I am going to make the garden as nice as possible. Father took a turn outdoors; he walked out the front door and round to back of house and sat and watched me working for a while and then took another similar stroll. A neighbour, Mr Reynolds, went off in his Fire Service uniform. He said some haystacks were ablaze at Biddenham.[9]

According to Aunt T's latest letter to Father Jessie would be made Mrs Maguire today, only she said '10th February'. We presume she meant 10th March. She is the only blood relation who has ever married twice.[10] The letter also said she (Aunt T.) was staying with my cousin John and his wife Edith (John is Aunt Sarah's son) until she gets somewhere to go. There has evidently been a big upset of some sort.[11]

Sunday, 18 March.

Jim has been at work a week [he was a bricklayer] and seems none the worse for the experience. The weather certainly was very favourable for the venture. Father is a lot better too and has advanced as far as walking round the block leaning on his walking stick only. I would never have believed it possible a few weeks ago.

In England, while we are employed, we are compelled to pay Health and Pensions insurance (also Unemployment if you are a full-time worker). Since I have given up going to work, of course that is finished. On Friday I went to the office of my Society to see about becoming a voluntary contributor, and I find that by paying 8½ pence a week for the next 17 years I will get 10 shillings per week at 60. Worthwhile. You can only become a voluntary contributor if you have formerly been employed and been a compulsory contributor. If I later take up employment I will automatically go back to the former arrangement, which also includes medical benefit and an allowance if out of work.

---

[9] 'Two straw ricks, estimated to contain about 80 tons, situated in a field off Biddenham Turn, belonging to Mr Rawlins, were burnt out', and three fire engines were called out. It was understood that two boys were being questioned by the police. (*Bedford Record*, 13 March 1945, p. 1).

[10] Jessie Hugill (née Aynsley), widowed in 1943 and mother of a toddler, married Erik Maguire in Sunderland on 10 March 1945. He was three years younger than her and a warehouse inspector for the Ministry of Food. His father was a staithes master – a staithe was a wharf, especially a waterside coal depot for loading vessels. At the time of their marriage they were both living close to each other on Melbury Court in Sunderland; perhaps they met as neighbours. (Ann Stephenson kindly helped us with this research.) According to Leah's later notes (BARS, Z1606/13), Jessie and Erik went on to have at least four children together.

[11] Aunt Tiny, whose full name was Justina Kate Aynsley (b. 1878), lived a rather perilous life, as Leah observed in her final book of writing (no. 13), where she recorded some details of family history. Aunt Tiny, she said: 'Never married. Was never trained to earn her living, and after nursing both aged parents had a difficult time to make ends meet. Took in lodgers, then ran what is called a "box", an annual savings club in which she kept so much for her trouble. This she extended to a sort of clothing club on the same system. Not being an employee, she got no pension until she was 70, which taught the writer [i.e., Leah herself] a lesson.' Leah, clearly, was prudent and careful in managing money; she also deplored waste (10 June 1953).

Jessie was duly married on 10th March, and Aunt T. has got fixed up with some nice people, so all is serene at present.

It was lovely at the garden this afternoon – primroses and daffodils in bloom. Crowds of people going by on way to woods.

Saturday, 24 March.
Jerry is still making himself felt round here. Early on Friday morning I heard a loud rumble and Jim heard that a rocket had fallen between Willington and Mogger-hanger. This latter has the san[atorium] where so many of the Youngs stayed. Last night there was an alert and there was a loud thud quite near and then immediately the 'All Clear'. That denoted a fly-bomb as you know there is no more danger once they've fallen; whereas a plane might drop 3–4 bombs.[12]

Thursday, 29 March.
I seemed to spend all this morning shopping. The fishmonger was shut and had a notice 'No wet fish today. Very little expected for Good Friday.' So I went on to P.O. [Post Office] for Father's pension and then for my ration. When I was well loaded up I passed the fish shop again and found a very long queue of people being served with herring only. I was too loaded up for queueing so went home and got on with housework. Then I found they had omitted to give me any sugar with rations so back I went and thought I would get some herring and hot cross buns at the same time but all sold out. I expect I will have to spend an hour in the queue for fish tomorrow. I had a nice time at Luton on Sunday. Their garden is very pretty with lots of flowers and a cherry tree in bloom. Janet is going with some other school girls to Stratford on Avon during the Easter Holidays. They are to stay with a French lady for a course in French language. Lucky girl. The place, of course, is Shakespeare's birthplace.

Good Friday, 30 March.
Not been a very nice day for holiday makers. The best weather was while I was in the fish queue; I stood from 9.20 to 10.15 a.m., 5 minutes longer than last Good Friday. Just after lunch there was a thunderstorm with heavy rain and the water came pouring through my roof just where they were supposed to have repaired it again last January. After Father had had his nap he allowed me, under great protest, to wash his hair. Then, for an airing, I posted some periodicals to Stella, had tea, cooked Jim's dinner, did a little gardening, had a bath, and thus spent a very quiet day. The scullery doormat is really worn out. I have looked in the shops for a new one but have not seen even one mat, and there were so many notices about various furnishing articles being for 'priority' purchases only that I thought there was small chance of my buying one, so I intend making a rag mat. Today I washed a sack and chalked out a design. I have dyed a creamy jacket of Father's [a] rose colour

---

[12] Except for the V-2 attack on Luton on 6 November, Bedfordshire suffered little damage from aerial attacks in 1944–45. There were only thirteen reported incidents in the county involving V-1 flying-bombs and V-2 rockets, ten of the former, three of the latter. By contrast, Hertfordshire to the south reported 116 incidents (O'Brien, *Civil Defence*, p. 682).

(I had some old dye in the house) and an old brown skirt of my own will do to make a start.

The Allies are making great strides east of the Rhine – but oh! when will the war end!

Wednesday 4 April.

Well, Easter is over once again, and one of the most quiet I've spent in my life. As I had to stay at home on account of Father, I had a big wash day as I did none last week on account of spring-cleaning Father's bedroom upstairs. He is agitating to get back there again, but I will wait awhile to see if his improvement is lasting enough to make it worthwhile Jim's moving all the furniture about again. On Monday Father wanted a bus-ride to the town so after an early tea we went as far as the market, walked across the square and High Street to the river and back again and caught the next bus back to Queen's Park. He was so exhausted we sat on a seat near the bus stop about 10 minutes before he could walk the few yards home. We were out exactly an hour and it was the first time he had been to the town since before Xmas.

Last night I was at a 'Crazy' whist-drive at the Adult School. Have you been to one? They made us do such things as pass our cards to our neighbours after the 6th trick, winners of round to swap scores with losers etc. Trixy's Aunt will be 90 on Friday, and Trix is making it the occasion of another party on Saturday. They have a cake and want to put her age on it so I have sent some of the decorations you sent on Xmas, as they have nothing like that. I still have one little phial left.

Sunday, 8 April.

Afternoon got out fine, and I went to meet Flossie out of her Sunday school class. We walked round the Embankment gardens, which were brilliant with flowers, and came back the other side of the river, where we saw a swan sitting on her nest in a back-water. It is not unusual to see American soldiers out with their wives and babies, but this afternoon I saw one wheeling his baby (presumably) all alone as though he had lived here all his life, and nobody took any particular notice of him.[13] Flossie's sister joined us. She was home for weekend from a hospital for Services at Watford (14 miles from London) and she said last week was the first time for months they have not had either fly-bombs or V-2s fall near them – sometimes 12 a day. That is because Allies are driving Germans out of Holland where the despatching sites are. I have started to make a fruit-tree net.

Tuesday, 10 April.

Turned out 3 bedrooms this morning and this afternoon sat in the garden working at fruit-tree net. It has turned out such a beautiful evening that I think I will go to garden instead of to business meeting of Adult School. As I am 'Auditor' I ought

---

[13] In a long article on the presence of US servicemen in Bedford, the *Bedfordshire Times*, 6 October 1944, p. 5, remarked on the many Americans 'marrying Bedford girls' since 1942. As Leah indicated, by late in the war this American presence in Bedford was more or less taken for granted.

to put in an appearance but I did the auditing on Saturday evening and there is nothing I need to do at the meeting except vote.

Thursday, 12 April.

I wished afterwards I had not gone to garden on Tuesday. After doing the 3 bedrooms I was too tired for the garden and could hardly sleep at night. However, it was a beautiful day yesterday so I sat in garden for 2 hours after dinner, and again today. The apple tree is covered with red buds which are just bursting into full bloom, the 4 red tulips which Jim sent from Belgium are fully open to the sun and look as though a breeze would shatter them, but they will probably close up again at sunset. The golden alyssum is in its glory and the lily of the valley beginning to bloom. While in bed this morning I heard a cuckoo; this must be about the earliest in the year I've heard it. The laburnum growing against the trellis, which I am training espalier-wise, is going to bloom for the first time this year.[14]

I must say I like this life – sitting in the garden – better than grinding away in an office. I am getting on with the fruit-tree net, and have just shortened a pair of Jim's army socks by 2 inches.

Saturday, 14 April.

President Roosevelt died yesterday, just on the eve of victory over the Germans. It will be a great blow and loss to Mr Churchill, who will have to carry a greater portion of the burden of the 'peace'.[15] In a measure Roosevelt is lucky to have passed on before all the wrangling and worries of the victors begin.

Trixy called late on Thursday and asked Father and me to tea today. I woke very early this morning full of the idea that this might be V-Day, and what a worry it would be if Father insisted on going out to tea through all the town gone mad! What a thing to have worried about. We got there and back without a mishap and had a game of cards after some other visitors had left.

Monday, 16 April.

Today it has been sweltering, the day I elected to spring-clean the middle room. The sweat poured off me. Father *seemed* very exhausted with the heat and by teatime changed into holland jacket [of smooth hard-wearing linen fabric] and panama hat. I was so exhausted I lay down after tea to try and regain some energy

---

[14] Leah, in taking great pleasure in the beauty of her garden, was in the company of generations of her countrymen and countrywomen of all ages and income levels (Willes, *Gardens of the British Working Class*, chap. 4, 'A Passion for Flowers').
[15] The US flag was flown at half-mast in Bedford; the BBC Symphony Orchestra, conducted by Sir Adrian Boult, broadcast a memorial programme on Friday evening from Bedford School Hall; Americans in uniform attended an open-air service on Sunday evening; and a memorial service was held on Tuesday, 17 April (*Bedford Record*, 17 April 1945, p. 1). This memorial service in honour of the President was described in the *Bedfordshire Times*, 20 April 1945, p. 7, as a 'profoundly moving act of thanksgiving for the life and example of a great man'. He was 'one who was Britain's best friend in the darkest hour of the war and without whom freedom might never have survived.' (The former claim, given American isolationism before Pearl Harbor, is debatable, though Roosevelt personally was long on Britain's side.)

before ironing and rehanging curtains. Jim came in and said Father had slipped out with his bike, tried to mount and fallen on the road and Harold [Bradley] next door [no. 68] had picked him up. Then Jim went off to the garden. I thought to myself that would give Father a lesson before much harm was done. About 10 minutes later I heard an altercation between him and the neighbour (Harold) and when I looked out of the window behold Father was wheeling out his bike again. I struggled with him to prevent his attempting to mount it but had to call Harold, who confiscated the bike and took it into his house. I am now waiting for Jim to come home to see what is to be done in the matter. To any ordinary eye Father is plainly unfit to ride a bike.

Saturday, 21 April.
We have had a real sweltering hot week and have sat in the garden most days with no stockings on. It is cooler today, and a good job too as it made me feel ill to work, and twice the milk turned and I made cheese of it. We partly dismantled Father's bike, but he has not thought much about going out on it again. He was 75 on 19th April. I have finished the net and started the doormat. I only do it out of doors so the bits do not litter the house. It is not a clipping mat but the rags are cut into long strips and pulled through the foundation in little loops. It is not so clumsy and heavy as a clipping mat, but even so I think I'd rather have factory-made mats. Cissie, in Sunderland, seems always to have a mat on the go. I think she must be fond of toil.

I had a long letter from Stella. She has been home since 8th March. She rises at 11 a.m., prepares dinner for Uncle A. and herself, washes up and tidies room and back to bed about 2 p.m., up at 5 for her Father's tea and bed at 9.30. I hope she sticks to that routine until she is much stronger. She is not sure whether the last operation is a success and has to have an X-ray in 3 months' time and then at 6 monthly intervals. She seems very pleased to be home again and what she calls 'free'.

There have been some awful pictures and accounts in the papers this week of German concentration and foreign workers' camps. I am glad Allied soldiers made German civilians come and look inside them and help to bury some of the corpses. I have just opened the tin of marmalade you sent a year last Xmas. It is delicious. It is '3 fruit' by E.D. Smith.

Did I ever mentioned that a party of caravanners had taken over a plot of ground at Thistley Green which once belonged to an enthusiastic little old lady who only once ever put in an appearance? They are a very rough lot with 3 caravans, and I believe 8 people sleep in one of them. They are usually very noisy but last Thursday there was an unusual quiet in their quarter and [I] thought the hot weather must be the cause. Also, on Bromham Bridge were lots of people that I thought had come for a cooler, but it turned out that two boys of the caravan company had been drowned on Wednesday and they were still dragging the river for them. The second boy was not brought up until about 10 a.m. D.S.T. [double summer time] this morning.[16]

---

[16] Two boys, aged sixteen and seventeen, from Thistley Green drowned. Both were said to have been poor or non-swimmers (*Bedford Record*, 24 April 1945, p. 1).

Monday, 23 April.

Cold and bright and ideal weather for work so I turned the contents of the kitchen-scullery out of doors and cleaned the room thoroughly. The lilac and laburnum are exceptionally good at present, and so are lilies of the valley. I have started to hemstitch a handkerchief of fine linen obtained from engineering drawings given me by Flossie Clarke (a tracer) from which I soaked the wax.

Saturday, 28 April.

After having no rain for a fortnight it poured during the night, and is bitterly cold today and has been snowing. I got your letter dated 20th March today; and Olive's dated 22nd March yesterday – with all the news of the adopted baby (abridged and otherwise). No wonder you had no time to write to me 'after the holidays' as you said on your Xmas card. Olive has had a rough time with that operation and has a sorry 2 years ahead if it was anything like mine. I could never have looked after a young baby during it. I don't like the idea of Bill joining the Paratroops.

The great news today is of the 'Link-up' between USA and Russian troops somewhere near Berlin. This actually occurred last Wednesday. Also Mussolini has again been captured and Goering is dead. Those prison camps at Belsen, Dachau etc. are hellish. I must admit that at one time I did not greatly fear if we *were* conquered by Germany. But now, although I do not suppose they would have done much to such as myself, it would have been insupportable that such fiends became masters of Europe, and further. I am thankful there were people with different ideas from mine.[17]

Monday, 30 April.[18]

Not having wireless (or radio as you probably call it) I often look forward to Monday morning for a double amount of news, and today I was not disappointed.[19] But first I must remark that when I woke this morning I saw through the window a lilac tree with its bloom fading, a laburnum in full glory, and *snow on the roofs beyond it*. I remember snow on one 19th April, but I think never so late as this. Jim said he saw today a field of peas so damaged by frost that men were ploughing them in and going to plant potatoes in place.

The news was that Himmler has offered to surrender but ignored the Russians so was not accepted. The paper seems to expect complete surrender in a few days. Mussolini is killed and his body lies on show in Milan and people have spat on it. Hitler is thought to be dead. Or very near it.

I received another letter from you with 3 snaps of Bill. He looks fine. I can see a likeness to you but even more to Roland when he was young.

I have had a busy day spring-cleaning the front room just vacated by Father who now sleeps upstairs again. I feel spent.

---

[17] Leah's admission of previous and mistaken defeatism is very unusual in private wartime papers.

[18] This entry marks the beginning of volume/workbook IV of the diary.

[19] She apparently took no Sunday newspaper. The liberal-leaning *News Chronicle* was her daily paper.

Thursday, 3 May.

Before I proceed further I must state that whereas for months (and years) we have been having only about one shell egg per person a month, since before Easter we [have been] having 2 and 3 eggs each a week. We feel we are in the lap of luxury, and the girl next door today says she is going to pickle some of hers!! And I know one woman who has bought a bucket for the same purpose, but the latter is understandable as on account of kidney trouble she must not eat them at present. Well, I myself could consume more than 3 eggs per week. The reason given at first for this increase was that Canada was sending us a shipload of eggs, but one shipload cannot have given all England 2–3 eggs a week for 2 months and I am wondering if it is because all the troops are abroad and we are getting their share of eggs.[20]

Yesterday the news was that all Germans in Italy have surrendered, and that Hitler has either been killed, died or commit[ted] suicide, but no-one seems to have seen his body and people here are dubious. Last night after I'd gone to bed there seemed such an air of excitement outside I thought it might be V-Day and expected church-bells to ring out, but it was only my imagination ran riot. I paid bill for ceiling this morning – £6 15s 0d – and impressed on them the leak was not cured.

No news of final victory yet, but shops have notices on the doors that they will close within an hour of official announcement and all the following day unless it should be Saturday, when they will close on Monday instead. I want a small wringer or mangle, and as you can only get secondhand I have been studying advertisements. There was nothing of that sort but a portable typewriter was for sale. I thought it would be useful to complete copying this diary and also to keep in practice in case I must go out to work again. I had to cycle at least 3 miles to a district I did not know existed. The man was taking offers and the best offer so far was £10. I offered £12 and he took my address and will let me know. I'd really like a better one and hope someone over-bids me, but they are very scarce and it would do for the present.[21] Then I cycled another 3½ miles to the garden and planted asparagus seedling, and was grieved to see all the gooseberries fallen through frost.

Monday, 7 May.

After a very wet day on Saturday, which was a godsend for the gardens after such a dry spell, it has been very hot and close. The news said this morning that Victory would probably be announced this evening, but has not been up to 6.30. This promise of 2 days holiday as soon as it happens has put everything at 6s and 7s. One does not know whether to lay in stocks or not. The butcher and fishmonger are closed today in any case. The baker said he won't do any business tomorrow if the announcement is made tonight and all the shops will be shut. I could not get any green vegs and the shops said they don't suppose there will be any delivered tomorrow if it is a general holiday. So the housewives and shopkeepers are grumbling; it would have been better to let victory come and then fix the two days' holiday.

---

[20] 'Only in the spring of 1945', according to one authority 'when rather more feedstuffs were made available, did the curve of sales [of eggs] at last show signs of turning upward.' (Hammond, *Food and Agriculture in Britain 1939–45*, p. 63).

[21] She was offering to pay around four times what had been her weekly wage when she started her diary.

Tuesday, 8 May.

V DAY. Well, the day is nearly over now. Very quiet around here. I have not heard any victory bells. The street has blossomed out into flags, bunting and fairy lights. The local shops were open – even the fish shop – and the baker called as usual. (His wife told me yesterday he would not.) Churchill broadcast at 3 p.m.[22]

Jim and I went [for] a walk up the riverside, past where I watched the tobogganing in January. There were a few punts on the river and a few bathers, white hawthorn bushes and buttercups and daisies all over the grass. A very pleasant day in May.

Thursday, 10 May.

I spent a quiet afternoon yesterday by the river and went to the garden in the evening. There the quietness ended for the day. As darkness fell they started a party in the street [Marlborough Road]. I heard they were going to burn an effigy of Hitler at midnight, but our family went to bed at 10.30 as Jim had to rise at 6.30 a.m. After about half an hour I heard such a terrific din I thought they must be burning the guy. I got up and went downstairs to peep out. Upstairs windows were lit up all along, which lighted the street, two loud-speakers provided music and people were dancing and shouting at the tops of their voices. I went back to bed but the noise went on until 1 a.m.

Today great preparations were made to give the children and old folk a tea in the street. At 2.30 John and Lily arrived by tandem. We went to the riverside and on the way passed a couple of streets where tea parties were going to be held and one lot of tables was already set out and beautifully decorated with flowers. Alas! it came to pour with rain and on our return journey we found all the folk carrying the stuff to the West End Club [84 Ford End Road]. Our street had not started setting out, so on account of the rain they used an empty motor coach garage. As soon as it became fine they brought all the chairs into the street and started party games. After the children had had enough they introduced a jazz-band and the older ones danced. The band, if you please, was next door's piano (Bradley's) in the bay window and the rest of the instruments were in the front garden!! Luckily for us they later got a piano on to the road and the band moved further away. The Mas and Pas that weren't dancing were sitting all around and no end of refreshments were handed about by little boys. The lighting, which last night I thought was from bedrooms, was from floodlights from next door (Lizar)[23] and another house.

---

[22] In his speech to V-E (Victory in Europe) crowds in London, Churchill highlighted national unity and the: 'victory of the great British nation as a whole. We were the first, in this ancient island, to draw the sword against tyranny. After a while we were left all alone against the most tremendous military power the world has ever seen.' He celebrated Britons' defiance of 'a terrible foe' and resolve to defend freedom (James, ed., *Winston S. Churchill: His Complete Speeches*, vol. 7, p. 7155).

As for mundane local facts, it was reported this day in the *Bedford Record*, p. 4, that: 'Every food trader is asked to display in his shop a notice telling his customers at what hours his shop will be open during the V Holiday, together with any further details useful to his customers.' Most households were dependent on almost daily access to local shops, and the dates of this two-day holiday were announced only at the very last minute.

[23] The next door neighbours at 64 Marlborough Road were Kenneth Lizars (he was a fitter) and his family. Leah misspelled his surname on a couple of other occasions (which we have corrected).

Next day.

When I got upstairs I found that the next street was also having a party, and between the two streets the noise was now deafening. They were burning *their* Hitler (which this afternoon we saw slumped in a doorway and I thought it was a man who had collapsed) and singing choruses even louder than our street did the night before. Our street closed down at 11 p.m., it being their second night of festivities, but Westbourne Road kept on until 1 a.m. Wasn't I thankful when the last God Save the King was sung. When I peeped out the last time lots of better-class strangers were looking, obviously come to see how the 'lower orders' were celebrating victory; which made me remember that when we lived in Sunderland on occasions like this some people liked to go down to the East End to see the fun, so I expect they acted like our neighbourhood is acting now – regularly slummy. Some of the neighbours are very disgusted at it all. I certainly hope that there is still a shortage of drink when Japan is beaten, or that it is very bad weather so they cannot all get together in my hearing.[24]

Friday, 11 May.

I bought a second-hand typewriter this evening, £17 10s 0d, so I will be able to complete typing out this diary. I had to stop when I left the office.[25]

Monday, 14 May.

Yesterday there was a violent rain storm after tea so I decided not to go to the garden but to meet Flossie out of Chapel instead. She came out and saw me but said she was staying on for a 'Faith for the Times Campaign' service and asked me to come too. She sings in the choir and took me to where she usually sits, in a balcony near the organ. It was Bunyan Meeting House [on Mill Street], a rather popular chapel in the town, and became packed. It was the first time I'd ever attended a service there, and rather astonishing that I should sing in the choir above all those people. My lips kept twitching at the humour of it. It turned out to be a revivalist meeting, and the preacher spoke as though none of us knew about Christ. However, about a dozen women came up to the altar during the last hymn to 'make the choice', as the preacher said, and he took them into the vestry to talk to them. This is the first time I have been to such a meeting.

---

[24] The *Bedford Record*, 15 May 1945, p. 1, offered a more charitable – indeed, effusive – view of the celebrations: 'On VE Day and all through Victory Week most of Bedford's small side-streets held high festival in a delightfully spontaneous manner and the typical English barriers of shyness were soon melted by the gay sunshine and colours and joyousness. There were to be seen long rows of tables, brightly decorated with flowers and coloured paper devices, and piled high with dainties, some of which had probably been saved for this glorious Day, while bunting and flags of the Allied Nations, and different patterns of fairy lights added to the pretty picture.' Later, after the eating, 'gramophones and loudspeakers sprayed music out into the streets so that dancing could take place.' Leah's last remarks testify to her disengagement from the raucous and 'rough' dimensions of working class culture and her preference for good order and decorum.

[25] This major investment confirms the importance Leah attached to her diary. No typed version of it is known to have survived.

During the evening I saw more fighter planes at once than ever I saw during the war with Germany.

Wednesday, 16 May.
I heard that those planes were making a salute before going off to the Far East. The weather at present suits me exactly; sometimes dull, but mostly sunny, with sufficient cool breeze to prevent any feeling of lifelessness. Yesterday I took Jim's Unemployment Card to the Food Office and made arrangements for him to have extra cheese ration. I think the clue on the Unemployment Book as to whether he was entitled to it was the words in it 'Industry Letters: ZZ'. So I suppose it would be of no use for any and every man just to produce his card and expect extra cheese.

Whit Monday, 21 May.
5.30 p.m. and a violent rain and thunderstorm. I sat by the riverside with my sewing this afternoon and it was very pleasant. I wonder how the various boating parties are getting on in this deluge; we were all warned in the newspaper of thunder showers for the holiday, but it is a pity, as this afternoon's sunshine must have tempted many abroad. Jim spent all Saturday afternoon and evening at Ickwell May Festival,[26] so I left him to get dinner ready and I spent Sunday morning at the garden. I enjoyed having a morning clear of Household cares. I spent the afternoon on the bed with *No Place Like Home* [1936] by Beverley Nichols[27] (it being a wet afternoon) and later I met Flossie as she came from Chapel and took a walk with her. She has invited me to have tea with them next Sunday. This morning arrived an invitation for tomorrow from Rose Stapleton 'to view the presents and partake of wedding cake'. She married Fred Stapleton on 10th May.[28]

Wednesday, 23 May.
We continue to have sharp showers with bright intervals, which is very good for the garden. We are eating our own spring onions, but they are rather small as yet. I made a gallon of herb beer yesterday. The instructions said ¾ lb. sugar for this amount but I only used ½ lb and ½ oz. yeast. I keep the bottles in the bath in case the corks pop. I have had some catastrophes in that line in the past.

---

[26] Ickwell is a hamlet in the parish of Northill, some nine miles south-east of Marlborough Road. It was famous for its maypole on the village green.
[27] This is a travel book. The places visited include Vienna, Rumania, Istanbul, Athens, Alexandria, Cairo and (most notably) Palestine. Nichols, a prolific author, was a keen gardener and wrote numerous books on gardening, including *Down the Garden Path* (1932), *How Does Your Garden Grow?* (1935) and *Green Grows the City* (1939). It is likely that Leah knew of him primarily as a writer on gardening and on this occasion sampled one of his other books.
[28] The wedding, at the Howard Congregational Church, was reported in the *Bedford Record*, 15 May 1945, p. 2. Both the bride and groom 'are well known as active members of the Bedford Adult School.' She 'is the School's Tennis Secretary, a keen worker in the Girl's Life Brigade, and is a member of the Organists' Association.' He 'is a member of the Workers' Educational Association, the Society of Friends, the local Labour Party, and the Bedford Rambling Club.' In other words, they belonged to the self-improving part of Bedford's working people to which Leah regularly attached herself.

Jim and I duly arrived at Rose's. She had some nice presents. There were 22 of us 'partaking of cake' in a little room no bigger than ours and all windows tightly fastened.

Thursday, 24 May.
Received an air letter from Winnie. She is sending us another parcel when she gets it made up. Billy has been in hospital 2 weeks with steel in his eye. The early part of the day was really cold and I lit the fire at dinner time, but I wrapped up well and sat in the garden this afternoon and worked at the rag mat. It was a beautiful evening while at the Thistley Green garden, but the Scotchman said there was going to be a frost so I covered one row of potatoes and one of haricots with straw, and left the rest to take a chance. On the way home about 9 p.m. I heard a woman call to her husband in front garden 'Himmler has commit[ted] suicide.' He replied 'Good.'

Monday, 28 May.
Had a good washday, including the last 2 pair of curtains after the spring-clean. This afternoon I collected the new ration books for the family from the Wesley Hall [Ford End Road], a place of worship which houses a temporary office near the organ. It has been a showery weekend with thunderstorms but I managed to get to the garden twice without a wetting. I received an extra letter from Celia with a pair of kid gloves.

Sunday, 3 June.
Been a very showery week. On Tuesday I called at the home of the Secretary of the Bedford Literary Society but she was away for the day. However, she posted me full particulars of the new Society. In the evening I attended the Adult School lecture on 'Our Cultural Heritage' by Mrs Matkin. She used to be a mistress at the Girls' Modern School.

Yesterday evening, instead of going to the garden, I witnessed the crowning of a May Queen (in June) at Kempston. It was very interesting and pretty and there were fold and sword dancing and of course maypole dancing. In the latter was performed The Spider's Web, which was new to me. The showers held off all the time of the festival.[29] Afterwards a man accosted us, and Jim mentioned his name – Reg Elstow. I remembered the name and face but couldn't place him. No wonder, as it must be about 15 years since our paths crossed. In those days he and Jim were very keen St John's Ambulance workers, Jim being secretary, and he used to call at our house. He joined the London Fire Brigade and passed from our lives. Now he is married and has a girl of 11 and lives at Kempston. He has lost an eye recently, but still he knew Jim and me after all those years.

---

[29] The festivities were described in some detail, and accompanied by three photographs, in the *Bedford Record*, 5 June 1945, p. 1. Before this fete, children under ten who wished to take part in the procession were asked to assemble 'at 6.15 p.m. at Hill Grounds, wearing cotton frocks and carrying wild or garden flowers.' (*Bedfordshire Times*, 1 June 1945, p. 10). 'Twenty four years ago today I was May Queen', Leah had written on 1 May 1935. She would have been nine years old; presumably this occurred in or near Sunderland.

Wednesday, 6 June.

Anniversary of D-Day. So far, it has been what you might call 'dripping June' and today it has rained steadily most of the day. Peggy, next door, has gone to Northampton to try to get a costume to fit her; she has tried all over Bedford without success. She rarely gets a day away from her family. I think this is the first during the 6 years she's been married. So of course it would rain. I went out at 9.45 a.m. to see the state of the fish market. The announcement on Bridgeman's door [fishmonger, 66 Iddesleigh Road] was 'Plenty of Cod, Hake and Skate at 11 o'clock', so I returned at 11 and found a long queue. When I had stood nearly half an hour Eric Bridgeman declared there was nothing but skate left. That is not suitable for Jim so I left the queue and went round the back of the premises and Les Bridgeman let me have a cutlet for 6d. I did not dare return past the front of the shop as the others were grumbling as there was only skate and would have guessed what I'd been up to, so I slunk round a back alley, down which I had never been before, in order to reach home. Such are the arts of shopping in these days of shortage.[30] I have completed the central diamond of the rag mat I am making (rose pink) and started the dark brown next to it.

Friday, 8 June.

Yesterday evening I went to the garden as usual on Thursday. My bad tyre went flat just as I reached Berry Farm, but I pushed on to the garden and gathered various vegs. The place was very quiet as all the noisy caravan folk had gone to the village [Bromham] to see the May Day (P) celebrations on the green.[31] I left at 8 o'clock and it took me 50 minutes to push my bike home. I was amused to see, at the turning to Bromham village, a horse-drawn lorry laden with the returning caravan dwellers. They were doing things in style. Good old Jim repaired my tyre before he had supper, but on his advice I have bought a new outer cover today (6s 3d). I went round registering at the shops with new ration books.

Monday, 11 June.

On Saturday I missed the cucumber plants that Jim has been raising in pots at home. They were there safely on Friday night. When Jim came home for his dinner I asked him about them and he said he'd given them away but would not say to whom. I was very annoyed as they were much in advance of those at the garden and I thought he might have left at least one so that we could have an early cucumber. When I arrived at the garden in the evening there they were, all planted out! It transpired that instead of going to work, Jim had played truant at the garden all the morning. I picked 4 lb. gooseberries which, with 2 pies we have had, is the whole crop. I bottled 3 jars yesterday and made jam mixed with rhubarb this morning.

---

[30] It is almost certain that such ruses occurred routinely in Bedford and elsewhere as women struggled to feed their families during a time of scarcity and rationing.

[31] 'Two masked "highwaymen" headed the carnival', a new May Queen was chosen, and 'there was traditional dancing and other happy events.' (*Bedfordshire Times*, 15 June 1945, p. 3). The celebrations were described, accompanied by two photographs, in the *Bedford Record*, 12 June 1945, p. 1.

Yesterday evening Doff and I walked over Foster Hill and across Clapham Park and what used to be the Golf Course [2½ miles north of Marlborough Road]. It is now partly under crops and contains the outposts of an American aerodrome [at Twinwood Farm]. This year the wild roses, also garden roses, are a very deep pink. I think this must be because of all the rain and very little sun. After crossing the erstwhile golf course we turned into a deep lane leading to the village of Clapham. It was very deserted but we were struck by the quantity of comfrey in bloom; it looked very pretty in the mass. We walked for 2½ hours without resting, although we stood once to shelter from a sharp shower.

Saturday, 16 June.
Last Tuesday evening I picked 2½ lb. blackcurrants and boiled them that night and left them to strain until next day. There was only 1½ pints of juice expressed, from which I made 3 lb. jelly, so I stewed some of the residue with sugar and water to eat with milk puddings, and made a drink by simmering some of it with sugar and a quart of water. Both concoctions were enjoyable. I obtained a form from Insurance Society to have dental benefit, but I want to change my dentist as my fillings only stay in a few months. So I have been making exhaustive enquiries regarding dentists.

Today I have been attending the Folk Dance Festival on the Castle Mound. This afternoon I was a spectator only, and among others the St Albans men performed an attractive Morris Dance in which they twizzled sticks instead of hankies. It was called 'Constant Billy'.[32] Flossie was there too, and we arranged to go to a concert by [pianist] Louis Kentner on 29th June. He is playing Beethoven's 'Pastoral Sonata' which I have for years longed to hear. I joined in the dancing after tea. The arena on top of the Mound is ideal for dancing; the grass is so fine and short, and as it is entirely surrounded by tall trees it is just like a green room. I only ever come here once a year to the Folk dancing, and I asked a gardener working down below if it was used for many functions and he said 'No, only once a year for folk-dancing but there is going to be a garden fete next week for Civil Defence people,' so I have been very fortunate to see such a beautiful and exclusive place. The house is going to be made into a museum, when I expect the grounds will become more public [later the Higgins Art Gallery and Museum].

Tuesday, 19 June.
Summer has really come. 2 p.m. DST and I am in the garden under the apple tree. Luckily, the season of caterpillars is over and past for this year, but the restless shadows of the branches are a bit tiresome for writing. Yesterday I noticed they were reaping oats along Bromham Road and this reminded me of a song I learnt at school 30 years ago called 'The Old Green Lane' and which I have long thought contained an anachronism, but now I know is truth as the cuckoo is still calling and some fields are red with poppies. The first verse is as follows:

'Twas the very merry, merry summertime that garlands hills and dells,
And the south wind rang a mystic chime upon the foxglove bells,

---

[32] *Bedford Record*, 19 June 1945, p. 3: 'A large crowd watched the proceedings.'

And the lark sprang o'er the village church and whistled to the sky,
For we had come from the harvest fields, a blythe and tawny train,
And tracked our path with poppy leaves, along the old green lane.

Living, as I did, among the bricks and mortar of a large dirty town [Sunderland], this song presented a picture of Heaven to me, and it was not until we came to live at Bedford 24 years ago that I had doubts about cuckoos singing in harvest time. It was evidently the oats harvest in a year like 1945. I wonder who wrote this song. The second verse brings coolness:

'Twas a pleasant way on a sunny, sunny day, and we were a happy set
As we idly bent where the streamlet went to get our fingers wet,
With a dogrose here and an orchis there, and the woodbine twining through and
through
With the broad trees meeting everywhere and the fern still dark with dew
Ah! Ah! I shall ne'er forget ... all free from care and pain
As we lay on the bank by the shepherd's cot to rest in the old green lane.[33]

I made an appointment with another dentist to have a tooth refilled. Also I procured two tickets for a Louis Kentner concert on 29th June. In the evening I picked 4 lb. blackcurrants and hope to bottle some when I return from the Literary Society's meeting this evening. Wrote and asked Lily when it would be convenient to take Father to stay a few days.

Thursday, 21 June.
On Tuesday I went to the Literary Society's meeting at 6 p.m. It was held in the drawing room at 43 The Grove [home of Stanley Goodman], looking over a beautiful lawn with a large cedar beyond, so it must have been an old garden. Only ladies present, and almost the first face I saw was that of Constance Cannon who was at the Midland Motor Company when I worked there 10 years ago[34] – in fact I employed her as junior typist. I remember she was very fond of reading then, when in her teens. A Miss Benest gave a talk on Elizabeth Myers' book *The Basilisk of St James*, being the life of Swift, at least 2 years of his life. I must read the book as it describes a period I don't seem to have read much about.[35]

On Monday evening I picked 4 lb. blackcurrants and on Tuesday, after the meeting, I bottled 2 jars full and made 5 lb. jam; there were still some left for stewing.

It was delightful at the garden this evening after the morning's rain. I have a favourite spot on a hillock against the high hedge, whence I can see the garden spread out, also right beyond the caravans, across the valley to Stagsden church.

---

[33] Presumably Leah had committed this verse to memory (more or less) as a schoolgirl, though she had forgotten a few words from the second last line.

[34] One of its works was in Old Ford End Road, not far from Leah's home.

[35] This 1945 book is subtitled *A Romance*. It is a novel set in the London of Queen Anne and centres around the gilded, gossipy and sometimes flirtatious society of the court and some of its most colourful characters, particularly Jonathan Swift. This was one of three well-regarded novels that Elizabeth Myers wrote, along with numerous short stories, during her short life (1912–47).

Tuesday, 26 June.

We have had some glorious June days and I have not worn stockings for over a week. The back garden is resplendent with roses, sweet peas and larkspurs along the trellis, and flame snapdragons and clouds of yellow daisies on the other side of the path.

I had tea at Clarkes' on Sunday and we spent most of the time sitting in the garden. I sported my pink and black crepe frock I only wear about once a year and Flossie had on a new pink crepe frock. We were very interested in a bee, or bees, carrying bits of leaf into a hole in the bottom of the clothesline post. Although I saw a bee five times go into the hole, none of us ever saw one come out.

I practically stripped the blackcurrant bushes on Saturday evening and bottled another 2 lb. jam jarful. I took some to the Clarkes and sent a boxful to Cissie in Sunderland; also gave a few to Doff. I am rather tired of them for the moment and find the art of bottling a great boon as one can spread the various fruits over the year. One Kilner jar[36] has proved rather expensive, however. The seal broke after 48 hours so I heated it in a pan of water instead of putting it in the oven. The instructions said the water must be 160 degrees Fahrenheit and I foolishly tested it with the room thermometer we have had as long as I remember. Of course it burst. I see new ones cost 13s 9d. I still do not know whether that particular Kilner jar has sealed properly, because if, when I test it, it has not I will use the fruit straight away and I don't want to do that for a week or two. I am hoping the tight screw band will preserve the fruit so long.

I have been emptying a postcard album to give it to Jacqueline. Some of the cards were sent over 30 years ago when it cost a halfpenny to send one. One was from myself at the age of 10, which I thought well written. I certainly squeezed a lot of news into the half side allotted for it. In some cases it was difficult to remember who the senders were.

Friday, 29 June.

I have had an acknowledgement from Canada of the instalment of this diary which I sent off about VE Day, so I will send some more.[37] Yesterday I took Father to Luton and left him there for a few days. What a performance it was getting him there. The train was more than ¼ [hour] late and the platform was packed. Father could not endure standing towards the end, and left his place at the front to sit on a trolley. A porter immediately took it away. Of course there were no seats in the train but an airman gave up his to Father. Janet met us at Luton and again there was trouble as he had to be fairly carried on to a seat in the bus. I wish he would not have these urges to travel these days. He has even talked of going to Cambridge soon. However, perhaps the change to Luton will do him good. All the family there are going to Clacton for a week on 21st July, along with their Aunt, Uncle and cousins, so there will be a lively party. Afterwards John is cycling to Lake District.

I went to a fresh dentist to have a tooth filled, but when he found I wanted it done through the National Health he would not do it until he had sent a report to

---

[36] A Kilner jar is a rubber-sealed, screw-topped jar used for preserving food. It was produced until 1937 by Kilner Brothers Ltd at Conisbrough, Yorkshire.

[37] One infers from this remark that she had mailed her typed version of the diary to Canada.

them and had their confirmation. So I am no farther forward. I made good progress this afternoon with the rag doormat I am making. I am really getting interested in it. Going to Louis Kentner [piano] concert this evening [at the Corn Exchange].[38]

Saturday, 7 July.
We have just had tea and Father rushed straight away afterwards to John Bull's to see about having his watch repaired, which stopped while at Luton. I hope the rushing will do him no harm, as it is very hot and only 3 o'clock G.M.T. He came home from Luton last Tuesday.

Thursday was general election day, but we will not hear the results for 3 weeks. I cannot think why.[39] Yesterday we received a delightful parcel from Canada containing tins [of] fruit, puddings, chicken, jelly etc. and some pan scourers that make aluminium shine like silver. I was startled to read today the double summer time ends next weekend.

Monday, 9 July.
This must have been a tantalizing day for astronomers. It has been warm with small clouds all over the sky and the eclipse of the sun could be seen in the gaps between clouds, but these views could not have been much use scientifically.[40] Yesterday I made up half a raspberry jelly I received from Canada a year gone Christmas. It did not set so Mrs Lizars [next door] put it in her refrigerator for me. After tea yesterday I went [on] a cycle ride through Stagsden and took a turn to the left about ¾ mile beyond the village and circled back to Stagsden and then to the garden. It was a lovely evening and the undulating country looked rich and peaceful. I was armed with a book on wild flowers and managed to identify 3 I'd never noticed before: goat's beard, angelica, hedge bedstraw.

---

[38] Classical music was on the verge of receding in Bedford, as the BBC musicians returned to London. A little over a fortnight later, on 16 July, the BBC gave a 'Farewell Concert' at the Corn Exchange, which was not broadcast. This performance was a kind of public thank-you, for, as a senior BBC manager observed 'our relations with the town have been exceptionally friendly and harmonious.' Sir Adrian Boult's speech on the occasion was warmly appreciative. He recalled that, in 1941: 'the Mayor of Bedford said "Yes" to the BBC envoys after a number of others Mayors had shown them the door. Their requests were considerable: 7 or 8 studios of varied sizes, a block of about 40 offices with telephone and catering facilities, and, in addition, a matter of some 250 beds, and it is not to be wondered at that many evacuee-packed towns found it quite impossible to consider such an invasion.' He was 'deeply grateful' to the local authorities. And he wanted to: 'make a special mention of the Corn Exchange staff who have done so much to make us comfortable, often doing rush conversions of the building on which we and many others have made such heavy demands.' (BBC Written Archives Centre, file R35/123).
[39] Time was needed to collect and return all the ballots cast by service men and women around the world. Leah's unawareness of this suggests that she did not follow the political news particularly closely – and she wrote nothing at all about the electoral campaign in Bedford. See also below: 25 and 30 July 1945.
[40] While in some parts of the world there was a total eclipse of the sun, the eclipse in Britain was only partial. *The Times*, 10 July 1945, p. 4, confirmed that it was not well seen: 'High clouds generally interrupted observation, although at some places visibility improved for short periods. But radio experiments are reported to have been successful.' A total eclipse was observed in the Canadian Prairies.

Friday, 13 July.
A Very hot day and this afternoon when I was in paying for the newspapers I found them doing a roaring trade in ice cream. I bought some for Father and me, but it was a waste of 1 shilling; not sweet and with lumps of dry starchy substance in it. I called at dentist's to see why he had not fixed up an appointment for me. No reason was given but appointment fixed for 23rd July at 10.30. All day Tuesday and part of Wednesday it rained so the gardens are growing well.

Tuesday, 17 July.
There was a thunderstorm during Saturday night, which the newspaper described as the worst for 20 years. It must have worse elsewhere than it was at Bedford as though the storm lasted many hours and the lightning was brilliant and constant, the thunder never equaled it and only rumbled instead of giving sharp, satisfying cracks. Double summer time ended that same night [the clock was moved back], so we had an extra hour to make up for lack of rest. The morning was fresh and as it was my free Sunday morning (occurring once a month)[41] I took my lunch and spent a few hours at the garden. It was serene and beautiful; birds singing and church bells ringing and the semi gypsy crowd had 'folded their tents like the Arabs and silently stole away' and therefore there were no squalling children to disturb the peace.

Sunday, 22 July.
Last Tuesday I went to a meeting of the Literary Society and Miss Arbon read a paper on Winifred Holtby. Never having read anything of W. Holtby's I primed myself by reading Evelyne White's book on her and luckily I did as the paper was very poor, but the discussion which ensued was lively and enlightening.[42] Flossie Clarke came too and I passed to her *The Compleat Angler* [by Izaak Walton, 1653], which one of her draughtsmen had asked to read. Afterwards I called at Adelaide Square and met Billy Cuthbertson's sister and family, who are on visit from Newcastle. Jim went camping at Bromham Park yesterday with some Scouts but he has arrived home for tea today.

Tuesday, 24 July.
After tea on Sunday I cycled to the Arnolds' smallholding hoping to find Flora there. There was no lock on the gate so I easily got in, but there was nobody there; they have evidently grown tired of spending every Sunday there. There were some fowls for evidently Bernard comes to feed them, and I see he has a glasshouse installed.

Yesterday I had two teeth filled at [George] Royle's [6 Goldington Road] the dentist. I was not in the place 25 minutes, and 5 minutes a previous occasion

---

[41] She probably means that her brother Jim looked after their father one Sunday morning each month.

[42] Author Winifred Holtby (1898–1935) was best known for her novel published posthumously, *South Riding* (1936). She was a close friend of Vera Brittain (*Testament of Friendship*, 1940). Evelyne White's *Winifred Holtby as I knew her. A study of the author and her works* was published in 1938.

for exam, and the charge was £1 16s 6d – that is, 10s 6d each tooth, 10s 6d for cleaning front bottom teeth only, 5s for exam. Reckoning 16s 6d for material and overheads, he must value his time at £2 per hour.[43] One of the teeth he filled had already been done 3 times and I strongly objected to having it done a 4th time. It is just as I feared; when I eat it makes me wince every now and then whereas it has been easy during the last 18 months without any stopping.

It was such a lovely afternoon I took my sewing to the riverside and got chatting with a North Country woman who knows Sunderland well. After tea I went to library, and as next meeting of Literary Society is on Samuel Johnson [1709–1784] I tried to get one of his books, *Rasselas* [1759] for preference, but could only get his *Letters*. There was Boswell's *Life* [1791] but the printing was so tiny I couldn't stomach it.

Wednesday, 25 July.
I had a vivid dream this morning. I dreamt the election ballot boxes were opened and it was announced that *I* was the Conservative Member for Bedford. At first I was elated and felt important at the idea of putting MP after my name, and thought how impressed the folk at Igranic would be. I expressed my surprise at not even knowing I had been nominated and why people had voted for me when I had never once addressed them. Then I suddenly realized it meant I would have to attend Parliament frequently and perhaps make speeches, and I immediately refused to be M.P. Those around me said they would decide between the Liberal and Labour candidate as to who should be member, but I said that Mr Wells (Conservative) might have the next number of votes. Up spoke a female and said 'No, I have only 79 votes.' I replied 'You mean 79,000.' She said 'Only 79.' Some little men busy with the ballot boxes then announced to me 'You had ¾ of all the votes' and it was explained to me that the reason I was nominated was that it was desperately urgent that neither Liberal nor Labour candidate should get in, but nobody wanted Mr Wells (Conservative), so they pushed my name in as Conservative at the last minute. Ralph Sage was a prime mover in this. I should say he is out and out Labour. The Election results are to be announced tomorrow.

Monday, 30 July.
Well, the election results bore no relation to my dream; 79 never came in it anywhere. Labour got in for Bedford after Mr Wells (C) had sat 24 years.[44] The overwhelming Labour majority must have been a great shock for Mr Churchill, but they ought never to have called for an election at this stage. On Saturday the 3 noisy families nearby went for a week's holiday, and all is peaceful and serene. Next door went to South Shields. Yesterday evening I cycled to Milton Ernest

---

[43] By these calculations, if correct, this dentist would make about as much in an hour as a working man would earn in half a week.

[44] Sir Richard Wells, Baronet (1879–1957), son of the founder of the brewery Charles Wells Ltd, had represented Bedford since 1922. At this summer's general election Labour's Lieut Thomas Skeffington-Lodge (b. 1905), R.N.V.R. (Royal Naval Volunteer Reserve), took 19,849 votes, Wells 19,561 and the Liberal candidate L. J. Humphrey 8,183. This was an unexpected, albeit very close, Labour victory.

with intent to see whether blackberries were as abundant by the riverside as they were 20 years ago. I found the village a military centre and the Hall taken over by Americans, so I did not dare wander round the hedges alone. I returned via Oakley and Bromham, and a very pleasant ride it was, but tiring. I do not like Virginia Woolf's novels, even if they are supposed to have style. I do not think I'll trouble to finish reading *The Voyage Out* [1915]. We have had lots of flies this year which I put down to: poultry kept nearby, dust-bins only emptied once a fortnight, food-bins in street,[45] and I wonder whether the new aviary built against house next door has made it worse this year.

Wednesday, 1 August.
A cold cheerless afternoon, but I took my needlework to the riverside just beyond the spot where there are children's amusements such as swings. Bye and bye a small boy came to see me and asked me to go and see what he thought was a child dead in the bushes. He 'thought she had been murdered.' I looked round for someone else in sight but there was only an old man on the next seat, so with a bounding heart I went to investigate. Well hidden in the scrub under a low bush were a soldier and what I am almost certain was a child of not more than 12, locked together and motionless. I could see neither face. There were some more children looking on and assuring me they were not breathing. I could see they were alive all right and when the man made a slight noise in his throat we all quickly retreated. I felt very disturbed, however, as judging by the thin little bare legs the girl seemed to be a child, but the time I had looked had been so brief I may have been mistaken. I decided to do nothing about the matter, but after warning the children to keep away from the couple I went home, as the place suddenly seemed desolate and sad in spite of many children on the swings etc. shouting and laughing. It was the boy talking of 'murder' and the greyness of the afternoon that took away all pleasure.

Thursday, 9 August.
A momentous week, one might say an ominous week. On Tuesday morning, the 7th, the papers gave the shocking news of the atomic bomb and that one had been dropped on Hiroshima. It sounds to me almost like the 'abomination of desolation' spoken of by Daniel the prophet.[46]

    Last Saturday was very hot, the hottest day this summer I think. Flossie came to tea and then we cycled to Pavenham. It was a beautiful ride and we stopped at Stevington for a lime drink. After this exertion I spent a restful day on Sunday, mainly occupied in answering an important letter which arrived from Canada on Saturday. I had just posted a long letter to Winnie on Friday in answer to her

---

[45] These bins may have been for pig swill – cottage pig-keeping was probably fairly common outside the town centre.
[46] 'The use of atomic power', thought the *Bedfordshire Times*, 17 August 1945, p. 7, 'which brought the war against Japan to so abrupt a conclusion, has revealed as nothing ever did before the stark alternative with which the human race is faced: either we learn to live at peace or this new mastery of undreamed-of power will bring about a collapse of civilization that will be complete and final.' This was at the time a common response to the atomic bomb.

comments on my diary. On Monday Jim and I intended cycling to Old Warden and having tea at Hare and Hounds, but weather was too bad. We did manage walk across fields to Clapham, and promised ourselves the ride on Tuesday. Weather worse still. On Tuesday afternoon I went to Luton and brought home 3 lb. Victoria plums. John brought in the news that Russia had declared war on Japan. Jacqueline has not passed for the High School. The weather was bad again today, so Jim and I went to Pictures – the first time for more than a year. I acquired a bad headache, so it will probably be a year before I go again. I hunted for fruit bottling jars this morning, without success.

Wednesday, 15 August, V.J. Day.
The children have been making great preparations for burning an effigy tonight. At present (6 p.m.) it is pouring but it may only be a shower. I have been working harder than usual today because I am expecting Jacqueline to come and stay for a few days on Monday, Janet the following week. I turned out my bedroom, front room and stairs and passage, and then before tea I tried my hand at wall papering the passage near the door where it was very shabby.

We have had wretched weather lately, but last Friday, the day Flossie, her sister and I had arranged to go to Aspley Heath, was perfect. We went by 3.11 train to Woburn Sands, had tea there and then strolled on to the Heath. It was sunny but the air was cool and fresh and the sandy roads firmed by recent rains. We went by pinewoods and bracken to Bow Brickhill Church for the view, as we did a year ago, gathered heather, and returned by 8.15 train from Woburn Sands. On Sunday afternoon Jim took me [for] a walk, part of which I have never been before, i.e. straight across fields to a point of the river midway between Kempston and Bromham, where we sat in the shade of a willow and watched cattle on the far bank.

Saturday, 18 August.
Cold and drizzly day but at 10 p.m. there are sounds of revelry and fireworks from Westbourne Road street party [immediately to the west]. Our street had a jumble sale last evening in the Blue Coach garage to raise money for their Victory tea. Honey Hill Road and side streets seem to have outshone all. They collected £45 for their party and had a good supply of free beer.[47] Father seems to be failing again. Rather a pity with the girls' visits ahead.

Wednesday, 29 August.
Well, Jacqueline has had her visit, and Janet arrived yesterday. The weather was atrocious during Jacqueline's stay but we managed to take her on the river, to the garden, to the fair and to see Newnham [Swimming] Baths [in Goldington, now the site of the Aspects Leisure Centre]. I heard her telling Tony [next door] that she wishes she was staying longer, so she must have enjoyed herself. We had two perfect summer days over the weekend but it turned dull and showery yesterday,

---

[47] Bedford's victory celebrations were described at length in the *Bedfordshire Times*, 17 August 1945, p. 7.

and rained a good deal this morning. We managed to get a trip on the river with Jim and Ron Appleby who is home on leave after more than 4 years in Africa, Italy etc. He stayed for dinner.

Sunday, 2 September.
Janet also had bad weather for most of her stay. Friday was better and we went on bikes to gather blackberries, and on the river again in the evening. Janet also had an hour on the river all alone on Saturday morning. She is used to rowing. Since so many strangers have come to Bedford it has become usual for boatmen to demand £1 deposit on letting out craft. The man asked Janet for £1, which she told him she had not got. He said '10s then?' She told him she had only 3s so he let her go without paying any deposit. I found Janet very 'heavy weather' in entertaining her. She never acknowledged enjoying anything and only spoke when spoken to. Also she was not so eager to help us as Jacqueline was and took no interest whatever in other individuals, whereas Jacqueline was interested in everyone she came in contact with. Jacqueline is decidedly the better company in our family although no scholar. Janet will wake up some day. Jim and I went blackberrying this afternoon and I hope to do some bottling tomorrow. I have begun to harvest lavender. We are getting a good many of our own tomatoes.

Monday, 3 September.
Did washing this morning and bottled blackberries and apples this afternoon. Father brought up his dinner before I had finished mine. I am glad this did not happen while either of the girls was with us, as I partly expected, seeing he did the same thing the day before Jacqueline arrived.

Sunday, 23 September.
Father has been very ill, but is on the mend now. He has been much weaker this time and submitted to stay in bed more. He gets up to tea. Janet has passed her school certificate with 7 distinctions and 3 credits and has most marks for her school. Joyce Bowyer (Mrs East) had a baby girl last Wednesday (19th). On Tuesday I enjoyed very much Miss Lee's talk on the book *Moby Dick* [by Herman Melville]. The Literary Society are talking of having a dinner soon.

Monday, 24 September.
A cold squally day. Some firms had their VE 3 holiday today,[48] and Jim spent it in rebuilding the back shed. Yesterday I forgot to ask John to take the jasmine for Mrs Barton so today posted part of it to her. Also took Jim's trousers and my skirt to be cleaned. Father's health is improving.

---

[48] According to the *Bedford Record*, 25 September 1945, p. 1: 'some of the local engineering firms treated yesterday as the third VE holiday, in accordance with an agreement reached by the Bedfordshire Association of the Engineering and Allied Employers, and gave their employees their third VE holiday'. However, it was not an official holiday for all workers – and many smaller shops 'carried on business as usual'. There were no bus services, which inconvenienced those 'waiting at the stops only to discover that the buses were not running.'

Tuesday, 25 September.
It has been a bright, sharp day; just the weather I like, although it makes my joints stiff. I peeled and cored apples that when prepared yielded 4 lb., and put sugar, water and vinegar with them to make jam tomorrow. I feel dubious about putting vinegar into an aluminium vessel and hope no harm is done. The doctor gave Father a 4th injection this afternoon, and is not coming again for a week. Flossie has sent a seed-time hymn of her own composition for me to type copies.

Wednesday, 26 September.
Made 7 lb. apple jam. The mattress that Jim took to be re-made on Saturday, and which they said would take 3 weeks, arrived completed this morning! I went to garden this afternoon and collected at least 10 lb. tomatoes, the last of the lavender, blackberries, beans, cabbages etc. My bike felt top-heavy with the load. After tea I sealed the jam, cleared top shelf in cupboard, made an inventory of jams and jellies (26 lb.) and stored it all away. A good hard day's work.

Friday, 28 September.
Flossie called yesterday evening and brought Father some *Methodist Recorders* to look at.[49] I gave her the two typed copies of her hymn. She is sending it in for a competition. The weather being very fine, I was able to get on with the mat-making out of doors this afternoon. I sent some bits of the jasmine tree to Mrs Barton, but while thanking me say they would like the whole tree and have offered to come through for it. It is the tree we are doing away with.

Tuesday, 2 October.
Father continues to improve. I am concentrating on finishing the mat but am very hard up for the last few rags. I may have to put it by for a while. Jim got all the potatoes dug up on Saturday and concreted the floor of the hut he is building on Sunday afternoon and then sang in a harvest cantata in the evening. This evening in the Adult School there was a discussion on Town and Country. It was quite

---

[49] Leah's diary indicates that she almost never went to church, and during the 1940s she wrote nothing about her religious beliefs (or lack thereof) or those of her immediate family. The sole occasion when she addressed the subject was very much later, in her diary for 19 July 1956, when she was strikingly revealing: 'The horror of my childhood was the family's religion. My parents belonged to a very peculiar sect, The New and Latter House of Israel, the men and boys of which had to have long hair! I hated to be seen with my Father or brothers and this poisoned all my childhood. At the same time I despised myself for this attitude. My Father had his hair tucked away in an elastic band, but the boys had ringlets hanging down their backs. I dreaded what it was going to be like when they were in their teens, and I was immensely relieved when it was revealed (not before the time) that it could be cut at 12 years of age and then grown again when they officially entered the church. There were other horrors for a child in that religion: such as never being allowed to go to parties in case there was any lard in the pastry or other "unclean" food.' If Leah retained any religious inclinations in her middle age, they were almost certainly vague and muted. Her father's firm beliefs were probably rooted in an absolute trust in God's will.

Given the apparent forcefulness of her religious upbringing, it is remarkable that Leah says nothing about it or her own views on religion earlier in her writings. Her nephew, John Aynsley, reports that his uncle Jack was openly hostile to religion.

interesting and George Sutcliffe was amusing. No definite decision was arrived at but I do wish they had Women's Institutes in towns.[50]

Thursday, 4 October.
Nothing much to relate. Just as I was setting out this evening for Adelaide Square Mabel arrived at our house. I was going for a library book I had lent to Billy, but Mabel brought my ticket, and also dried milk, and southernwood [a flowering plant] from Stella. Billy and Sybil have been up North and seen Stella. She looked very well but easily tires. We had beefsteak pudding for dinner today, which Jim seems to have digested.

Sunday, 7 October.
On Friday I made an appointment with Mr S. Sanders to have an impression taken for some false teeth (24th October). He will provide them through National Health Insurance. As Brinklow's [baker and pastry cook, 59 Ford End Road] were not making any cakes last week owing to shortage of fat, I set to and made oatmeal scones with sultanas in, and apple-sauce cake. The latter is an invention of my own, the only moisture in the mixing being sweetened stewed apple, but it was quite undiscernible in the cake which was just like coarse-grained Madeira. Jim has been busy all this weekend with the hut and place looks more ship-shape. I went to Folk Dance party at Physical Training College, and to garden this afternoon.

MONDAY, [51] *8 October.*
It is now 'wintertime'. I rose at 7.15. As soon as I got downstairs I set some sliced onion to simmer for my breakfast, and then fried potato, tomato and dried egg for Father. I made some sage tea for my first cup and ordinary tea for Father and my second cup. I read sage is good for rheumatism. I gave Father his breakfast in bed, and then transferred onion from the frying pan with tomato and dried egg. Had breakfast and read paper until 8.30, when I took it to Father and also his medicine. Made 2 beds etc. Washed breakfast things. Set out last picking of tomatoes to complete ripening upstairs. Swept cobwebs from corner of kitchen, cleaned top of gas stove, turned out pantry (floor and shelves), saw to Father and gave him a snack. Now 11 a.m. Set towels to boil and sat and prepared vegs for dinner. Swept living room, did the small amount of washing, washed scullery and lavatory floors, made custard, cooked vegs, warmed apple tart. Sat and read for ¼ hour and had dinner, to which Father came in his dressing gown. Washed dishes and myself, took in dried clothes at 1.50, went to bed with the book *Moby Dick*. Soon fell asleep, roused at 3 o'clock but did not get up until nearly 3.30. Felt very tired. Changed, took in rest of clothes and line. Went to Post Office and baker's, had tea and am writing this while waiting for Jim [to return from work].

---

[50] The Women's Institutes were established and active largely in rural districts. If its urban equivalent, the Townswomen's Guild, played any role to speak of in Bedford, there is no evidence that Leah was associated with it.

[51] These were her capitals. It appears that she had decided to compose a detailed log of her household activities this day, up to late afternoon.

Thursday, 11 October.

Tuesday was the day the Literary Society had a dinner at the Dujon restaurant. There were 19 of us, including only one man. After a good meal (the usual English Sunday dinner) we discussed the business of the Society, the new secretary, Mrs March, wishing to bring it into some regularity of form by introducing a few rules etc. A large dinner at 7.30 p.m. does not suit my digestion and I had the wakeful night I anticipated. I suppose the others must have eaten lightly at teatime but I am afraid I had my usual tuck-in at 4.30.

Yesterday and today have been real summery and I spent both afternoons at the garden, harvesting and doing a little digging in the rhubarb plot. On the tiny green in front of the Bromham Swan [public house] there is a host of caravans and they have even erected a roundabout and swing boats. The whole collection seems overflowing the little green space and as lots of heavy traffic tears by the caravan homes are in a precarious position.

At the dinner-cum-meeting they impressed that everybody should take a turn at reading a paper, so last night I made a start on one. I very much wanted to write on modern Chinese writers I have enjoyed, but that subject was too wide and my knowledge not deep; then I thought of W.H. Hudson, but could not do justice to him; so I trimmed down to W. Fortescue's book *Sunset House*, which is simple for a first attempt.[52]

Sunday, 14 October.

All the last week the weather has been sunny and dry. I went to garden yesterday and today, digging and tidying the plot I call the rhubarb patch, but it also has various herbs, asparagus, an apple tree etc. The advantage of tidying a garden at this time of the year is that it stays so for a few months. There has been a slight frost at night and since Thursday the trees have turned to vivid colours. Made tartlets with a filling I invented: soya flour and treacle with a drop of milk

---

[52] W.H. Hudson (1841–1922) was an ornithologist, naturalist, novelist, and well-known author of books on the English countryside; Leah read three of his books in 1944 (see Appendix, 'Some Books Read by Leah Aynsley'). *Sunset House: More Perfume from Provence* (1937) was written by the much less prominent Winifred Fortescue (1888–1951). Lady Fortescue lived in Provence for many years and wrote several books about her life there. This volume tells a heart-warming story – with accompanying frustrations – of transforming a derelict country cottage into a home for herself (she had been widowed two years before); her dealings with cunning and sometimes bewildering locals; and her delight in creating a garden on the hillside behind the house (which no doubt appealed to Leah). Her passion for Provence foreshadows the later and bestselling writings of Peter Mayle, notably his 1990 book, *A Year in Provence*.

This paragraph testifies yet again to the range and often quality of Leah's reading – in June 1947 she was reading Anthony Trollope's classic, *Framley Parsonage* (mentioned 23 June). The paragraph also speaks to her interest in topics relating to rural life. This interest reappeared in a diary entry on 2 February 1947: 'I am reading a book, *The Rabbit Skin Cap* [1939], being recollections of an old countryman's childhood.' The book was edited by Lilias Rider Haggard and subtitled *A Tale of a Norfolk Countryman's Youth*. It records the author's recollections of a mid-Victorian childhood, including boyish scrapes and adventures, local dialect and customs and details on agricultural tools and crafts, and is charmingly illustrated. 'How miserably the poor lived at one time', Leah remarked. 'We working folk live like lords nowadays; we have not cause to grumble.'

to mix it easily. Tasted very like dates. Made a plain cake this morning with almond flavouring.

Thursday, 18 October.
The plain cake just referred to was not sweet enough and was not sufficiently flavoured with almond. Yesterday we had 3 visitors from Luton; Mrs Barton, her daughter Vera and the latter's husband. They came for the jasmine shrub. I was expecting Lily, and not the husband. He is on 12 days' leave from Germany.

This afternoon when I arrived at the garden I found the north-east corner buried in a heap of fresh clay and a large pit dug just outside the hedge. I learned from enquiring of neighbours that the War Agricultural [Executive Committee] are ditching the farmers' lands further up the hill and they were probably responsible.[53] I walked nearly to the wood and came to some German prisoners and saw another man further off. I asked the prisoner if he was English (i.e. I pointed to him and said 'English?' in a querying tone) and they chorused 'Yes.' So I went and tackled the man. He said that a yard of the land outside the hedge belonged to me and that when the ditch is made or deepened all the clay will have to go on to my garden!! And what is more, I shall have to pay for the ditching along my plot!!! I am going to see the War Agricultural [Executive] Committee about the clay thrown on the garden [see below, 29 December].

Saturday, 27 October.
This has been a week of high winds and rainstorms, and mines have been washing up on the sea coast. Uncle A. came south on Thursday for a week's holiday and called this morning with plants from Stella, seakale, alpine pink, seedling hawthorns; also bulbs. I took the plants to the garden and was surprised and amused to see that someone had broken through the hedge and removed the clay. I had called at the War Agricultural Offices a week ago and the man there said they should not do any damage in spreading clay and would see into it for me. I did not expect such prompt action.

Sunday, 28 October.
Wind got into south again and has been damp all day. I prepared a mature marrow for jam this morning, and what a difficult job it was to peel it; like clipping off horn. I acquired a blister at the root of a finger when I had finished. To the garden this afternoon, and although too wet for digging I got rid of a lot of chrysanthemums I have long intended to, but the blooms had usually faded off when I could tackle the job, and I never know which were which, but now I have got rid of those I consider 'no class'. Mr Barrett called this evening to see Father. I have started to make lavender sachets for Xmas gifts.

Monday, 5 November.
The first peacetime Guy Fawkes day, and well we know it – bangs and children knocking at the doors for 'penny for the guy'; also they have been collecting

---

[53] This committee was tasked with managing effectively the agricultural production of the county, and possessed considerable powers.

rubbish for a bonfire as for the victory celebration.[54] Had a big washday but no weather for drying. Had a surprise visit from Maud Summerfield Saturday morning. She looked very well, and intends leaving Vauxhall at Xmas and going back to dressmaking business.

Wednesday, 7 November.
Doctor called yesterday and gave Father an injection and also a prescription for digestive pain he has been having. I asked if he could have any extra milk and he said if I went to surgery he would give me a certificate. Today I went to Food Office about it and Father is to have a pint per day for 4 weeks. I also collected my new false teeth. They felt as though I had a plum in my mouth, but when eating my tea it seemed as though I had several plum *stones* in my mouth.[55] It has been a very fine autumn day.

Sunday, 11 November.
My mouth has become so sore with those teeth that I removed them today. I am trying to harden the gums with alum. Yesterday Cissie's 2-monthly letter arrived with a shopping bag she knitted me with string. It is a very nice one. I have been to the garden these last 3 afternoons and am gradually getting the flower beds tidied. Stella has sent me lots of snowdrops for planting in the grass. I have also got the back garden into a trim state and Jim has finished the hut.

Monday, 12 November.
Most of the day dry and breezy, which would have been good for washing clothes, but I elected to scrub the middle room and polish, an operation which has not been done completely at one time since spring-cleaning; also turned out Father's sleeping room. After tea went to the library and renewed [John] Masefield's *In the Mill*.[56] Father was sick after supper.

[54] This was the first 'bonfire night' since 1938, and throughout the county, according to the *Bedfordshire Times*, 9 November 1945, p. 7: 'the evening, for which thousands of children, many of whom had never seen the effigy [of Guy Fawkes] seated placidly on top of a roaring bonfire or heard the "swish" of a rocket shoot up into the sky, had waited for weeks and queued for hours on end, was full of bangs and flashes, strangely reminiscent of the war years.'
[55] It was common for people in their thirties and forties to get false teeth. Those around fifty years of age who still had most of their own teeth were in a distinct minority.
[56] John Masefield (1878–1967), the Poet Laureate, published this coming-of-age memoir in 1941. The 'mill' was a carpet factory in Yonkers, New York, where he worked for nearly two years in the 1890s. During this time he read widely, discovered the attractions of North-East America's natural environment and its greatest city, wrote a huge amount (which he later burned) and found his life's work as a writer and poet. He had mainly happy memories: 'I felt that indeed my lot had fallen on fair ground and that I had a good heritage; beauty all round me, leisure, such as I had not thought possible, books, so cheap that I could have a library of them, and a great, vivid, romantic capital City only half an hour away.' (p. 43). This was when he resolved to devote himself to poetry – though not without self-doubts: 'Very likely I wasn't good enough for poetry, but the extraordinary beauty of that promised land was enough to call out all my hope and all my courage.' (p. 126).
    While Leah gave few hints as to her political views on labour and capital, it may be noteworthy that Masefield's portrait of factory labour a half-century before said little about

Tuesday, 13 November.

Quickly procured fish etc. so easily got through my housework this morning, including the weekly do of 2 bedrooms. Thoroughly sponged Father's navy suit. Called at Adelaide Square for a chat after tea. They advise me to have my false teeth adjusted slightly.

Wednesday, 14 November.

Rather a cold day. After spending nearly an hour shopping for fish etc. I got home about 10 and got on with housework and cooking. I soaked the curtains I have made for Jim's room in soda, soap and warm water and half intended to dye them daffodil, but there still seemed too much of the blackout dye in them so did not bother. I may later. Father and I arranged to go to town about 3 p.m. to get him some slippers. Just as I was getting ready Ron Appleby called; he is on 10 days' leave. I asked him to come and spend tomorrow evening with Jim. He told me he is of a family of 11 children, 2 being a half-brother and [half-] sister. He is a fine tall fellow himself, with a slightly nervous impediment. He says his Father is 68 and still working, but years ago he spent a year and another long period in a sanatorium. Pa and I got to the town and got some slippers at Draper's, an old-fashioned little firm I have never entered before,[57] but Father seems well-known there, and the stately greetings all round and the attention paid to him made me think of Jane Austen's *Emma*. The post brought an invitation to tea on Sunday from Flossie, which I have accepted.

Thursday, 15 November.

A real November day – hardly any daylight. A cold clinging fog all the morning but the sun showed as a disc towards noon. Afterwards was so dark and chilly that I spent most of the afternoon on my bed under the eiderdown. Ron Appleby came to have a chat with Jim while I went off to a folk-dance class. We did 'The Russian Dance', 'Old Noll's Jog' and 'St Martin's'. I left just as they were starting Running Set as I wanted to get home to give them supper. The Shieling is a cake shop [96 Bromham Road] to beware of. Some of their goods are very nice but others are wretched. For supper I bought some bright pink jellies made up in paper cases, but they were hard as jujubes and tasteless.

Sunday, 2 December.

On Friday Father went himself to draw his pension and he also drew £3 from the Post Office [savings account]. When he got home he said he'd left his purse, with all the money in, on the counter. About ¾ hour later I went for it but it was not

---

workers' unrest or alienation. Indeed, he recalled (p. 34) a non-unionised workplace where: 'We were all well content with our lot. In all my time there I heard no serious complaint against the management or the conditions of service. …We knew that we were getting a square deal; in return we gave our best.' (He was less buoyant when the factory later closed, with unhappy consequences: pp. 103–4 and 135–6.) Contentment of the sort Masefield remembered probably met with Leah's approval. Her diary reveals no serious disapproval of the social order as she found it or anger about social inequalities.

[57] Draper's shoe shops were located at 8 Midland Road and 7 Gwyn Street.

there and none of the assistants had seen it. I posted a notice of the loss on our front window and after dinner I took a notice to be inserted in the newsagent's window; they were closed so I went to the butcher's and on returning to the newsagent's the manageress of our grocer's (Pearks' [62 Iddesleigh Road]) called out 'Has your Father lost his purse?' It appeared he had dropped it just at their door, a lady picked it up and took it into the shop. They opened it and found his name on his sweet ration points. They don't know who the lady is. He is very lucky to have found it so easily. I was also going to enquire at the police station.

This morning was very wet. I washed fruit to make a Xmas cake next week. The sun got out after dinner and I did quite a bit of tidying the chrysanthemum plot. The War Agricultural [Executive] Committee have had our bit of ditch deepened 2 feet.

The week before last Father had diarrhea and I had a rare old time with his washing.

Monday, 3 December.
A very good day for washing, so washed the tablecloth on which Pa spilt the ink but have not improved it much. As Jim has finished concreting etc. I thoroughly washed the yard. Also tried to get the dandruff out of Father's hair, but it really requires a thorough shampoo. Have sent order for 3rd lot of rheumatism tablets.

Tuesday, 4 December.
A very thick white frost this morning. I was kept in all morning as we were expecting the doctor to pay his monthly visit. He came while we were at dinner and gave Father an injection. Not being able to get out while fish was being sold in the local shops I had intended to give Jim soup for his evening meal, but as I was free in the afternoon I made a bus trip to the town and got some fish. It was raining all the time and I had to walk home.

After tea I went to meeting of Literary Society. Mrs Clark spoke on Hugh Walpole. As a matter of fact she spoke of his works only, but she started off with the words 'I am dividing Hugh Walpole into six parts ...', which tickled my fancy. She gave a very good talk and there was a good discussion, the general opinion being that he was not a genius and his work would not last.[58] Two or three weeks ago I attempted to read *Mr Perrin and Mr Traill* [1911] and gave up after about three chapters. It appears that it was Walpole's first novel and Mr Garrett, who is a schoolmaster, said it is an exact description of school life (mainly hates) even to the battle for the newspaper. I went to the Adult School expecting to hear a talk on Christmas music, but no speaker had been procured so Arthur Bues gave a cinematograph show. Much to my surprise I saw myself folk-dancing in Castle Close, and Trixy playing tennis.

Wednesday, 5 December.
A nice windy morning so just before dinner I washed and tinted the short curtains of the bay window and this afternoon replaced them and also the long lace curtains

---

[58] This critical prognosis has been proven accurate. Hugh Walpole (1884–1941) was a prolific and popular story-teller for over thirty years, including numerous novels set in the Lake District, notably the *Harries Chronicle* series.

with green heavy ones. This is a job I dislike and am glad it is over for Xmas. Also washed my hair this evening, another job I dislike.

Before dinner Father felt ill with the cold and his left hand was dark blue, so I packed him off to bed with a hot [water] bottle, but at 3 p.m. he went to the town to get some violin strings and also to have the bow re-haired. I prophesied a collapse, there was such a cold north wind, but he was none the worse for his outing.

Sunday, 9 December.
There is ice on the water today. I finished pruning the Laxton's Superb [apple tree] this afternoon, a job to make the feet cold, so I dug up all the spinach to get warm. Mrs Thomson told me that Hughes' cottage went under the hammer last week and was sold (with land) for £50!! A great loss for them. Mrs T. makes mats the same method as I do. The one she was finishing looked very nice. She sold the previous one for £35 – dirt cheap for a hearth-rug these days. I made a Xmas cake on Thursday and it *looks* very nice. I went to a folk dance party last evening and came away at half time to get Father's supper as Jim was also there. I enjoyed my share of it.

Thursday, 13 December.
I feel very disinclined to continue this diary. I have just finished reading Rom Landau's book *The Wing*, a very interesting account of his year in the R.A.F. which is half diary. I should say the man has a very obstreperous ego.[59] Father is keeping very well. He eats much better, which makes it so much more worth while my cooking meals. I bought a breast of lamb, or part of one, for 6½d. It was a lump of meat. We had it baked with potatoes and onions yesterday and stewed with the same today. We feel we have had an orgy of meat. I made a Xmas pudding today, also bought one. Had our 2nd allocation of oranges today and have been debating on keeping them for Xmas. Jim wants his now.

Sunday, 16 December.
A very wet morning. Jim could not go to the garden so he sawed away the second head of the apple tree at back of house. This makes the tree more cup shaped and will allow more light to reach the fruit (when any). He and I went to hear *The Messiah* at the Bromham Road Chapel this afternoon. It is nearly 18 years since I was last inside this chapel, and that was to hear *The Holy City*. I believe that is the last oratorio or cantata I have listened to other than broadcasts.

---

[59] *The Wing: Confessions of an R.A.F. Officer* was published by Faber and Faber in 1945. Rom Landau (1899–1974) was a prolific author, educator and foreign service officer who specialised in Arab and Islamic culture. A British citizen of Polish birth, he volunteered to serve in the RAF. This book is an account of his experiences at many air bases, his forceful efforts to achieve an active military role, his activities as liaison and interpreter between Polish pilots and the RAF, and eventually his training as an air gunner that gained him his 'wings'. However, when he was denied an active combat role – he was over forty and lacked perfect vision – he resigned and returned to civilian life. His book shows him to have been highly opinionated and very assertive in striving to get what he wanted.

Saturday, 29 December.

A very quiet Xmas but plenty to eat. The chicken, or fowl, lasted 4 days. John came to tea last Sunday and brought our gifts and returned with a parcel from us. The War Agricultural [Executive] Committee have not gone any further than our plot with the ditching. There was a lot of rain during Thursday night and yesterday morning and the result is that the ditch overflowed all across our garden and over Mrs Thomson's caravan site. They are in an awful mess. Cabbages in our garden are standing in water this afternoon and a stream was still trickling merrily to the road. When I signed the agreement to have the work done I stipulated verbally that they were not to stop short at our plot where the land dips, as I foresaw such a flooding, and the representative assured me the ditching would be completed. It is a month since they stopped working that I can see. As it was impossible to do any gardening I fell to tidying the hut.

Sunday, 30 December.

Very white frost this morning which in some places lasted all day. Jim says the floods are all out at Bromham and Oakley Bridges. Yesterday I noticed extra streams coursing across the meadow at Bromham; I expect it is one sheet today. This is a sight worth viewing but instead I went exploring streets in Bedford I have never been in before, not new streets but the area between Kimbolton Road and Goldington Road. It is a rather genteel district going to decay. The inhabitants were noted for running up bills with tradesmen and then being very slow to pay. It appeared to me as though many of the houses had several tenants so perhaps these smaller people pay as they go along. Having made this tour I met Flossie out of Sunday School and we walked and chatted. I gave her my old *Pears' Cyclopedia* [in one volume] for office use. I find I have had it 20 years. Jim went to see Jim Lowe and family.

*   *   *   *

1946 and After

Tuesday, 1 January.

Yesterday the weather was vile – foggy and freezing. However I washed. The lorry never turned up to bring Jim and company home from work at the brickworks. They trained and he was an hour late for his meal. Today it is still freezing, but bright. Healthy weather to be out in but I was tied to the house as the doctor never arrived until nearly 4 o'clock. I gave him as a New Year gift a jar of blackcurrant jelly and one of apple ginger jam as I much appreciate his calling monthly and keeping Father in order. Father asked him if he enjoyed Christmas; he replied 'Had the 3 kids in bed with flu.' Rather a sad state of affairs in a doctor's household.

Thursday, 3 January.

Yesterday was very dull and still freezing. On account of Mr Smith calling late Tuesday evening and saying he wanted his hut for his own use (that we use at the garden) I called at St Andrews Road to view a hut advertised, but it was not very suitable and was priced at £10 – 10 feet X 6 feet. I also went to Food Office to have Jim's milk and eggs continued but they told me to call next week as period was not up till then. Our usual chemist could not supply Father's liquid paraffin so I had to go to Boots who would not let me have it until 2 hours ahead, which meant another journey. It seemed altogether a fruitless morning but I did luckily get some frozen cod for dinner. After dinner I went to garden to carry away as much stuff from the hut that I could manage, and I must have looked like a tinker laden with pots and tins and other old junk. This morning I went to War Agricultural [Executive Committee] to see about the flooding from the ditch. The man was very sympathetic and said he would soon have the trouble attended to and even said he was glad I called and let him know the state of affairs. Of course fair promises are cheap, but they certainly soon disposed of that unwanted clay the men threw over my hedge, so I have hope.

Today is the 4th day of frost and has been sunny all day. I am now getting used to the frost and enjoying it. Brought home another load of tackle from the garden hut, and have advertised for another hut in Kimber's window [56 Iddesleigh Road, newsagent and confectioner] and our own front window.

When busy at the garden yesterday I heard a loud rending noise and thought someone must be hurling something large through a hedge. When I investigated I found it was the ice in the ditch sinking and cracking, the supporting water having drained to a lower level. I have read of the thunderous noise when thaw comes to great rivers; I can well believe it when a 2 foot deep ditch made such a noise.

Saturday, 5 January.
Thaw set in yesterday and today it is quite mild. I went to the garden this afternoon but did little work. First I had a long chat with Mr White, who planted a whole gallon of early peas. He says if he sold his 30 foot X 20 foot plots he would want £150 for them!! He paid £15 10s 0d for the 20 foot plot after we acquired ours nearly 5 years ago. Then I had another long chat with the Thomsons. I asked if they knew of a garden hut for sale. They kindly offered to house our tools while we are without a shed. I discovered the man's name is Thomson; his sister's is Mrs McFee – she is known as Mrs Thomson. Have just finished reading a life of Thomas de Quincey by Edward Sackville-West called *A Flame in Sunlight* [1936].

Tuesday, 8 January.
On Sunday Flossie came to tea and stayed on for a little supper. We'd had the Peak Frean Xmas pudding for dinner and I cut rather large pieces of Xmas cake for tea, and what with mince pies, jelly etc. again I ate more than was comfortable. I only slept in snatches the night following. On such an occasion we missed having access to the piano in the front room, as on Monday I took up the carpet in Father's upstairs bedroom preparatory to spring-cleaning the room a little at a time, and he can sleep upstairs again as soon as the weather is warmer.

In the *Bedfordshire Times* an advertiser required a typewriter and I offered mine; but no reply. I have an advertisement in front window, and also one in newsagent's window for a garden hut but no offers as yet.

Sunday, 13 January.
A beautiful bright cold day. The river has risen since yesterday and was flooding across the meadow at Bromham Bridge again. The ditch has evidently not yet been attended to and the garden is very wet after Friday night's rain; Thomsons are within a swamp. The hut has been taken away. On the whole, however, the garden looks very trim at present: digging done, grass shorn, trees pruned. Summer with its rush of life will soon alter all that. Last evening I began machining the gray [her spelling] skirt I am making out of an old coat. Also I made 'fruit fluff' from a Food Facts recipe. It is compounded of fruit juice – I had opened a bottle of gooseberries – gelatine and dried milk.

Tuesday, 15 January.
The usual day of frost. Yesterday was spent in spring-cleaning Father's bedroom!! At least I did the worst part: dusted ceilings and walls, washed paint and floor. I was interrupted for an hour by a visit from the Pensions Officer, come in response to Father's application for supplementary pension. His comment during the interview was 'Why haven't you applied for it before now?' so he evidently thinks Father qualifies for some extra pension.

Today I was at both the Literary Society and the Adult School. The former meeting was disappointing as the lecturer did not turn up and we had a discussion on 'Are Women Qualified to Wield Authority?' I thought they would have chosen a subject more 'literary'. My disappointment was more than compensated by Dr Metcalfe's talk and slides on Birds and also two cinematographs in colour: one showing birds, bees, butterflies, flowers and blue sky, including a long stretch of a busy kingfisher;

and the other of a holiday in North-West Ireland, including a rainbow and finishing with a gorgeous sunset. It was a most delightful entertainment.[1]

By the way, Mr Garrett, who is a member of the Literary Society and a master at Bedford School, is producing *George and Margaret* showing at the theatre next week.[2]

Wednesday, 16 January.
3rd day of frost, although there was a little thaw at mid-day. I continued spring-cleaning Father's bedroom. It sounds a ridiculous procedure but I can work better now than in warm spring days, and at my rate of progression it will be some months before I get through the house. Jim is working in the town [at brick-laying] and came home for dinner at middle of day, which gave me a longer afternoon. It is my birthday. I am 44. We have had a 3rd recent allocation of oranges this week and I also got 2 lb. lemons. I hardly know what to do with the latter. They would have been useful in the Xmas cooking.

Thursday, 17 January.
4th day of frost, but bright sunshine. A note arrived from the Old Age Pensions Office advising that Father is not eligible to any supplement. I called to see Flossie's mother and took along the mat I'd made. She was very interested in it. Marjorie Maynard has invited me to tea next Saturday. I wonder what is wrong with Celia. Heard nothing from her at Xmas and her December is long overdue. I am afraid there must be grave illness. Went to Folk Dancing class in evening.

Friday, 18 January.
5th day of frost and a very bitter east wind. There is skating on the flooded field at Goldington.[3] I went to the school department at Hockcliffe (!) [booksellers] for an exercise book and picked up a second-hand copy of Chaucer's *Canterbury Tales* (i.e. tales in modern English) which I have long been wanting to read. Also called at dentist's and find I do not need a stopping but only a sharp edge of enamel drilled smooth, which he did in a moment. When I arrived home at 4.30 I found Father in a sorry plight. Blood was streaming from his head on to his collar and jacket. He had slipped, with a kettle of water in his hand, on the tiled floor of the scullery. He had been trying to mop the water from the floor while the blood was running from his head and there were traces of it everywhere. I used two basins of water trying to clean his hair but as I could not stanch the flow of blood it was useless. I put some iodine and sticking plaster on and waited for Jim, who bound up the head and said we'd better wait till Father got over the shock before we cleaned him up.

[1]   Colour film of any sort had been virtually unobtainable during the war, though some American servicemen had it from home and their photographs are the basis for the appealing book by Roger A. Freeman, *Britain, The First Colour Photographs: Images of Wartime Britain* (London, 2003; first published 1994).
[2]   A comedy by Gerald Savory, presented at the Royal County Theatre on Midland Road by the Bedford Telephone Area Dramatic Club.
[3]   It was reported that on Thursday afternoon (early closing day), 17 January, a flooded field at Goldington and the lakes at Longholme and Bedford Park were crowded with skaters and small children who revelled in the joys of sliding and wearing out their precious skates (*Bedford Record*, 22 January 1946, p. 1).

Saturday, 19 January.

6th day of frost. There was a thin covering of snow this morning and a slight thaw when the sun shone during the morning. I met Marjorie at 3 p.m. and while walking around she told me all the Igranic news she could think of that might interest me. Then we went to her house for tea. Her father is a barber and they have a very cosy sitting room behind the shop. He kept dashing in for a cup of tea between serving customers – which it appeared was his usual procedure on Saturdays, his busiest day. My Father seems none the worse in his general health after his fall yesterday. His head is still bandaged and, having pushed it askew, he looks rather jaunty.

Sunday, 20 January.

7th day of frost. They are skating on Longholme Lake. This afternoon I went to the Adult School to hear our M.P., Mr Skiffington-Lodge. He came from London, spoke for ½ hour, answered questions for ½ hour and then went back to London by 4.17. I thought it a farce for a man to come all that distance to say those few words, which have been said many times lately: that we must return to religion to set the state of the world aright.[4]

Wednesday, 23 January.

Monday was frosty and foggy and it was impossible to hang out the washing but yesterday partial thaw began. It is very dull and dreary, however. Last night I went to Adult School. Mr Maude talked on Tolstoy and very interesting the talk was. He enlarged upon the fact that Tolstoy was a thinker and sketched for us his philosophy. He also expounded T's interpretation of some of the sayings in the Sermon on the Mount, one of which had a very salutary effect on me.

Nothing much to write about today except that we had another allocation of oranges. They were such big Jaffas that 5 of them weighed more than 3 lb. and cost 1s 11d. We divided them: 2 to Jim and 1½ to Pa and me. Also I called at Adelaide Square and Sybil, who gets many more oranges than the rations, sold me 2 lb. She wanted to give me them. I have not told the family of them yet.

Sunday, 27 January.

Last evening Jim and I went to the Folk Dancing annual ball at the Dujon Restaurant. It was packed and we could have done with a bigger room. It was very enjoyable and people who have not taken part for many years put in an appearance (or vice versa I should say). Mr Parris, treasurer for over 20 years, was presented with a cheque on his retirement. I left before the end, on account of Father, but he had enjoyed himself playing draughts next door.

---

4   The title of his talk was 'The Importance of Ordinary People': 'He stressed the importance of sound Christian religion and principles as being the fundamental basis of understanding between the peoples of the world, and expressed the conviction that the future peace and security of the world depended on their adoption.' He indicated his willingness 'whenever possible' to address local Christian organisations (*Bedford Record*, 29 January 1946, p. 4). Leah's rather sharp response tends to confirm her lack of enthusiasm for religion.

I have been troubled lately by what I think might be neuritis in my right hand. Three nights I have wakened with a numb, yet tingly burning pain. Each time it did not last long but I feel the numb yet tingling sensation during the day.

Tuesday, 29 January.
Spring-cleaned Jim's room yesterday and called at Doff's in the evening to arrange about going to the Anglo-Russian Ballet [at the Royal County Theatre on 11 February]. Today the doctor called just as we were beginning dinner and gave Father an injection, so I was able to get out in the afternoon to go food hunting. I have started to knit a pretty coloured cardigan – bought the wool at the Jews' market stall on Saturday – it is the only place you can get a good choice of wool.

The news at the weekend was of earthquakes in Switzerland; it must feel more fearsome having them in mountainous districts than on plains.[5]

Friday, 1 February.
Last night Father got what I can only call 'the shakes' and I thought I would have had to get the doctor today, but he has recovered.

Sunday, 3 February.
Too wet for garden yesterday, and so wet today that I have not been out of doors till today. I wrote Stella and packed up the book *Garden That I Love* [by Alfred Austin, 1907] for her.

Sunday, 10 February.
Garden very flooded. Yesterday Mr Chambers came along to investigate and was of the opinion that the pipe outlet from our ditch was stopped up and that all the water was steeping through the soil across the garden. Nevertheless I transplanted chrysanthemums etc. to borders alongside the main path, and various plants that Stella sent, into old chrysanth plot. There was a sale of 3,000 blankets during the week and I got 2 @ 10s. Also sent form to get licence for timber for hut.

Tuesday, 12 February.
Had a busy day spring-cleaning my bedroom yesterday; then I went to the Anglo-Russian ballet in the evening. It was enjoyable, but a very small corps. *Les Sylphides* was danced in a very dim light, I suspect to veil the shabbiness and drabness of the costumes that should have been glistening white. It was the first time that Flossie and her sister had seen a ballet and [they] were very enthusiastic. Doff never turned up at all, and was waiting outside at the end. Her mother is ill and she could not leave her all those hours.

---

5   The earthquake on the evening of 25 January was felt most severely in Sion, capital of the canton of Valais, and at Sierre. The earthquake was said to be the strongest in Switzerland since 1855 and was felt throughout the country. Falling rocks disrupted rail traffic, buildings were damaged, numerous houses had to be evacuated, church steeples in some villages were on the verge of collapsing, and a few people were injured by falling chimneys (*The Times*, 26 January 1946, p. 4 and 28 January 1946, p. 3).

Today I again went to the War Agricultural [Executive Committee] about the ditch. The ultra-charming youth who had inveighed me into signing consent to have my part of the ditch deepened was standing among a bevy of pretty female office staff with the very air of an Adonis among nymphs. After a lissome blonde had told me Mr Lear was not in, I said 'This gentleman will do as well' and tackled him and I was pleased to hear from him that German prisoners were on the job and were continuing the ditch down the lane as first intended instead of piping it via a private pond. Jim was able to corroborate that Jerries were working in the lane and had come to where he is building and asked for petrol to start their lunchtime fire!! Jim is working [as a bricklayer] for Sid. Smith building houses near Thistley Green Lane [in Bromham].

Mary Wilkinson, Probation Officer, gave a very interesting talk on her work, at the Adult School tonight, and then brought the Burtons and me home in her car. I remember her as a slip of a girl in the tennis club and I judged her to be 8–10 years younger than I, but now she seems older by far.

Wednesday, 13 February.
Mrs Matthews asked if her hen house would make a garden shed for Jim – but of course it is too low. Trixy called with my umbrella which I had left at Adult School last night. Washed hair.

Thursday, 14 February.
An exceedingly dark day, but Princess Elizabeth visited the town and in her tour passed by our house in a car!! I just managed to distinguish her in time by a sharp nod she gave in our direction, and then she was by. Her nose was much more retroussé [turned up] than I had imagined, and I would not have recognised her but for the nod. Her manner is like Queen Mary's [1867–1953, her grandmother, widow of George V].[6]

Saturday, 2 March.
A miserable day, snow and sleet falling all day but not lying, just as it was on Tuesday. However, there are 2 feet of snow in Paris!! Last Sunday, a beautiful day sandwiched between very high winds of the previous week and sleet and frost of the week just past,[7] I went to Luton and spent a very enjoyable day. We had Xmas

---

[6] The Princess opened a three-day exhibition in the Corn Exchange of agricultural and handicraft work by members of the Women's Land Army (*Bedford Record*, 19 February 1946, pp. 1 and 3). A commentator in this paper ('The Stroller') reported that local ladies: 'have been generous in their praise of her charming appearance and the becoming simplicity in the style of her clothes, which I gather met with general approval in these days when we are all a little down-at-heel and feeling the draught in our coupon book as well as in our pockets' (p. 5). The Princess viewed in the parade on High Street 600 Bedfordshire land girls, many of them on the final day of their service (Antrobus, *'We Wouldn't Have Missed it for the World': The Women's Land Army in Bedfordshire 1939–1950*, pp. 71–7).
[7] A photograph of a woman with a pram against a background of coal in the *Bedford Record*, 19 March 1946, p. 1, was headlined 'Housewives Throng Coal-yards' and its caption reported that: 'The shortage of coal became acute during the late cold spell, and all kinds of trucks and perambulators were brought into use to serve as transport from the coal yard.' The

pudding for dinner and rich birthday cake for tea. Janet was doing homework morning and afternoon; Jacqueline had just been enrolled a Girl Guide and went to a special Guides' service at Luton Parish Church in the afternoon; John and I listened to a concerto but he was soon snoring. After tea we had piano-playing and then John put on his latest records. One which they called *Night on the Bare Mountain* [by Modest Mussorgsky, 1867] was deafening.

Yesterday I made two choker necklaces out of a long rope of ivory beads.

*   *   *   *

While Leah continued with her diary, her subsequent writing was very intermittent. After a brief entry for 6 March, the next three entries in 1946 were on 13 April, 17 July and 8 December, concluding that year with entries for 18, 19, 23 and 26 December – so for most of 1946 her diary virtually ceased to exist. She offered no comment on the sudden silences. She resumed writing with more frequency in January 1947, and then made numerous remarks about that year's exception-ally – indeed famously – bitter winter. On Wednesday, 5 February she reported that: 'The last snow had not got completely away when we awoke to a fresh fall this morning; quite dry snow too and more ice. The roads and railways in some parts are in a worse state through snow than they have been for years. In this very cold weather we seem to just eat and sit about.' Severe cold and snowy conditions persisted. Temperatures dropped to record lows.[8] For weeks life was a struggle. Rugby matches and other public events had to be cancelled or postponed; some schools were closed. 'Yesterday was the first day of the big electricity cut', she wrote on Tuesday, 11 February: 'that is, none for industry and none for domestic users during the hours 9–12 and 2–4. In our district yesterday the power was cut off from the main during those hours, but today it was not and we were on our honour not to use it. ...There have been long queues at the gasworks for cinders – apparently no coal is being delivered.' The following day she observed that: 'On account of fuel crisis street lighting is reduced to wartime condition. There were many German prisoners strolling around the town and in Bromham Road I saw one pick up a little girl aged 6–7 and carry her a few yards, until her mother came and claimed her. It will be a good thing when they can all get back to their homes.' Milder weather did not prevail until the second half of March, when people then had to contend with floods.

Leah continued to write, intermittently, until the middle of 1957, and hardly at all thereafter. Sometimes her diary is fairly full; at other times there are gaps. After July 1957 there are only a handful of entries – none at all for 1958, 1960, 1961 and 1962, and only one for 1959, which recorded the birth on 8 January of her nephew,

---

supplies of coal could not satisfy the demand: 'Coal merchants are allowing the Housewife a maximum of 28 lb. (ten-pennyworth), which in the average household lasts less than a day. More than that they cannot provide unless the purchaser can produce a permit.... Much of the coal at present available is poor in quality, but even that, say Bedford's housewives, is better than no coal at all.'

8   *Bedford Record*, 25 February 1947, p. 1.

John, son of Jim, who had married just before his fifty-second birthday.[9] The diary revives modestly in 1963, but speaks mostly of the weather. On 14 March 1965, after a two-year silence, Leah wrote of the: 'urge to continue diary to leave some record of my beloved nephew John Aynsley, at present aged 6.' However, her resolve was not sustained and, after some sixteen pages of further writing, the diary ends for good on 27 June 1965.

*   *   *   *

---

[9]   Folk dancing continued to be a significant feature of the Aynsleys' lives. Jim met his wife, Nellie Wilkinson, folk dancing, and in the 1980s their son, John, met his wife, Margaret Elliott, at a folk dance (information courtesy John Aynsley).

Epilogue

Leah Aynsley's life embraced many of the everyday experiences that would have marked the lives of tens of thousands of English women during the 1940s. There was, in particular, the prominence of time-consuming housework and the provisioning of food and drink (though not, for her, the duty of child-care).[1] A degree of self-sufficiency through gardening was a common and widely promoted ideal, though Leah certainly came closer than most women to realising this ideal. Caring for an ageing relative, as she did for her father, was also commonplace. Keeping tabs on a loved one in the armed forces, and often writing to him, as Leah followed her younger brother's travels and wrote of his welfare during his months of service, was a central feature of many women's lives. Recreational activities varied widely in wartime – and they were fairly abundant, partly because the government acknowledged that they played a role in sustaining public morale, especially as the war dragged on and on and on. Books played a reasonably prominent role in Leah's life, musical performances some role, the radio almost none at all. Her travelling was almost entirely local, and never – with one exception – involved sleeping anywhere but in her own house. Rural life and traditions meant a lot to her, as they did for other women at the time who were mainly town-dwellers. It was frequently easy to get from town to country – very easy for those living in Queen's Park, Bedford, which bordered on countryside – and rural outings in various forms were staples of life, and not only in the warm months of the year. Leah would have been classified as a town-dweller, but much of her energy and many of her thoughts were invested in cultivating the land.[2] While shopping was never easy in wartime, the shops that supplied life's necessities in urban districts were usually located close to home. Several that Leah relied on were located in nearby Iddesleigh Road.

---

[1] Very few diaries are known to have been kept by mothers with young and dependent children. Researchers in the Mass Observation Archive in Brighton, which holds some 480 wartime diaries, and other repositories, have discovered this reality. Few mothers had time to be conscientious diarists. Their lives were full of mandatory responsibilities. If they wrote at all, they were mainly letter-writers (especially to friends and loved ones living elsewhere, whose numbers grew significantly during the war: letters were a vital way to keep in touch, and it is likely that most sent to men in the Forces have not survived). So the individual experiences of mothers in their twenties and thirties have thus far been less well recorded than those of other women. One exception, edited by us, is *A Mother in Tadworth, Surrey in 1940: The Wartime Diary of Daidie Penna*, Banstead History Research Group (Banstead, 2019).

[2] Leah's liking for the countryside and gardening was shared by another wartime diarist around a decade older than her who spent most of the war in Morecambe, Lancashire (Patricia and Robert Malcolmson, eds, *A Londoner in Lancashire 1941–1943: The Diary of Annie Beatrice Holness*).

Diaries are rarely tell-all documents. Self-censorship has been common amongst diarists, and Leah was no exception. Some matters that were personally important to her were not fully disclosed (or perhaps not disclosed at all). Leah raised this question of discretion – or silence – in her entry for 2 April 1951: 'All through the years I have kept a diary (about 20) I never[3] mention my inmost thoughts, i.e. on spiritual matters or affairs of the heart. People seem puzzled that Jane Austen never mentions religion or passion in her novels, but I can well imagine that these matters went too deep for her to dig them out and display them to the public. If I had no notion of anyone reading my diaries I might have been less reticent, but I hope they will be read after my death as I have never read any published diary by a working-class person.' It was her class identity that especially fuelled her determination to document and preserve. Temperamentally, she was inclined to reticence, and her diary-writing displays this disposition. It was not, for the most part, intended to be therapeutic. It could even be said that her diary probably concealed more than it revealed, at least psychologically.

There was, however, one moment in her writing when, unusually, Leah did dig deeper into her feelings. This happened much earlier, on 13 October 1935, when she was 33: 'I often wonder why I was ever born. I am not beautiful and not particularly useful. I make no great effort for good in the world – and yet I am happy. I have sometimes thought the reason why I am so happy and fortunate in life is that I appreciate so much the pleasures that God gives, so because I am so appreciative of them He keeps heaping them on me. If nobody appreciated all the beauty on earth and in life, it would be wasted effort; and therefore such as I am born.' Leah was not ambitious or driven. She accepted much of life as she encountered it. She endorsed the merits and satisfactions of 'a simple life' (16 March 1948). No doubt these were features of hundreds of thousands of respectable, well-ordered working-class women's lives. Leah Aynsley mainly stood out in her desire to record such a life – that is, her own.

*   *   *   *

---

[3] 'Rarely' would be more accurate.

Appendix

Some Books Read by Leah Aynsley

At the end of volume two of her diary, which concludes in the middle of her entry for 1 June 1944, Leah compiled two pages under the heading 'Books I have enjoyed this year' [1944].[1] They were:

Home is the Sailor [1940], by [William] Blain. The reminiscences of a sea-captain [William Brown]. Very interesting and thrilling.
I Know a Garden [1933], by Marion Cran. About gardens, not a gardening book. Most beautiful, and lovely illustrations.
Magic Gardens [1939], by Rosetta Clarkson (I think), an American. All about herbs, parterres, knot gardens, etc.
Memoirs of a Highland Lady, being the Autobiography of Elizabeth Grant, afterwards Mrs Smith of Baltiboys [1911]. Edited by Lady Strachey. This is one of the best books I have read. The period is about 1800 onwards, and the book is full of interesting and charming episodes.
My Country and My People [1936], by Lin Yutang. A very good book on China, both ancient and modern.
A Shepherd's Life [1936], by W.H. Hudson. About the South Wiltshire Downs.
Far Away and Long Ago [1918]. W.H. Hudson's boyhood in Argentina.
Idle Days in Patagonia [1893]. By W.H. Hudon.
My Garden by the Sea [1936[, by Robert Foster-Meillar; about a garden in Cornwall.
Chinese Childhood [1940], by Yee Chiang; very charming and well and profusely illustrated.
In the Heart of the Country [1942], by H.E. Bates. Each chapter has two beautiful woodcuts.
A Childhood in Brittany Eighty Years Ago [1919], by Anne Douglas Sedgwick, afterwards de Sélincourt. This is very interesting and charming, being the childhood of a French aristocrat about 100 years ago.
Lark Rise [1940], by Flora Thompson. Describing life in an Oxfordshire hamlet in the 1880s.

[She then added to this list four books read in 1945.]

Over to Candleford [1941]. Somewhat of a sequel to the above.
Candleford Green [1943]. Life in an Oxfordshire village in the 1890s.

---

[1] It is not possible to know how many other books she may have read but did not put on record.

Bridge of Heaven [1944], by S.I. Hsiung. Autobiographical novel. Very good.

Moby Dick [1851], by Herman Melville. All about whales and whaling. Some very delectable descriptions: '...one serene and moonlight night, when all the waves rolled by like scrolls of silver...', and top of page 110, chap. 28.

Bibliography

Primary sources

Bedfordshire Archives and Records Service

Z1606 Diaries of Leah Aynsley, 1930–1983

BBC Written Archives Centre

R13/223 Departmental London Area: BBC Club Bedford 1941–1943

R35/123 Premises: Kingsley Hotel General 1945

R61/17 American Liaison Unit: Censorship – Origins of Programmes 1939–1944

Mass Observation

Diarist no. 5423, Annie Schofield

Diarist no. 5451, Dorothy Walklen

Royal Voluntary Service Archive and Heritage Collection

Bedford Narrative Reports, 1943–44

Newspapers

Bedford Record

Bedfordshire Times

The Times

Secondary sources

Antrobus, Stuart, '"Holidays at Home" in 'Bedford during the Second World War', *Bedford Local History Magazine*, no. 100 (September/October 2017), pp. 41–50

Antrobus, Stuart, *'We Wouldn't Have Missed it for the World': The Women's Land Army in Bedfordshire, 1939-1950* (Copt Hewick, 2008)

Barker, Herbert Edward *A Bedford Diary of Four War Years* (np, 1943)

Bates, H.E., *The Tinkers of Elstow: The Story of the Royal Ordnance Factory run by J. Lyons & Company Limited for the Ministry of Supply during the World War of 1939-1945* (privately printed, 1946)

Beck, Earl R., 'Under the Bombs', in Igor Primoratz, ed., *Terror from the Sky: The Bombing of German Cities in World War II* (New York and Oxford, 2010)

Bedford and District Directory 1939 (Bedford)

Boult, Sir Adrian, *My Own Trumpet* (London, 1973)

Bradford, Sarah, *King George VI* (London, 1989)

Brewer, David, *Greece, the Decade of War: Occupation, Resistance and Civil War* (London, 2016)

Briggs, Asa, *The History of Broadcasting in the United Kingdom, Volume III: The War of Words* (Oxford, 1970)

Buchan, Ursula, *A Green and Pleasant Land: How England's Gardeners Fought the Second World War* (London, 2014)

Dundrow, Michael, *A Lasting Impression: One Boy's Wartime in the Country* (Dunstable, 1981)

Ferguson, Sheila and Hilde Fitzgerald, *Studies in the Social Services* (London, 1954). A volume in the *History of the Second World War, United Kingdom Civil Series*, ed. by W. K. Hancock

Freeman, Roger A., *Britain, The First Colour Photographs: Images of Wartime Britain* (London, 2003). First published 1994

Gilbert, Martin, *The Road to Victory: Winston S. Churchill 1941–1945* (London, 1986)

Hammond, R. J., *Food and Agriculture in Britain 1939–45: Aspects of Wartime Control* (Stanford, 1954)

Hargreaves E. L. and M. M. Gowing, *Civil Industry and Trade* (London, 1952). A volume in the *History of the Second World War, United Kingdom Civil Series*, ed. by W. K. Hancock

Hart-Davis, Duff, ed., *King's Counsellor: Abdication and War: The Diaries of Sir Alan Lascelles* (London, 2007). First published 2006

Hill, Maureen and James Alexander, *The Blitz on Britain* (Croxley Green, 2010)

Hyams, Jack, *Bomb Girls: Britain's Secret Army: The Munitions Women of World War II* (London, 2013)

James, Robert Rhodes, ed., *Winston S. Churchill: His Complete Speeches 1897–1963* (London and New York, 1974), 8 vols

Kershaw, Ian, *The End: The Defiance and Destruction of Hitler's Germany, 1944–1945* (London, 2011)

Laird, Dorothy, *Queen Elizabeth the Queen Mother* (London, 1966)

Lande, D. A., *From Somewhere in England: The Life and Times of the 8ᵗʰ AF Bomber, Fighter and Ground Crews in WWII* (np, 1991)

Lutt, Nigel, *Bedfordshire at War* (Stroud, 1997)

Lyons, J., *Rules of the Danger Area, Elstow Ordnance Factory* (np, 1942)

Lyttelton, Oliver, Viscount Chandos, *The Memoirs of Lord Chandos* (London, 1962)

Madge, Charles and Tom Harrisson, eds, *First Year's Work, 1937–38, by Mass-Observation* (London, 1938)

Malcolmson, Patricia and Robert, eds, *A Londoner in Lancashire 1941–1943: The Diary of Annie Beatrice Holness,* Record Society of Lancashire and Cheshire (Liverpool, 2016)

——, eds, *A Mother in Tadworth, Surrey in 1940: The Wartime Diary of Daidie Penna*, Banstead History Research Group (Banstead, 2019)

——, eds, *A Shop Assistant in Wartime: The Dewsbury Diary of Kathleen Hey, 1941–1945,* Yorkshire Archaeological and History Society (Woodbridge, 2018)

——, eds, *A Soldier in Bedfordshire, 1941–1942: The Diary of Private Denis Argent, Royal Engineers*, BHRS, vol. 88 (Woodbridge, 2009)

——, eds, *A Vicar's Wife in Oxford 1938–1943: The Diary of Madge Martin,* Oxfordshire Record Society (Woodbridge, 2018)

——, eds, *Warriors at Home 1940–1942: Three Surrey Diarists*, Surrey Record Society (Woking, 2012)

——, *Wartime Cumbria, 1939–1945: Aspects of Life and Work*, Cumberland and Westmorland Antiquarian and Archaeological Society (Carlisle, 2017)

——, *Women at the Ready: The Remarkable Story of the Women's Voluntary Services on the Home Front* (London, 2013)

McCooey, Chris, ed., *Despatches from the Home Front: The War Diaries of Joan Strange 1939-1945* (Tunbridge Wells, 1994)

Middlebrook, Martin, *The Berlin Raids: RAF Bomber Command Winter 1943–44* (London, 2000). First published 1988

Moore, Bob and Kent Fedorowich, *The British Empire and Its Italian Prisoners of War, 1940–1947* (Basingstoke, 2002)

Mortimer, Gavin, *The Blitz: An Illustrated History* (Oxford, 2010)

Murray, Keith A. H., *Agriculture* (London, 1955). A volume in the *History of the Second World War, United Kingdom Civil Series*, ed. by W. K. Hancock

Nossack, Han Erich, *The End: Hamburg 1943* (London and Chicago, 2004). First published 1948

O'Brien, Terence H., *Civil Defence* (London, 1955). A volume in the *History of the Second World War, United Kingdom Civil Series*, ed. by W. K. Hancock

Ondaatje, Michael, *Warlight* (London, 2018)

Origo, Iris, *War In Val d'Orcia: An Italian War Diary 1943–1944* (London, 2017). First published 1947

Peniston-Bird, C.M., '"Yes, we have no bananas": sharing memories of the Second World War', in Mary Addyman, Laura Wood and Christopher Yinnitsaros, eds, *Food, Drink, and the Written Word in Britain, 1820-1945* (London, 2017)

Ramsey, Winston G., *The Blitz Then and Now* (London, 1990), 3 vols

Risby, Stephen, *Prisoners of War in Bedfordshire* (Stroud, 2011)

Shawcross, William, *Queen Elizabeth, The Queen Mother* (Toronto, 2009)

Smith, Daniel, *The Spade as Mighty as the Sword; The Story of the Second World War 'Dig for Victory' Campaign* (London, 2013)

Smith, Graham, *Hertfordshire and Bedfordshire Airfields in the Second World War* (Newbury, 1999)

Soames, Mary, *A Daughter's Tale: The Memoir of Winston Churchill's Youngest Child* (New York, 2011)

Stacey, C. P. and Barbara Wilson, *The Half-Million: Canadians in Britain, 1939–1946* (Toronto, 1987)

Summers, Julie, *Fashion on the Ration: Style in the Second World War* (London, 2015)

Webster, Wendy, *Mixing It: Diversity in World War Two Britain* (Oxford, 2018)

White, Doris, *D for Doris, V for Victory* (Milton Keynes, 1981)

Willes, Margaret, *The Gardens of the British Working Class* (New Haven and London, 2014)

Williams, Michael, *Steaming to Victory: How Britain's Railways Won the War* (London, 2014)

Wood, Ian S., *Britain, Ireland and the Second World War* (Edinburgh, 2010)

Woolven, Robin, ed., *The London Diary of Anthony Heap 1931–1945*, London Record Society (London, 2017)

Websites

North-East Diary 1939–1945, www.ne-diary.genuki.uk

W.H. Allen Engineering Association, https://www.whaea.co.uk

Index

There are three subjects that appear on almost every page of Leah Aynsley's diary, often with little or no elaboration: illness, housekeeping (mainly cleaning and food preparation), and family members and relations (usually named). For the most part we have indexed these subjects only when something noteworthy is said about them, or when they appear in some sort of larger context. Many weather events (another repeated subject) are indexed indirectly, mainly when they bear on human activities.